Character Toys

and Collectibles

Second Series

by David Longest

COLLECTOR BOOKS

A Division of Schroeder Publishing Co., Inc.

The current values in this book should be used only as a
guide. They are not intended to set prices, which vary from
one section of the country to another. Auction prices as well as
dealer prices vary greatly and are affected by condition as well
as demand. Neither the Author nor the Publisher assumes re-
sponsibility for any losses that might be incurred as a result of
consulting this guide.

Printed in Singapore by Singapore National Printers Ltd.
through Four Colour Imports, Ltd.

Acknowledgments

The author is greatly indebted to a host of devoted toy lovers, collectors, dealers and friends who helped to make this book possible. Without their toys, which are the real "stars" of this book, this endeavor would have been impossible. Together, they have proven that "toy people" are friendly, enthusuastic, caring and very hospitable. They made me feel at home in their residences, shops or even booths at antique shows. They fed me dinners and ice cream sundaes during photo sessions when my vision was getting blurry and my spirits tired. For these many kind courtesies so often extended, I say "thanks."

I would personally like to thank the following toy contributors to this book: Joel Allan, Allan Beckman, Marc Belich, "Doc" and Julia Gernard, Harry and Jean Hall, Tommy Hall, Dennis Hasty, Dave Harris, Louise Henderson, Jim and Sue Miller, Doug Moore, Helen and Foster Pollack, Terry and Jeannie Quadnau, Joe and Juanita Reese, Michael Rittman, Ken Schmitz and Donna Walker.

An additional special note of thanks goes out to Violet Meier, curator and owner of the Memory Lane Antique Doll and Toy Museum in Mystic, Conneticut. She and her husband retrieved dolls from hard to reach areas and helped to set them up before my camera. Violet embodies the very best of what is in all collectors. Also, Bill and Mary Furnish deserve a very special thanks for their contributions to this book. Dr. Furnish and Mary bring a wealth of knowledge to all aspects of toy collecting that is often mind-boggling and truly amazing. I am looking forward to the day when Bill decides to write his own book.

Also, for certain kind hospitalities and courtesies offered to me in the course of the production of this book, I would like to thank David and Jane Eberle, and Steve Quertermous, my most understanding editor at Collector Books. In addition, I would like to thank Mary Jane Augenstein who, many years ago, made me much of the writer that I am today. Also, I thank Martha Saunders who helped me to get my very first piece of writing published some fifteen years ago.

And to Elmer and Viola Reynolds of Indiana, I offer a world of thanks. Their toys appear in every chapter of this book and they are continuing to build one of the finest character toy collections in the country. Their toys are the true heart of this book and their enthusiasm for collecting helped to drive me toward the production of this second volume. The Kewpie chapter of this book is dedicated to them, for they initiated me into the wonderful world of Rose O'Neill and her Kewpies. Elmer and Vi are very special friends and equally special collectors. I hope their dream of a museum comes true someday.

Finally, I thank my wife, Ann, for being tolerant of my shifting moods and reclusive writing habits. She brought me those kindly cups of hot chocolate and plates of doughnuts with perfect timing - just when I needed them! I offer her a special thanks for keeping a smile on her face through most of this. I also thank her for all of her efforts in bringing about the newest future collector in our family. It's an interesting phenomenon when your firstborn and new books are due in the same month! So, to Claire or Clay, whoever you will be, enjoy this book filled with lots of pictures of old toys . . . your Dad was thinking of you all the while he wrote it.

I dedicate this book to the memory of Linda Ann Newton, my sister.

Table of Contents

Introduction

This book is intended to be a companion volume to the first edition of *Character Toys and Collectibles* published by Collector Books in 1984. It is not intended to replace that volume. Every attempt has been made to avoid duplication of any items pictured in the first book or described in the text of that work. In rare instances, when a different variety, size or color of a particular toy described in Volume I has been discovered, then such interesting variations have been pictured here.

The format of Volume II remains the same as that used in the Volume I. Collectibles have been grouped by general areas of collecting specialties, i.e. "Western Heroes", "Disney Comic Character Collectibles" and many others. Some books and price guides choose to lump together items by chronology or by type. The emphasis here has been upon grouping the toys and collectibles in an interesting and presentable way in order to be helpful to both toy collecting specialists and generalists in all toy fields. The toys are put into chapters by category; they have not been grouped by chronology or manufacturer.

Character Toys II pictures toys, in all instances, that are the property of private collectors, museums or were currently for sale from dealers at the time of the original photography. These are all toys that exist today and are actually "out there" in the collecting world to be found. We have all seen antique and toy guides that picture reproductions of old toy advertising catalogues and promotional literature as a basis for reference. This approach is fine if the author's intention is solely to produce a reference book on the advertising and promotion of old toys. In this author's opinion, such efforts that reprint catalogue pages from Sears Roebuck over the years are not half as satisfying or pleasing to the collector as pictures of toys that HAVE REALLY BEEN FOUND by some collector out there.

This author's intention, then, is to present pictures of toys which actually DO EXIST and can be found by today's resourceful collector. A catalogue of impossible-to-find-toys serves only as a frustration to both novice and advanced collectors.

Several contacts with amateur photographers who are also toy collectors have always brought up the subject of photography and processes used for this book. Since the photographic procedures for this book and the first one were identical, one answer will address both. Toy photography is always done at a host of locations under a tremendous variety of lighting conditions. Some of the pictures were shot on tables in museums, some on carpeted floors in collectors' homes, and in one of the most convenient spots in one advanced collector's home – right in the middle of his pool table!

To insure uniformity of all backgrounds, a sky blue display board supported by a wooden frame was used as the base and backdrop of all photographs. Frames were shot without the use of flash photography and utilized 35mm ASA 400 film with supplemental incandescent lighting of approximately 400 watts.

Blue filters and polarizing filters were used in some instances. The basic camera used was a Pentax K1000 with attachments and a tripod for some shots. Because my photographic crew consisted of one – me – equipment was kept very portable and confined to all that I could carry in two loads. The most difficult photo assignment was carrying my entire array of gear in one huge load for three blocks in downtown Chicago about two blocks from Lake Michigan. I could state in near honesty that at one time the blustery winds caught my background apparatus and both author and equipment were almost airborne.

Each of the photographs here is captioned with basic information to help the reader identify the toy by a second means other than the picture itself. Certain features of toys are discussed along with measurements to give collectors an overall view of the toy. The chapter texts and discussions of toys are designed to inform the reader about each individual specialty area of collecting. Entirely new areas for this volume are "Hollywood Personality Collectibles" dealing with character toys inspired by movie stars, and "Kewpie Collectibles" which introduces the collectibles inspired by Rose O'Neill's Kewpie characters.

A slight change in character groupings has taken place from the first volume to this one. Popeye and Dick Tracy appeared in Volume I in a chapter titled "Comic Character Superstars." In this volume, they, along with several others, have been grouped in a chapter titled "Heroes of Earth and Space."

Additionally, characters inspired by both radio and television programs over the years have been placed into a chapter titled "Radio and Television Characters." This chapter begins with characters who made their fame on radio and continues on through Howdy Doody and the young years of television.

Of course, two chapters on Disney Character Collectibles have once again been included. Since the Mickey Mouse renaissance and craze of the 1960's, Disneyana collectors have been on the forefront of character toy collecting. Two national fan club organizations now exist and these chapters should be a welcome sight to those loyal followers. (Addresses for these clubs are listed in the Disney chapter).

The chapter on "Western Heroes" has not been reorganized, but the toys are all new and so is the text! Western hero collectors remain a character collecting group all their own, and this section of western "goodies" is for all those childhood cowpokes who just can't lay down their six-shooters.

The new "Kewpie Collectibles" chapter has been added for coverage of those lovable, impish little creations of Rose O'Neill just after the turn of the century. This author is aware that there is a large fan club and following of Rose O'Neill and all her characters who gather each spring in Missouri for the annual "Kewpiesta". To all those who annually meet to share the passion and enthusiasm for Rose and her creations, this chapter is intended as a tribute to both O'Neill and her fans. A full-color chapter in a toy book devoted simply to Kewpies and Rose O'Neill's characters is long overdue.

Another innovation in this second volume is the "Collector's Resource Guide." In the travels associated with the preparation of this book, I have constantly heard from collectors that their weeks and months are often filled with both "up" and "down" periods in collecting. Occassionally, some collectors feel that there "just isn't any good stuff left out there." Obviously, that point is relative to where the individual collector lives and how resourceful he is. This author realizes that there are sometimes months and even entire seasons when a collector goes "dormant" simply because the opportunity to collect doesn't seem to present itself.

In response and to remedy to this, the Resource Guide is filled with information useful to collectors interested in general toy collecting and within the specialty areas. This chapter is devoted to the toy collector who seeks some new insights into collecting or one who just needs a guiding hand.

"The Collector's Resource Guide" also gives some personal "pointers" to both novice and advanced collectors. Every toy collecting enthusiast has his or her own style and system of acquiring items for collections, but this chapter offers several new ideas for those who seek other angles on collecting.

The author encourages readers to respond to this book openly. In all inquiries, please include a self-addressed, stamped, legal size envelope with author's business address: David Longest, CHARACTER TOYS & COLLECTIBLES, Series II, P.O. Box 2183, Clarksville, Indiana 47131-2183.

Input as to "fantastic finds," price updates, notes on specialties, questions about character toys and general comments are always welcomed and can be used to help with any further updates of the first two volumes.

Toy collecting in itself is not an art; it is a hobby. However, the collector becomes the artist when he assembles the most aesthetically pleasing collection pieces into a reflection of his own personal tastes. When a collection becomes a real expression of the collector's own likes, tastes and individualism, then the collection in itself, is a type of self-portrait.

Finally, speaking now as the author of two books on character toys, I would like to thank all of those friendly collectors who have stopped to talk with me at toy shows and conventions. Contrary to what the general public might believe, toy collectors are not quiet people. They are still filled with enough of the child in them to make a most interesting group. A wealth of knowledge has been passed directly on to me as a result of these conversations, and to this bunch of friendly people, I tip my hat.

Readers will find this volume somewhat different in style from the first book on character toys. The first volume presented the material in a more textual, matter-of-fact style discussion. In this book, I have decided to write a little more personally, as one collector speaking to another. I hope such a differentiation will help to complement the first volume and add collector interest and readability to this second one.

Character toy collecting is one of the fastest growing areas of toy collecting today. It is also one of the most publicized areas, so thrifty collectors have a tremendous challenge facing them if they seek only bargains in the marketplace. Aside from the personal tips offered here on collecting, this volume also includes some collector anecdotes within the specific chapter discussions. Like the prize inside the box of Cracker Jacks, I hope these little tidbits will add to the reader's enjoyment of the book.

Enjoy *Character Toys and Collectibles, Volume II*. If it is as much fun for the reader as it has been for me to write, then we will both be well pleased.

Happy collecting!

David K. Longest

Character Toy Hall of Fame

Every area of collecting must have its origins and the origin of character collectibles undoubtedly comes from mass media offshoots of the Industrial Revolution. Did you ever try to stop and think what are the collectible character toys of the 1820's or even 1860's? There are none. Character collecting seemed to begin when characters, in any manner, shape or form began to be reproduced into the print media.

Our chapter begins with the interesting characters created by Palmer Cox late in the 19th century called "Brownies." The first Brownie character books date from the late 1880's, so this volume begins a little earlier on the time table than its Volume I counterpart. The early Brownie collectibles which date mainly from the 1890's are usually paper-type toys or printed matter. The figure sets in Plates 1 and 4 are unusual in that they are more dimensional than most Brownie collectibles. When collectors are lucky enough to find such examples, they are usually no longer grouped in sets but are simply odd, lonely figures.

The Brownie character wooden puzzle shown in Plate 2 is a more typical Palmer Cox character collectible. It is fiberboard backed and features bright paper lithography. The reproduction of the Cox characters is detailed and the colors

are similar to those found in the Brownie books.

Soon after the Palmer Cox characters made their successful debut onto the American scene, Richard Outcault found success with his "Yellow Kid" comics which are noted today as America's first popular on-going comic series. With the Yellow Kid being America's first comic strip character, whenever examples of him are found in toys, it is a real rarity.

From scanning the classified pages of several noted monthly toy publications over the years, there are collectors "out there" who specialize in collecting nothing but Yellow Kid memorabilia. My hat goes off to them for will power and perserverance. In my annual travels to toy shows around the country, I seldom if ever, run acrosss Yellow Kid items. They are quite few and far between since not only specialists are out there scouring the shows for the good pieces, but also just about every comic character collector who's worth his weight in toys wants to add a Yellow Kid piece to his collection. Note the Yellow Kid sheet music in Plate 8.

Another Richard Outcault creation was Buster Brown and his dog, Tige. Although Buster Brown dates from just a little later than the Yellow Kid, his toys are no less significant on the collecting scene. Collectors should be aware that two classifications of Buster Brown toys exist. Those that are most rare and extremely valuable are the Buster Brown character items that date from the turn of the century. These are the toys associated with Outcault's early comic series.

Later Buster Brown items are those not actually inspired by or associated with the original comic strip. Since the popular brand of shoes for children often promoted itself with premiums and advertising items, many Buster Brown character items of the 1940's and the 1950's are often confused with such items much earlier. Both classifications of Buster Brown are collected today and both have value. But it is the early Buster Brown toys that most of today's advanced collectors are searching for.

Another early character on the American comic strip scene was Foxy Grandpa. Although seemingly less popular among today's collectors than the Yellow Kid and Buster Brown, this early character is still highly collectible. The Foxy Grandpa and Foxy Grandma dolls pictured in Plate 11 are extremely rare and were photographed as a part of a museum collection in Connecticut. This author has never seen examples of these dolls for sale anywhere.

The "Toonerville Trolley" comic strip created by Fontaine Fox first appeared in 1915, but collectors usually place toys from this series high on their priority lists. The madcap antics of the creaky old trolley and its oddball skipper and patrons made the strip a monumental bit of American comic character history. Volume I showed many of the most desirable of all the Toonerville toys. This volume pictures the Toonerville Trolley candy container that is popular today among comic character collectors and candy container collectors alike.

Other early comic strip characters introduced here into our "Hall of Fame" are the "Katzenjammer Kids" created by Rudolf Dirks in 1896 and "Happy Hooligan" first penned by Fred Opper in 1900. Both of these characters have an intensely recognizable association among serious toy collectors as being early collectible characters. The Happy Hooligan planter pictured in Plate 13 is a particularly beautiful example of an unusual character item. The pastel finish is so subtle and the design so pleasing that a collector could proudly display it even on the dining room table. (It might be one of the very few comic toy items that a non-collecting wife or husband might allow in the non-collectible part of the house!)

The giant Happy Hooligan match or pencil holder is also a most impressive item. Pictured in Plate 14, its 8½″ height makes it one of the tallest bisque items among all comic character collectibles!

The cast-iron mechanical toy example of Dirks' Katzenjammer Kids can often be found with a skyrocket price tag at toy shows. Were the toy not mechanical, it would be most desirable because it is early and it is associated with a comic character. Add to it the fact that there is the mechanical action of the boy being spanked and it is clear to see why this cast-iron creation is a hot item among collectors.

Billy DeBeck's "Barney Google and Spark Plug" characters first appeared in 1922 and made the little bugged-eyed fellow and his delapidated horse a favorite among comic strip readers. The toys today among collectors still reflect that popularity.

Continuing on with the collectible characters of the early 20th century, Andy Gump rolled his way into the hearts of young Americans with the Arcade 748 roadster. This heavy iron toy is virtually indestructible and is heavy enough to be used as a doorstop, although few collectors would ever dare use it as one. A red version of the car was pictured in Volume I, and here an orange version of the same car has been pictured in Plate 22.

Another interesting "Gumps" item is the ginger ale bottle pictured in Plate 23. Collectors often search for such unusual oddities when trying to "round out" their collections. The strong appeal that this bottle has for collectors is its amber color and its very brightly colored paper label.

George McManus brought the feuding domestic couple into the limelight with his "Bringing Up Father" comic strip which featured the famous characters Maggie and Jiggs. Although some character collectibles from this strip date from the late teens, most Maggie and Jiggs character items date from the 1920's and the 1930's.

Plate 25 shows one of the many character books published by Cupples and Leon devoted to Maggie and Jiggs. The hilarious antics of the proverbial hen-pecked husband who was continually being sought by his domineering wife who wielded a wild rolling pin is today a popular subject for collecting. The Jiggs character chalk figure pictured in Plate 26 appears to be a companion figure to the Maggie pictured in Volume I.

The "Bringing Up Father On Broadway" sheet music book of an actual Broadway production featuring the McManus characters is another interesting collectible. In this particular piece of character memorabilia, Maggie is pictured only as a looming and threatening shadow in the background at a window as Jiggs meets in a restaurant with another lady.

The two rarest Maggie and Jiggs items pictured in this volume are the Maggie and Jiggs wind-up and the Schoenhut dolls pictured in Plates 28 and 30, respectively. The tin wind-up toy in Plate 28 features an unusual spring-middle design that allows the tin figures to swing their arms and bob back and forth towards one another when it is wound. The tin lithography on the characters is extremely detailed and attractive and this alone would make it very valuable to collectors. The fact that the toy also works with unusual action makes it all the more desirable.

The wood composition jointed Maggie and Jiggs dolls pictured in Plate 30 are also prized items among comic character collectors. The dolls were fashioned in a design that makes them surprisingly loyal to McManus's own artwork. Even their eyes look as if they just stepped off of the newspaper comics page. Notice also the cute salt and pepper set pictured in Plate 29 which was designed as Maggie and Jiggs. Although this little set is less rare than the other two toys, it is certainly a fine example of quality character toy design.

The nodder figures pictured in Plates 31 and 33 are only the tip of the iceberg in regard to what is available to be collected. Nodders are generally described as all those comic character bisque figures which were designed with a movable head attached to the body of the piece by an elastic string. Many collectors falsely assume that these toys are supposed to have some very special action because of their name. On the contrary, most collectors hope to find their bisque nodder character pieces with the elastic very much intact and tight. In more worn examples where the elastic string is loose, the character heads "flop" rather than nod and, subsequently, agile collectors have to balance the bisque heads onto the bodies as they are placed for display. This author has yet to see any of these pieces that actually nodded with any pleasant sort of motion. A note to the wise: when purchasing these bisque pieces, look for elastic strings which will hold the head onto the body firmly. If they wobble or "nod" too much, your figure may be permanently headless before he or she gets to your collectible shelf.

Most of these nodders were manufactured in Germany and have identifiable markings on the back. Each comic character is normally marked with his name on the back and the average size ranges from three to four inches in height. The bisque styling of most pieces is very true to the comic strip form of the characters and the painting detail and quality is normally very fine.

Pat Sullivan's famous cat, Felix, has a double appeal to today's collectors. In contact with collectors at shows and markets, this author has found that Felix not only strongly appeals to general comic character enthusiasts and Disneyana collectors who sometimes collect him for his look-alike association with Mickey Mouse; he also is very popular with cat collectors. Cat collectors? Yes, believe it or not, there are those who spend their free moments in an endless search for the world's most unique cat memorabilia, and who is a more prime target than the world's most famous comic character cat?

Although Pat Sullivan always gets the name credit for the Felix copyright and his name is usually on just about every Felix the Cat piece from the 1920's to the present, the actual animator of Felix was a man by the name of Otto Messmer. Since Messmer worked for Sullivan's studio, it was Sullivan's name associated with the Felix copyright and not Messmer's. A similar phenomenon took place in the Walt Disney Studios when Walt, famous for his creation of Mickey Mouse, employed a man by the name of Ub Iwerks who actually did most of Mickey's early design and animation.

Felix toys run the gamut of forms and span half a century. The original, earliest Felix dates from 1920 and his toys have continued to be produced since that time up to the present. The Felix dolls manufactured by Chad Valley of England are particularly rare and valued by today's collectors. And collectors should be forewarned that there are many Felix knock-off items which look identical to the cat but have no identification or copyright information. There's nothing wrong with collecting such items; the collector should simply realize that they were not copyrighted by Sullivan's studio or sanctioned in any way by the creators. A fine, early Felix piece pictured in this volume is the lithographed wind-up toy pictured in Plate 39. The high quality china pictured in Plate 40 depicts the very earliest style of Felix, and the game board in Plate 41 shows a much more recent-vintage Felix collectible.

The Happyfats characters are an odd lot that even the most knowledgeable of character collectors have never heard of. Very serious and advanced toy collectors who contributed many of the toys in this book had to fill this author in on their background. The Happyfats were characters based upon the drawings of Kate Jordan around 1914. Many persons believe that Jordan's effort was aimed at drawing from the tremendous popularity of Rose O'Neill's Kewpie characters. Granted,

the little Happyfats characters pictured in this book (Plates 43 and 44) do bear a family resemblance to Rose O'Neill's characters. But these odd little characters appear to be all-human and lack the wings always attached to the back of Kewpies. And as Plates 43 and 44 attest, where a Happyfat toy was manufactured had a lot to do with the way a Happyfat looked. The German tea set and the German bisque figures pictured in Plate 43 bear a strong similarity of design and resemblance. But the figures distributed by George Borgfeldt in the teens and probably of Japanese origin look very little like their German counterparts. (See Plate 44). Such a striking difference remains a puzzlement to collectors.

Yet another comic character here introduced into our "Hall of Fame" is the funny little fellow, Scrappy. Scrappy dates from the decade of the 1930's and had his origin in several Charles Mintz children's film productions which were released by Columbia Pictures. His little life was short-lived in the movies, and by 1939, America had seen the last of anything new dealing with Scrappy. He's one of the characters, then, that is quite easy to date chronologically. Find a Scrappy toy today, and it's a sure bet that it's from the 1930's. That was his one and only decade with any claim to fame. Plates 46 through 48 show some popular Scrappy collectibles.

Uncle Wiggily is a character newly introduced to Volume II. His origins are most traceable as a storybook character, and the 1939 Platt and Munk paperback book versions of Uncle Wiggily titles are probably the most popular. Among all of toy collecting, this humanized rabbit is a very minor character. Some very advanced toy collectors choose to overlook him altogether for his relatively meaningless historical significance. Although he is indeed not as recognizable or even desirable among collectors as a Bugs Bunny or Mickey Mouse, he does have two very nice tin wind-ups that stand as a lasting tribute to his little spot in children's literature history. The Uncle Wiggily's Crazy Car is the rare one (Plate 49) that seems extremely hard to come by. Our example here was borrowed from a dealer's table at a toy show. The color and detail of lithography are very attractive on this toy, and it's easy to see why it is desirable. Readers should not confuse this "crazy car" with the less rare Uncle Wiggily Crazy Car pictured in Plate 51. Both toys have a real value among today's collectors. It is a simple law of supply and demand that makes the rare one in Plate 49 so much more valuable.

As we reach well into the 1920's and the 1930's and head toward the decade of World War II, character toy production begins to move into full swing. A host of characters appear and flourish during this twenty-five year span. The "Gasoline Alley" comic strip created by Frank King introduced Uncle Walt and Skeezix to the world in 1921. The comic strip was most unique because King aged his characters as the strip grew older. Therefore, if a collector finds examples of toys where Skeezix appears as a very young boy, it's probably a 1920's example. By the 1940's Skeezix had grown old enough to become a soldier.

Betty Boop moves into the limelight in this volume as a popularly-collected character. During the 1970's and on to the present, she has enjoyed a sort of nostalgic revival, especially in regard to character merchandising. Her Boop-A-Doop style and her short little skirts made her nothing short of a phenomenon in the 1930's. Produced into cartoons by Max Fleischer and originally created by Grim Natwick, Betty was one of several memorable movie cartoon characters who made their claims to fame in the 1930's.

The Betty Boop string dispenser shown in Plate 58 is a most unusual item, although its date is uncertain as there are no markings. The boxed Bimbo musical figures pictured in Plate 59 give evidence to the popularity of the saucy sweetheart's little dog.

In Plate 60 we see Betty Boop as a subject of commercial art at its best. This box of Betty Boop Candy is covered with plenty of Boop-esque art designs. One of the rarest of the Betty Boop toys pictured is the celluloid wind-up nodding toy pictured in Plate 63. This rare toy utilizes an elastic wind-up mechanism which is attached to Betty's head and allows it to sway side to side with good animation. Since the toy was produced completely in celluloid with the exception of the tin base and metal mechanism, it is doubtful that too many of these little treasures survived. Celluloid was one of the most brittle, yet fragile substances that man ever created, and although many of the 1930's toys that were produced in it are wonderous, they are also frighteningly breakable and combustible.

The Betty Boop and Bimbo wall pocket shown in Plate 62 is one example of the many different character designs in which these were produced. There are Mickey Mouse and Little Orphan Annie versions of these which are often hung as sets by advanced collectors. This particular version of the wall pocket has a bright lusterware finish.

Carl Anderson's "Henry" first appeared in 1932 and he remains today a unique challenge for serious collectors. There were simply not that many fine Henry toys produced, so good toy examples of him are hard to find. Two rare and fine examples of Henry toys are pictured here in Plates 71 and 72. Like the Betty Boop wind-up nodder figure, both of these toys are manufactured in celluloid. The two-character figure in Plate 71 features a pull-along wind-up mechanism that allows the smaller figure to coast along behind Henry. The Henry and the Swan toy in Plate 72 is equally unique and rare. In this case, there is no hardware inside the swan. The cart under Henry where the mechanism is located does all of the drive work for the toy. Two of Anderson's Henry character books are pictured in Plate 73.

The decades of the 1940's and the 1950's continued to bring new characters to the collectibles scene. Joe Palooka toys are pictured in Plates 79 through 81 and are based upon characters from the strip by the same name.

Blondie and Dagwood Bumstead, creations by Chic Young who appeared as early as 1930, really seemed to swing into popularity during the 1940's and 1950's. Blondie's Jalopy pictured with its original box in Plate 82 is the rarest of the two "Blondie" toys pictured in this chapter. This toy is one of the largest of all tin wind-ups and it features vividly bright color lithography. The 1949 vintage Blondie doll stroller is also a large comic strip character toy. It pictures characters from Blondie on all sides of the seat and would have been a perfect doll accessory for any young girl.

Al Capp's "Li'l Abner and Daisy Mae" comic strip characters and Ernie Bushmiller's "Nancy" creations help to round out our "Hall of Fame." Although these characters are more recent in-popularity and creation than most presented in this chapter, character collectors still enthusiastically search for their toys to help complete their sampling of American comic character history.

Where comic character collecting in general is headed remains a mystery to most. Toy shows are still packed on opening dates with long lines of anxious, energetic buyers. Some come to specialize and purchase toys of only one particular character. Others seek out rare additions to their already massive collections. Still other collectors seek to uniquely sample ALL that is and was good among American comic character toys from 1900 until about 1960.

The 1960's bring us to an interesting discussion point in regard to character toy collecting. Obviously, comic strips have been loved, read and enjoyed by readers since their inception after the turn of the century. Likewise, character toys have been associated with these strips as long as the comics themselves have been around. Today's toy collector is usually a very knowledgeable person who seeks to broaden his knowledge base by reading up on character history whenever he's not out pounding the pavement or plodding the turf at antique shows.

If this hypothetical toy collector of the 1980's is very knowledgeable, then he should be able to recognize a similarity of both styles and prices of toys from each decade. For the sake of simplicity, this author likes to classify character toys based upon the comic strips into four basic categories.

The first category is what I like to call simply "Early." This includes those characters who made their appearance before or just at the turn of the century in 1900. It extends two decades through the 1900's and the teens and stops at 1920. In this category of collecting, we meet up with collectors of the Brownies, the Yellow Kid, Buster Brown, Barney Google and Spark Plug and many others. The thing that these toys have in common is that they were all inspired by the newspaper comics format and their appearance in the print medium. Some of the toys from this grouping are very rare today, and these are the toys that collectibles speculators are attempting to buy up for investments.

The second category of collecting I call "Pre-War." Many of the toys in this time period (1920 to 1940) were also inspired by the newspaper comic characters of the day, but a larger number who had won great fame as cartoon movie subjects also made their appearance in these two decades. Here we find Betty Boop, Scrappy, all of the early Disney characters (discussed in later chapters), Felix the Cat and many others. With the advent of motion picture technology, Americans, both young and old, went crazy over the movies - and that included motion picture cartoons. The movies made possible a toy production mass-marketing craze unlike anything that had been seen before. It was one thing to buy toys based upon your favorite newspaper comic strip characters. It was quite another matter to beg for toys in the likeness of your favorite movie characters! So the toys of the period from 1920 to 1940 have a very definite influence straight out of the Hollywood cartoon studios.

Another quality shared by many toys of this prime era of toy production is the fact that American toy manufacturing was probably at its best during these two decades and the workmanship, unique design, coloring and creative action of toys was unsurpassed. Tin lithographed toys in the United States really picked up in popularity during this time period, and generally, they got better. This period is also the one most generally accepted as the golden age of tin wind-up toys produced both in America and abroad. The collector who sets his sights only on this period could certainly do worse. The toys of the 1920's and 1930's will have a lasting value because of both their historical significance and their quality of workmanship. However, this also seems to be the period of greatest activity among collectors. Just like the teddy bear craze of the late 1970's and early 1980's when collectors who had collected old "Ted" over the years saw prices double in under five years, toys from the 1920's and 1930's seem to have currently caught the eye of serious collectors.

It seems hard to believe, but rare character tin wind-ups from the 1930's can often be double or triple the price of a fine cast iron toy that pre-dates them by 50 years! This "hang-up" with the 1930's as THE period for comic character toy collecting seems to have emerged during the mid-1970's and it has yet to let up.

One nationally known dealer in rare comic character toys (some of which are pictured in this book) wanted to go on the record as stating that the astronomical bubble of out-of-sight comic character toy prices has burst. He actually reported as much as a 20% drop in real values of rare toys that most collectors would assume could escalate forever. Whether or not this respected dealer's observation is a general one or just an isolated example of price fluctuations is uncertain. Regardless of this instance, serious collectors who collect only for the investment of it should be very knowledgeable and keep up with the most current trends in both pricing and collecting.

The third category of character toy collecting that I like to use as a rule of thumb is the "Post-War toys." Unlike their 1920's and 1930's counterparts, the toys in this category can still be found on the bargain tables in second-hand shops and at yard sales. The post-war toys are more influenced by all of the mass media together rather than from one direction of mass marketing. In the 1940's, collectors are offered the possibility of collecting toys inspired by radio, comic books, newspaper comic strips and even the movies.

With the end of the war, the baby boom and America's return to health, wealth and prosperity, the toys of the post-war period are unmatched by any other time period in regard to number, ingenuity and selection. What they lacked in quality and sturdiness, they made up for it with their unique and special appeal.

The post-war period of toy collecting ends, according to this author (and granted, quite arbitrarily) around 1961. By this time, the wonderful Japanese toys manufactured by the Line Mar Company (foreign subsidiary of Louis Marx) start to disappear. Also missing from the toy shelves as we move on into the decade of the 1960's are toys made of lithographed tin and hard rubber. Of course, occasional examples of these appeared, but not like they had before. The 1960's was the decade of futuristic design and that horrid word hardly uttered by any serious toy collector – PLASTIC!

Plastic was cheaper, more durable, lasting, non-biodegradable and highly workable. It was the answer to all toy makers' dreams and the nightmare of those of us who relish our nostalgic link with the past. Our own personal plastic prejudices aside, that substance is here to stay and this brings us to our final period in toy collecting – "the Plastic era."

From the early 1960's until the present, plastic and other man-made substances such as vinyl, latex, high impact resistant polystyrenes and just about every other concoction that could be poured into a toy mold have been used. There is certainly no need to debate whether or not today's character toys for the future "Hall of Fame" will ever have a value. Of course they will, for as soon as they are not around anymore - the children of the previous generation will want them!

But collectors of toys in the most recent period should consider one thought as a word of warning: Are today's knowledgeable parents still throwing out all of junior's toys with the wild abandon that they once did? When the toy collecting phenomenon of today started to build steam during the 1960's and 1970's, how many parents totally missed out on hearing at least one or two news notes about what toys from the previous generation were worth? In this author's opinion, very few. It is my belief that a substantial number of toys from the 1960's and the 1970's ARE being saved and the simple laws of supply and demand will hold prices down when they start to flood the collector's marketplace. (If they have not already started.)

So, it is up to the collector to decide which collecting time period will be his choice. There are bargains to be had in all periods, but today's collector of character toys, in particular, should decide where the focus must be. Snoopy is not pictured in this book, but he is a character of the 1960's and most certainly he is collectible because of the national popularity of the comic strip he is associated with. But what about all the toys associated with the cavalcade of Saturday morning cartoons that have flooded the toy shelves over the past three decades? Are all of these toys collectible?

The answer is certainly a qualified "yes." All of these toys are collectible, if we subscribe to the definition associated with the word as something that "can be collected." People can certainly collect flower pots, back scrubbers, vacuum cleaners and old dish pans if they have a desire, but the real question is "Will my collection have an increased value some day?" I don't think there has been a tremendous increase in the value of dish pans over the past fifty years.

Likewise, if a collector wants to build value into a character toy collection, he must be sensitive to what the public will still consider valuable decades into the future. That's not an easy job by any means, but an informed collector today can use his own knowledge of the past trends in toy collecting as his best advice.

"The Character Collectible Hall of Fame" has introduced readers to a broad sampling of what is actually out there in the marketplace to be collected. The toys pictured within this chapter span nearly 70 years! The intention, here, has been to give the novice collector some off-the-cuff advice about embarking upon a hobby in character toy collecting while at the same time whetting the appetite of already advanced collectors. The following chapters of the book will deal with toys associated with specialty areas.

PLATE 1
PALMER COX'S BROWNIES CHARACTER
BOWLING SET features beautifully colorful
stand-up musical Brownie character figures,
each measuring 12″ tall. All of the figures are
marked "copyright 1892 by Palmer Cox".

PLATE 2
BROWNIE CHARACTER WOODEN PUZZLE
copyright by Palmer Cox is an unusual early
character jigsaw puzzle. It measures 12″ x 10″
and is copyright 1891.

PLATE 3
Item A: THE BROWNIES AT HOME by Palmer
Cox published by the Century Company of New
York and copyright 1893. The book features a
colorful cover and black and white illustrations
inside. 144 pages.
Item B: ANOTHER BROWNIE BOOK by
Palmer Cox also circa 1890.

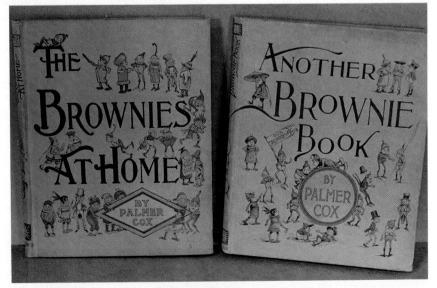

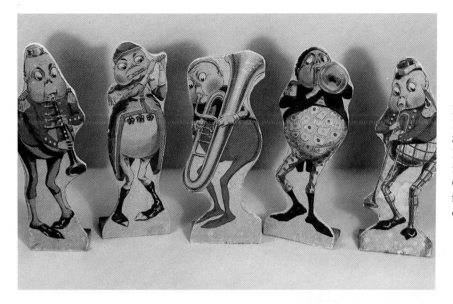

PLATE 4
BROWNIE WOODEN BAND FIGURES are all
8″ tall and based upon the Brownies created by
Palmer Cox. Although these figures bear no
identification markings, they are undoubtedly
Cox's creations. The first Brownie's books date
from the late 1880's, but this set is probably circa 1900.

PLATE 5
EASTMAN BROWNIE CAMERA No. 2A. This
camera was manufactured by the Eastman
Kodak Company of Rochester, New York and
its measurements are 5″ x 6″ x 3″. The box for
this camera is decorated with Brownie
characters inspired by those created by Palmer
Cox. The measurements of the colorful box are
5″ x 6″ x 3½″.

PLATE 6
BROWNIE CHARACTER PLATE, obviously
inspired by Palmer Cox's characters but with
no visible markings, measures 7″ in diameter.
The plate probably dates from the first decade
of the 1900's. It has a gold rim and various
Brownie characters.

PLATE 7
BUSTER BROWN AND TIGE cast-iron pull toy. This rare and early comic character toy is circa 1900 and measures 7½″ x 5½″. Since Richard Outcault's Buster Brown was one of the earliest comic characters just after the Yellow Kid, this is a prized toy among collectors. Buster Brown is being pulled by his dog, Tige, in this toy's design.

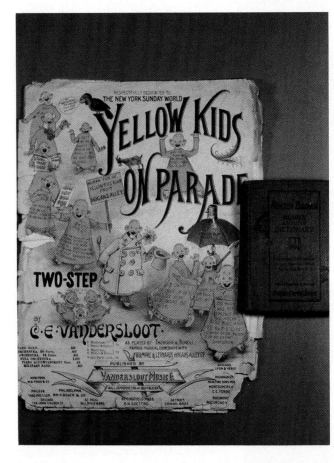

PLATE 8
Item A: "YELLOW KIDS ON PARADE" SHEET MUSIC, circa 1900 published by the Vandersloot Music Company. This is a very rare and early comic character sheet music piece. Based upon Hogan's Alley character by Outcault.
Item B: BUSTER BROWN DICTIONARY distributed by Buster-Brown shoes (later version of Outcault's original character pictured on cover.)

PLATE 9
BUSTER BROWN LOOK-ALIKE CHARACTER VALENTINE. Although this 8″ card bears no identification markings, there's no mistaking who he's supposed to be. When the nutshell is raised on this mechanical card, his eyes roll. Circa 1900.

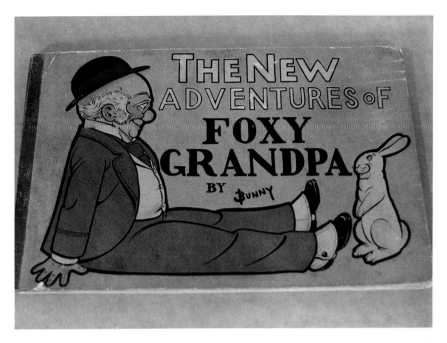

PLATE 10
THE NEW ADVENTURES OF FOXY GRAND-PA by Bunny early comic character book published in 1903 by the Frederick A. Stokes Company Publishers and also copyright 1902 by William Randolf Hearst. This book is in unusually fine condition for such an old copy. It measures 10″ x 15″.

PLATE 11
Item A: FOXY GRANDPA DOLL has a movable mouth like a ventriloquist's dummy but measures only 12″ tall. Composition construction.
Item B: FOXY GRANDMA, companion doll to Item A. Both dolls are circa 1900.

PLATE 12
TOONERVILLE TROLLEY CANDY CONTAINER measuring 3″ tall is a rare find among collectors today. Candy containers are increasing as an enthusiastically sought-after specialty. This particular Toonerville design is one of the more unusual character-inspired candy containers.

PLATE 13
HAPPY HOOLIGAN CHARACTER PLANT-
ER. This Majolica planter is circa early 1900
and is a colorful glazed ceramic piece. The
planter measures 5″ x 5″ and bears a wonderful likeness to the comic character Happy
Hooligan.

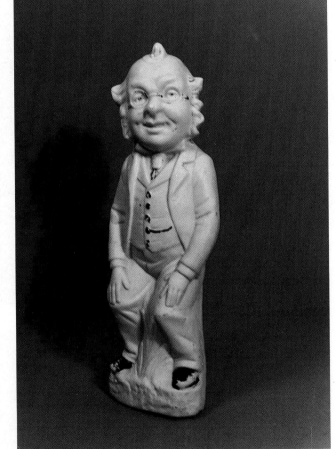

PLATE 14
Item A: HAPPY HOOLIGAN PENCIL HOLDER is a giant 8½″ tall
and manufactured in bisque. This is a rare piece shown with 98%
of its original paint. It is a "super" early character collectible.
Item B: KAYO CHARACTER WOOD-JOINTED DOLL, companion
character to Moon Mullins, it stands 4″ tall.

PLATE 15
FOXY GRANDPA BISQUE COMIC FIGURE is an excellent likeness
of the early comic character and it stands a full 8″ tall. Although this
example is missing most of its original paint, it is still a most impressive piece because of its large size.

PLATE 16
THE KATZENJAMMER KIDS CAST-IRON
PULL TOY manufactured by the Dent Company
and dating from 1906. The action of this toy
as it rolls along is that the baby on his mother's
knee gets spanked. This is a fine condition example of an extremely hard-to-find toy. Cast-iron
toys themselves are rare in good condition; a
cast-iron comic character toy in bright, working order is a real rarity.

PLATE 17
THE KATZENJAMMER KIDS HOCKEY
GAME licensed by King Features Syndicate and
circa 1950. This is a very fine, mint condition
example of a colorful boxed game. Although the
Katzenjammer Kids comic strip dates originally from the very early part of the 20th century,
the popularity of the strip and its characters has
been lasting. The box measures 7" x 10".

PLATE 18
THE KATZENJAMMER KIDS IN 4 PICTURE
PUZZLES published by the Saalfield Publishing
Company of Akron, Ohio. The puzzles are
copyright 1933 by King Features Syndicate. The
box and puzzles measure 8" x 10". Three puzzle styles are shown and the fourth puzzle included in the set is the same design as the box
lid. Price in guide is for complete set of all four
puzzles in the box.

PLATE 19
SPARK PLUG RACER PULL TOY bears no identifiable production markings but is copyright 1924 by King Features Syndicate. Construction is of vividly colorful lithographed tin with Spark Plug being ridden by a jockey. Spark Plug and Barney Google items are prized additions to comic character collections.

PLATE 20
ALL THE FUNNY FOLKS hardcover book featuring early renditions of a host of famous comic characters. Published by The World Today of New York, the book is copyright 1926 by King Features Syndicate. It features 110 full-color pages and has a wonderful cover picturing Barney Google and Spark Plug racing with Felix, Buttercup and Spare Ribs, Tillie the Toiler, Maggie and Jiggs and many other characters' faces around the cover. 9½″ x 12″.

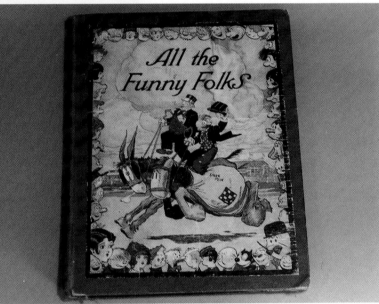

PLATE 21
BARNEY GOOGLE AND HIS FAITHFUL NAG SPARK PLUG soft-cover book by Billy DeBeck. The book was published by Cupples and Leon Company of New York and is copyright 1923. The cover shows Barney roller skating as he hangs on to Spark Plug's tail. The book contains 48 pages and measures 10″ x 10″.

PLATE 22
ANDY GUMP CAR manufactured by Arcade.
The car measures 7″ long and is constructed
of cast iron. Original paint is shown. (Another
color/paint version is shown in Vol. 1 of
Character Toys.)

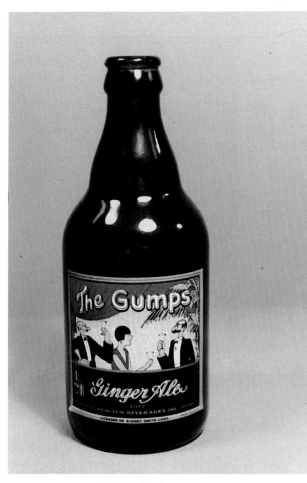

PLATE 23
THE GUMPS GINGER ALE was bottled by Bon-Ton Beverages, Inc.
of Chicago, Illinois. Marked on the bottle label is this information:
"Licensee of Sidney Smith Corp." The bottle is a dark amber color
and stands 7″ tall. The label pictures the Gumps toasting glasses of
ginger ale.

PLATE 24
MUTT SHELL GASOLINE CARDBOARD STAND-UP FIGURE
measures 23¼″ tall. This unusual display piece is marked "copyright
1934 by H.C. Fisher." The colorful figure is printed on both sides.

PLATE 25
BRINGING UP FATHER - SEVENTH SERIES
character book published by Cupples and Leon
Publishers. Collectors often try to obtain a complete collection of all books dealing with one
subject. ''Seventh Series'' means that at least
six other comic collections of this character were
published.

PLATE 26
JIGGS CHARACTER CHALK FIGURE is painted with nice detail and
measures 8″ tall. This is the companion figure to the Maggie chalk
figure shown in Vol. I of *Character Toys*.

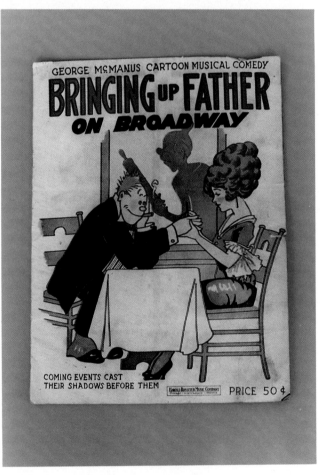

PLATE 27
''BRINGING UP FATHER ON BROADWAY'' SHEET MUSIC,
published by the Harold Rossiter Music Company, circa 1920. The
cover shows Jiggs courting a new flame with the shadow of Maggie
with the rolling pin lurking behind.

PLATE 28
MAGGIE AND JIGGS WIND-UP manufactured in brightly colored lithographed tin featuring a unique and funny arm-swinging action of the characters when the whole mechanism is wound. The toy is marked "c. George McManus, International Features Syndicate". This wind-up is 7″ long and the Jiggs figure is 5½″ tall. It is a highly sought comic character wind-up.

PLATE 29
MAGGIE AND JIGGS SALT AND PEPPER SET. This unusual set features two brightly glazed character figures, each 2½″ tall and a small tray. Both figures have cork stoppers in the base and are marked "Made in Japan". The holder is 3″ tall and marked the same. This is an uncommon, attractive set.

PLATE 30
Item A: JIGGS CHARACTER DOLL with fully jointed and posable legs and arms constructed of wood and composition by Schoenhut. Jiggs is 8″ tall.
Item B: MAGGIE CHARACTER DOLL with jointed legs and arms also manufactured by Schoenhut. This pair of dolls is highly prized among comic character collectors because of the distinct likeness in design to the original comic strip characters. Maggie is 10″ tall.

PLATE 31
COMIC CHARACTER BISQUE NODDER FIGURES made in Germany. Each of these figures has an elastic string that runs from its base through its body and allows the attached head to swivel or "nod".
Item A: CHING CHOW character bisque, marked "Germany" on reverse.
Item B: LORD PLUSH-BOTTOM character bisque stands 3½" tall.
Item C: MR. BAILEY, THE BOSS character bisque, 3½" tall.

PLATE 32
Item A: TILLIE THE TOILER book by Russ Westover and published by Cupples and Leon, 1930. The book measures 10" x 10". It is copyright King Features Syndicate.
Item B: MUTT AND JEFF Book 7. This book was also published by Cupples and Leon, but it is dated copyright 1920 by Bud Fisher. It measures 10" x 10".

PLATE 33
GERMAN BISQUE CHARACTER NODDERS based upon comic strip characters.
Item A: ANDY GUMP character bisque marked "Andy Gump" on his back. 4" tall.
Item B: RACHEL comic character bisque, 3½" tall, marked "RACHEL" and "GERMANY" on her back.
Item C: CHESTER GUMP bisque character figure marked "CHESTER GUMP" and "GERMANY" stands 2½" tall.

PLATE 34
Item A: FELIX THE CAT CELLULOID
FIGURE, approximately 6″ tall showing Felix
playing a violin. Probably circa 1920.
Item B: MICKY CHARACTER MOUSE TOY
often referred to as a very early Walt Disney's
Mickey Mouse toy. The misspelling may have
been to avoid coyright infringement, but this is
generally not considered a Disney character collectible. He does look like a mouse—just not
Mickey Mouse. The wood figure is 4½″ tall.

PLATE 35
Item A: "FELIX THE CAT" SHEET MUSIC, copyright 1928 by the
Sam Fox Company featuring Pat Sullivan's character on the front.
Item B: FELIX THE CAT JOINTED DOLL by Chad Valley showing
Felix with a snarl and a hump on his back. The doll is 12″ tall.

PLATE 36
Item A: FELIX THE CAT CHAD VALLEY DOLL, 8″ tall showing
Felix with a cat-like grin.
Item B: FELIX THE CAT CELLULOID FIGURE, 2″ tall.

PLATE 37
ITEM A: MAGGIE AND JIGGS VALENTINE measuring 8″ total length, marked only "USA".
Item B: FELIX THE CAT CHARACTER VALENTINE probably patterned after the popular wood-jointed toy of the 1920's and dating from the same. It is 5″ tall and marked "Germany".

PLATE 38
FELIX THE CAT JOINTED-ARM CHALK FIGURE stands 14″ tall and is an excellent likeness of the famous, sassy cat.

PLATE 39
FELIX THE CAT tin wind-up toy. No visible identification markings, but the toy is possibly by Nifty and of German origin. It measures 7″ tall and is probably one of the earliest Felix tin wind-up toys.

PLATE 40
FELIX THE CAT THREE-PIECE PLACE SET-
TING EARLY CHINA CHARACTER SET
marked "c. Pat Sullivan" and "Bennett-
Baltimore". The plate measures 6″ in diameter,
the saucer is 5″ in diameter, and the cup is 2″
high.

PLATE 41
FELIX THE CAT CHARACTER GAME
BOARD copyright 1960 by Felix the Cat Productions. The board pictures Felix and many
of his later associates.

PLATE 42
*Item A: BRINGING UP FATHER - SECOND
SERIES* SOFT-COVER BOOK by George
McManus. This book was published by Cupples
and Leon and is copyright 1919 by International
Features Service.
*Item B: BRINGING UP FATHER - THIRD
SERIES* BOOK by George McManus is also
copyright 1919. Both books measure 10″
square.

PLATE 43
Item A: HAPPYFATS CHARACTER TEA
SERVICE including the teapot and one cup and
saucer. The teapot is 6″ tall, the cup 2″, and
the saucer 4″ in diameter. The cups in the set
are marked "RUDOLSTADT - Made in Germany."
Item B: HAPPYFATS BOY BISQUE DOLL,
probably German, stands 4″ tall.
Item C: HAPPYFATS GIRL BISQUE DOLL,
mate to boy bisque, also stands 4″ tall.

PLATE 44
Item A: HAPPYFATS GIRL BISQUE FIGURE
with jointed arms; distributed by the George
Borgfeldt Company and dating from the 1910's.
These figures were all based upon drawings
made by Kate Jordan and were probably a spin-
off of Rose O'Neill's popularity with her
Kewpies. The doll is 3½″ tall.
Item B: HAPPYFATS BOY BISQUE DOLL also
with jointed bisque arms, 3½″ tall.

PLATE 45
REG'LAR FELLERS PENCIL BOX based upon
the Gene Byrnes comic strip measures 6″ x 11″
and was manufactured by the Eagle Pencil Company. It is decorated with characters from the
strip on the front and the back.

PLATE 46
BOX LID for Scrappy christmas tree light set
shown in Plate 47.

PLATE 47
SCRAPPY CHARACTER LIGHTS manufactured by Mazda and copyright by Columbia Pictures. As with many of the early character
Christmas light sets, the boxes were more
beautiful than the lamps themselves. The box
for these measures 6″ x 16″ and the light globes
with applied decals measure 1½″ tall.

PLATE 48
SCRAPPY CHARACTER BANKS based upon
the movie character created by Charles Mintz
in the 1930's. The banks are identical in size
and style to the Disney banks popular in the
1930's.
Item A: SCRAPPY BANK, beige, 3″ x 3½″ tall.
Item B: SCRAPPY BANK, green, 3″ x 3½″ tall.

PLATE 49
UNCLE WIGGILY TIN WIND-UP CAR marked as "Uncle Wiggily's Crazy Car" is a rare item among character toy collectors. Several versions of Uncle Wiggily cars were made over the years, and collectors should not confuse this one with the car pictured in Plate 51. This toy measures 8½" long and is copyright Howard R. Garis as marked on the front of the car.

PLATE 50
Item A: UNCLE WIGGILY AND THE RED SPOTS child's book published by the Platt & Munk Company, Inc. and copyright 1939 with illustrations by George Carlson.
Item B: UNCLE WIGGILY AND THE PEPPERMINT book published by Platt & Munk and copyright 1939.

PLATE 51
UNCLE WIGGILY CRAZY CAR copyright 1935 by Howard R. Garis. This brightly lithographed tin wind-up car features characters from "Uncle Wiggily" stories around its body and on the wheels. The car measures 7" long and 7" tall.

PLATE 52
PETER RABBIT LIONEL HANDCAR
manufactured by the Lionel Corporation of New
York. This was a companion toy to the Mickey
& Minnie, Donald & Pluto, and Santa & Mickey
Handcards produced by the company in the
1930's, although Peter Rabbit was not a Disney
character. This model bears no copyright information, although it was probably a take-off of
Beatrix Potter's famous character. The toy
measures 9″ x 6½″.

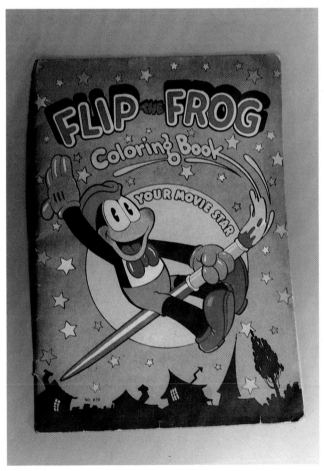

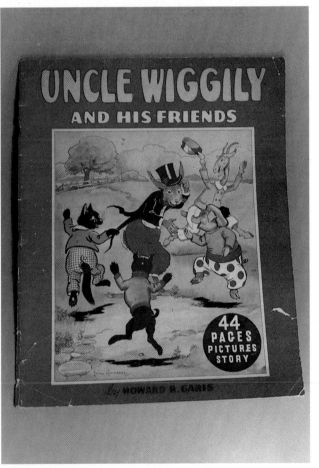

PLATE 53
FLIP THE FROG COLORING BOOK published by the Saalfield
Publishing Company of Akron, Ohio and copyright 1937 by Celebrity Products, Inc. Flip was created by Ub Iwerks, one of Disney's earliest
animators and artists.

PLATE 54
UNCLE WIGGILY AND HIS FRIENDS 44 Pages Picture Book by
Howard R. Garis measures 10″ x 13″ and was published by Whit-
man. The book is copyright 1933.

PLATE 55
GASOLINE ALLEY - A GAME OF WALT AND SKEEZIX AND THEIR FRIENDS is a beautifully graphic boxed card game manufactured by the Milton Bradley Company and copyright 1927. Pictured at the right of the box and below it are only a few examples of the attractive cards contained within this game set. The box measures 7½" x 5½".

PLATE 56
Item A: MOON MULLINS BISQUE COMIC CHARACTER FIGURE (left) measuring 4" tall.
Item B: UNCLE WILLY BISQUE CHARACTER FIGURE, 4" tall (right).

PLATE 57
SNUFFY SMITH AND HIS BROTHER SALT & PEPPER SHAKERS are each 4" tall and made of glazed ceramic. Each of the figures is marked "JAPAN" on the bottom. An uncommon set among character collectibles.

PLATE 58
BETTY BOOP STRING HOLDER. The date of this chalk piece is uncertain. Its age appears to be that of Betty Boop's original years of popularity, so it is probably circa 1920 or 1930. It is an interesting piece measuring approximately 10″ across with a chalk-like paint finish over the plaster.

PLATE 59
BIMBO BISQUE FIGURES from the Betty Boop comic series. These are shown in their original box and were made in Japan. Each figure measures 4″ tall. Note the three different musical instruments that each figure "plays".

PLATE 60
BETTY BOOP CANDY BARS ORIGINAL BOX is marked with copyright by Fleisher Studios, Inc. The candy bars were manufactured by the Schutter Johnson Candy Corporation of Brooklyn, New York. The box dimensions are 8″ x 11½″. Such a box would make an excellent background for smaller Betty Boop collectibles placed in front.

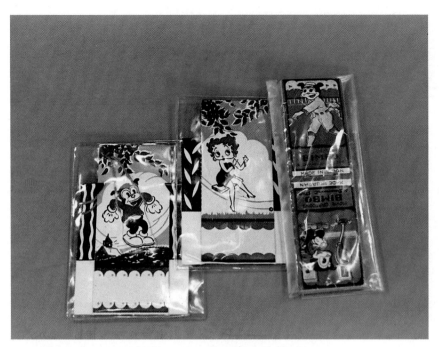

PLATE 61
Item A: BETTY BOOP & BIMBO BRIDGE CARDS are each 3½″ long with a place for bridge scores on reverse.
Item B: BIMBO CHARACTER FLIP CARDS packaged in a set of two, they measure 4¼″ long total.

PLATE 62
BETTY BOOP WALL POCKET made of ceramic lusterware stands 5½″ tall and shows Betty Boop and Bimbo on the front. Wall pockets were especially popular during the 1930's. On the back is marked "Betty Boop Des. and Copr. by Fleischer Studios Made in Japan".

PLATE 63
BETTY BOOP CELLULOID MEHANICAL WIND-UP TOY measures 7″ tall with a metal base. When the base is wound, the head mechanism will nod. Celluloid toys such as this one are rare since they were very fragile. Made in Japan.

PLATE 64
MOON MULLINS AND KAYO CHARACTER SOAP FIGURES are shown in original undecorated box. The character figure of Moon Mullins stands 4″ tall and the Kayo figure is 2½″ tall. These character soaps have an unusual amount of paint on them. Usually, character soap figures have only high-light paint. These figures are painted much like their bisque figure counterparts.

PLATE 65
Item A: BIMBO CHARACTER from the Betty Boop Fleischer Studios, is the smaller version, only 2½″ tall. The character was made in Japan and is bisque.
Item B: KOKO THE CLOWN CHARACTER BISQUE FIGURE measures 3″ tall and has the Fleischer Studios copyright on the reverse.
Item C: BETTY BOOP CHARACTER BISQUE FIGURE was made in Japan as marked on the reverse and is also marked Fleischer Studios. The figure is 3″ tall.

PLATE 66
Item A: BIMBO CHARACTER JAPANESE FIGURE is 4″ tall, circa 1930.
Item B: BETTY BOOP CHARACTER BISQUE FIGURE was made in Japan, circa 1930 and is 4″ tall.
Item C: BIMBO CHARACTER playing the French horn is made of bisque and stands 4″ tall. Each piece has the character name and the Fleischer Studio copyright on the back.

PLATE 67
BUTTERCUP CHARACTER COMPOSITION
FIGURE. This unusual and rare toy features the
baby character from the ''Buttercup & Spare
Ribs'' comic strip. The baby features a jump-
ing crawling action with spring bound legs and
it is entirely composition.

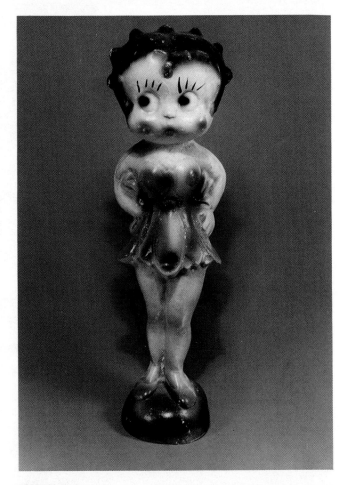

PLATE 68
JEFF COMIC STRIP FIGURE molded in plaster/chalk from the comic strip Mutt and Jeff. This may have been a carnival piece, but its
circa date is unknown. The figure measures 6″ in height.

PLATE 69
BETTY BOOP CHALK CARNIVAL PRIZE FIGURE measures approximately 14″ tall and is made entirely of chalk. No identification
markings are visible, as many of these mass-produced figures were
manufactured without paying royalties to the character licensees.

PLATE 70
BUTTERCUP & SPARE RIBS CHARACTER
WIND-UP TOY manufactured by Nifty and
marked "copyright 1925 by Jimmy Murphy".
The toy measures 7½" x 5½" and features two
hard-to-find comic characters depicted on the
toy. Comic character enthusiasts are always trying to add this one to their collections because
the characters here were so rarely produced in
toys.

PLATE 71
HENRY CELLULOID WIND-UP CHARACTER
TOY measures 6½" tall and features a fun two-
figure design. The wind-up mechanism in the
base of the Henry figure pulls along his tiny
friend (Snubby) whose base then coasts along.
The toy is of Japanese origin.

PLATE 72
HENRY AND THE SWAN CELLULOID
WIND-UP toy is a rare comic character find.
This toy measures 3½" tall to top of Henry and
9" long from back of toy to tip of the swan's
nose. Made in Japan.

PLATE 73
Item A: CARL ANDERSON'S HENRY PAINT BOOK published by the Whitman Publishing Company of Racine, Wisconsin and copyright 1951 by King Features.
Item B: HENRY GOES TO A PARTY BOOK published by Wonder Books and copyright 1955 by King Features Syndicate.

PLATE 74
HENRY DOLL is made of vinyl and was manufactured by Irwin. He is marked "MADE IN USA" and has a copyright marking on his back. The toy has a built-in squeaker and stands 8½" tall.

PLATE 75
DENNY DIMWIT COMPOSITION CHARACTER WOBBLER or sometimes referred to as a nodder because his head and body both wobble and nod. Copyright 1948 from the Wee Winnie Winkle strip. The toy is 11" tall and is often confused with and mislabeled as Disney's Dopey.

PLATE 76
Item A: YOUR FAVORITE FUNNIES JIGSAW PUZZLE, circa 1940 has a standard package box which would have included one of the several characters featured on the cover in a puzzle inside.
Item B: HAVE FUN WITH FUNNIES JIGSAW PUZZLE featuring characters such as Felix the Cat, The Little King, Tillie the Toiler, and Henry on the box lid. One of the characters shown would be represented in a puzzle inside.

PLATE 77
MOVIE KOMICS CHARACTER MOVIE VIEWER shown with original box has illustrations of Dick Tracy, Uncle Walt, Skeezix, Little Orphan Annie and Moon Mullins on the box lid. The viewer itself is lithographed tin with the movie character reel loaded inside. Probably circa 1940 from the apparent age of Skeezix in the illustrations.

PLATE 78
LITTLE LULU BOOK published by the Rand McNally Company of Chicago and copyright 1936. The book bears an additional copyright by the Curtis Publishing Company. It measures 6¼″ square.

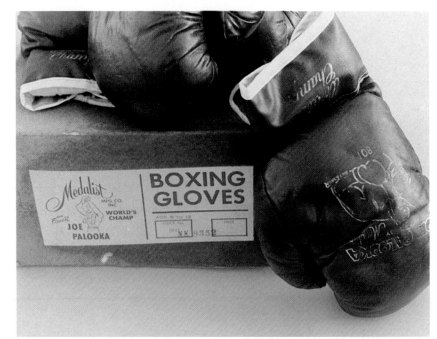

PLATE 79
JOE PALOOKA CHARACTER BOXING
GLOVES manufactured by the Medalist
Manufacturing Company, Inc. with Joe's likeness
screened on each of the four gloves packaged
in the set.

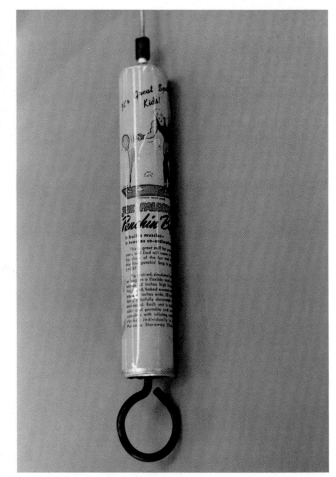

PLATE 80
HUMPHREY DOLL "THE HAPPY BLACKSMITH, JOE
PALOOKA'S PAL" character doll manufactured by Ideal Toy and
Novelty and circa 1940. This unusual doll has a brittle plastic face
and a stuffed body. He wears a button on his lapel that says "Hi!
Humphrey-Good Luck".

PLATE 81
JOE PALOOKA BICYCLE PUMP measures 9" in length and features
a colorful picture of Joe at his punching bag lithographed on the side.
This character toy had a most practical use and it came in a handy
size. It was manufactured by the Dodgers Sporting Goods Corporation of New York.

PLATE 82
BLONDIE'S JALOPY WIND-UP CAR shown with its original box in the background. This toy was manufactured by the Louis Marx Company and is copyright 1935 by King Features Syndicate. Daisy and Cookie Bumstead are pictured on one side and Blondie is on the other. Dagwood and Alexander "ride" with their moving action heads sticking out of the roof. This very colorful car features fun wind-up action and a very sturdy tin construction.

PLATE 83
BLONDIE CHARACTER STROLLER, copyright 1949 by King Features Syndicate. This pink and blue doll stroller measures 16½" to top of the seat and 27" to the top of the handle. It was manufactured by Nassau Products Corporation of Freeport, New York.

PLATE 84
COMIC CHARACTER OILCLOTH DOLLS:
Item A: UNCLE WALT DOLL 25" tall.
Item B: SKEEZIX DOLL, 12" tall.
Item C: CAMEL, 10" tall
Item D: PAL THE DOG, 6½" tall.

PLATE 85
TWO COMIC CHARACTER BOOKS featuring
Li'l Abner and Joe Palooka:
Item A: LI'L ABNER AND THE RATFIELDS
Item B: JOE PALOOKA'S GREAT
ADVENTURE
Both books are circa 1940 to 1950.

PLATE 86
LI'L ABNER COMIC STRIP CHARACTER DOLLS:
Item A: PAPPY YOKUM DOLL by Barry Toys and copyright Al Capp
Dogpatch Family.
Item B: MAMMY YOKUM DOLL by Barry Toys. Both dolls measure
14″ to 15″ in height.

PLATE 87
LI'L ABNER AND DAISY MAE COLORING BOOK, circa 1950 and
published by the Saalfield Publishing Company. There are no color
pictures inside as the children were to do these, but the covers are
extremely colorful.

PLATE 88
CHARACTER ITEMS FROM DOWN 'ROUND DOGPATCH:
Item A: LI'L ABNER AND DAISY MAE CHARACTER BOOKENDS, made of plaster and measure 9″ and 6″ tall respectively. The paint colors are bright, but the figures are not highly glazed.
Item B: LI'L ABNER CAN O' COINS with the words "It Sho Pays to Save" on the side, is copyright 1953 UFS (United Features Syndicate) and pictures various Dogpatch strip characters around it. The bank holds $53.00 in quarters.

PLATE 89
SHMOOS SALT AND PEPPER SHAKERS from the Al Capp Li'l Abner comic strip. These were made in Japan and they measure 4″ and 3½″ tall. The Shmoos were a later addition to the Al Capp strip.

PLATE 90
LI'L ABNER AND DAISY MAE PICTO-PUZZLES manufactured by the Plastrix Company of Brooklyn, New York. Each bag measures 11″ long and the puzzles are copyright United Features Syndicate. These are packaged in their store-display format on the picture card display.

PLATE 91
NANCY AND SLUGGO GAME manufactured by the Milton Bradley Company of Springfield, Massachusetts and copyright 1944 by United Features Syndicate. The game box measures 9″ x 15″ wide. Note the unusual graphic design of the concentric perspective pictures of the game box being held by Nancy on the cover. This is a very desirable piece of paper memorabilia for characters in a strip that was seldom manufactured in toys.

PLATE 92
COMIC CHARACTER CHRISTMAS CARDS, circa 1950. These cards came as a boxed set, but are often sold individually at today's flea markets.
All cards measure 4¼″ x 5½″.
Item A: LITTLE ORPHAN ANNIE CARD.
Item B: DICK TRACY CARD.
Item C: GASOLINE ALLEY CARD showing a grown-up Skeezix with his children.

PLATE 93
COMIC CHARACTER CHRISTMAS CARDS from the 1950's. All of the cards measure 4¼″ x 5½″.
Item A: NANCY AND SLUGGO CARD picturing them under the mistletoe.
Item B: COMIC HERO CARD.
Item C: THE GUMPS picturing Andy and Chester singing Christmas carols on the front.

Radio and Television Character Collectibles

Marconi gets most of the credit for its invention, but Little Orphan Annie is probably more of a household word associated with radio. We all either have vivid recollections of actually gathering around the old tall console radio with our families, or we can imagine what it must have been like from seeing it in the movies if we belong to a younger generation. Whatever is the case, there is probably nothing more worthy of being a Norman Rockwell scene or the all-American pastime of decades gone by than that of a family gathered in the living room to listen to an evening of radio.

The golden age of radio (the 1920's through the 1940's) was an interesting time. The movies of the day were great ones and everybody would flock to the theatres when they had the money and the chance, but it was radio that transmitted nightly into homes across America and became a very personal form of entertainment. Mom might knit, Dad might smoke his pipe and doze off occasionally, and the kids could probably be found on the floor messing with their Radio Orphan Annie decoders or coloring books. It was the great day of radio. It was a time when Americans used their mind's eye to visualize action rather than relying on a picture tube to beam the action before them. Some say that life was simpler then and it should have stayed that way. Others disagree and claim that radio was only a stepping stone for television transmission and the age of television was our true destiny. Whatever opinion the reader agrees with, it cannot be denied that radio programs brought about the production of some great toys.

Ask anyone on the street to name an old-time radio character and the random sample would probably produce more responses for Little Orphan Annie than any other character. Her radio show was a memorable one, but the premiums given away to push sales for Ovaltine thrust her into the limelight. The tie-in of tangible toys to play with in front

of the radio while your "favorite" program "Radio Orphan Annie" aired was sheer marketing genius.

Orphan Annie remains as a central character of the 1930's because by that time, she was popular both on the radio and in Harold Gray's popular comic strip. Along with her dog, Sandy, the twosome became as famous on the airwaves as they were in the comics. As a result of this, two distinct areas of Annie marketing emerged. One set of Annie collectibles belong to the family of items that were marketed, sold or given away as premiums for the Orphan Annie radio program. Another family of Little Orphan Annie collectibles is all of the comic character memorabilia associated with Harold Gray's successful comic strip characters. Both sets of collectibles are synonymous with the 1930's and the 1940's.

Nearly all of the collectibles devoted to Little Orphan Annie that appear in this chapter are part of one single private collection. The private collector began collecting Annie memorabilia because she was first a fan of the Broadway musical version of "Annie." The collection represents a blending of the dual categories of Orphan Annie on radio collectibles and Harold Gray's comic strip character collectibles.

Generally, serious collectors of radio premiums shy away from collecting any comic strip collectibles associated with Little Orphan Annie. They place their special emphasis on the things that could be purchased by mail order which were associated with the original run of Radio Orphan Annie. Collectors of this category are always on the lookout for decoder pins, secret decoder manuals, fan memorabilia such as cards and photographs and generally anything associated with the radio show. Although such items were manufactured because of the radio program which aired on NBC's Red Network during the 1930's, many of these radio items were printed or manufactured with the comic strip likeness of Little Orphan Annie as a part of their design.

Comic character fans who collect Little Orphan Annie toys are not as selective as fans of radio premiums. They normally collect samples of Annie toys and collectibles inspired by both the comic strip and the radio program. The greatest bulk of Annie character merchandise falls into the category of comic strip toys. There are far more examples of comic strip Orphan Annie and Sandy toys available to today's collector than there are radio-inspired items.

Bisque character figures were especially popular during the 1930's. Those who focus only on comic character bisque figures can find a lot of Orphan Annie styles in the marketplace to choose from. Plate 94 pictures a variety of sizes and styles that all appeared in the 1930's. Collectors of bisque figures, or those who plan to collect, should heed a word of warning. Don't buy figures with substantial amounts of paint missing. Bisque figures without paint appear flat and unfinished and they are simply not pleasant to look at. Collectors should demand at least 90% of the original paint in their bisque examples since anything less usually looks as if it was just dug up out of the sandbox.

Because Little Orphan Annie is most often remembered as both a radio character and a comic strip character, she has been placed into this chapter for discussion. The toys associated with her radio programs and her comic strip popularity are colorful, neatly designed and interesting collectibles today. The Little Orphan Annie sheet music displayed in Plate 95 is a rare and unusual early Annie piece. Note the early appearance of Sandy and Annie's polka dot dress, both trademarks of the early years of the characters.

Oilcloth was a durable material used to fashion dolls in the 1920's and 1930's. It was water and soil resistant and as a result, the toys were very easily cleaned up, plus they were quite sturdy. The oilcloth dolls pictured in Plates 98 and 99 are 50 to 60 years old, yet they still have a much nicer appearance than if they had been manufactured in regular cotton or velvet. As a result of their durability, oilcloth character dolls such as these Annie and Sandy examples make fine, permanent examples for collections. They are virtually maintenance-free and they will probably last for centuries. The oilcloth doll pictured in Plate 98 is one of the very earliest Little Orphan Annie dolls ever manufactured and she is circa 1926.

The Trixytoy Company of Boston, Massachusetts, manufactured some interesting wooden Annie toys during the 1930's. Although these toys do not match up to the exquisite design of some of the early Fisher-Price Disney character models, their simplicity and total wood look make them desirable. Fisher-Price toys of the 1930's utilized lithographed paper glued upon die-cut wood to achieve their design effects. The Orphan Annie Trixytoys used no lithograph paper. The coloring and effects are painted directly onto the wood producing a design of simplicity with a sturdy look. (See Plate 97.)

The Little Orphan Annie doll pictured in Plate 101 along with its original box is a particularly striking composition piece. The "Pop-Up Little Orphan Annie" shown in Plates 103 and 104 is also worthy of special note. In addition, the paper

tablecloth which was probably used for birthday parties (as shown in Plate 109) is a very rare collectible today since most of these were pitched into the garbage after a party. Finally, two styles of glazed ceramic wall pockets depicting Little Orphan Annie are shown in Plates 102 and 122.

The J. Pressman Company of New York was responsible for some of the very finest of all boxed play sets marketed with Annie designs on them. The knitting outfit pictured in Plates 110 and 111 show how colorful such toys could be. The same fine company also manufactured the embroidery set pictured in Plate 115 showing Annie leading a circus parade of wild animals in front of the circus tents. This particular set is extremely colorful and graphic, while its very large size makes it even more collectible. Yet another knitting outfit manufactured by the same company, J. Pressman, is pictured in Plate 116.

Over the years, Little Orphan Annie has had her ups and downs in regard to public recognition and popularity. The Hoosier poet from Indiana, James Whitcomb Riley, once wrote a poem describing an odd little girl who comes to stay with a family and spreads the fear that goblins may hoist little unsuspecting kids off in the middle of the night. Now, this isn't exactly the thing that Harold Gray had in mind for his character, and it is not exactly clear whether or not the fellow Midwesterner and artist had Riley's poem in mind when the character was created. Regardless of her exact origin, the strong-willed, independent and street-wise little moppet of a girl, Annie, has at the very least held her own over the years. She seems to have slipped in popularity during the late 1950's and on through the 1960's as a collectible character. Much of that slip was due to the disappearance of Annie from both radio programming and the comics scene. It wasn't until her great re-emergence in the late 1970's inspired by the popular Broadway musical, *Annie*, that collectors really began to sit up once again and take notice. To the faithful few who stuck by the little curly-haired carrot-top through the good times and the bad, the "Annie-craze" inspired by the Broadway musical and later the motion picture must have seemed a bit untimely. Why did it take half a century for her story to make it into a full-fledged Broadway and motion picture production? She was certainly not insignificant in her day. In fact, her worldly wisdom and candid commentary made her strip quite readable and occasionally controversial in respect to political overtones, not unlike the approach of Garry Trudeau's wonderful and timely comic strip "Doonesbury" of today.

One of this author's favorite Annie items pictured in this chapter is shown in Plate 126, the "Little Orphan Annie Bubble Set" manufactured by J. Pressman. The beautiful box lid is reminiscent of Art Deco styling and the colors are fantastic. A rare celluloid doll is pictured next to this set in Plate 125. Probably a Japanese piece, she has jointed arms and a paper belt which reads "Little Orphan Annie." Still another fine collectible set pictured here appears in Plate 124. The Little Orphan Annie boxed bisque character set contains figures of Annie, Daddy Warbucks, Sandy and an old upright, console radio. It is a most expressive set.

From Little Orphan Annie, we move ahead to another very popular radio character, Charlie McCarthy. Over the years, Charlie has had his imitators, but his general popularity has never been matched. As a radio celebrity, Charlie McCarthy and his more lowly counterpart, Mortimer Snerd are media oddities. How could ventriloquist dolls become so popular when their actual gag is visual and radio is a non-visual medium? That is a puzzlement. In fact, most fans of Charlie and Edgar Bergen would agree that they were at their very best on radio, and somewhat out-of-place on television. Radio was their own special medium, and Bergen's own voice characterizations for Charlie and Mortimer were at their best when we were allowed to supply all the visual cues.

In a recent high school English class, I played a vintage recording of a heated debate between Charlie McCarthy and W.C. Fields. Most of the sixteen-year-olds had heard of Fields, but few had any knowledge of Edgar Bergen or Charlie McCarthy. We were doing an assignment on the impact of radio, both past and present, and by the time the students had listened to the blistering arguments between Fields and McCarthy firing mutual one-liner insults as fast as bullets at one another, the radio pair had won them over. Radio was a powerful medium in the 1940's and the 1950's. When presented at its best, it still is today.

Many radio premium collectors often seek to add Charlie McCarthy and Mortimer Snerd items to their collections. There are also character toy specialists who today seek only toys and memorabilia associated with Bergen's puppets. Even general toy collectors are eager to jump on the Charlie McCarthy bandwagon because he was such a unique figure in entertainment history.

Interesting Charlie McCarthy and Mortimer Snerd toys pictured in this chapter are the Mortimer Snerd Crazy Car by Marx shown in Plate 133. The two composition dolls manufactured by Effanbee and shown in Plates 134 and 135 are equally impressive. A fine selection of Charlie McCarthy and Edgar Bergen items produced in paper are shown in Plates 136 through 149. The talking cards pictured in Plate 140 are worthy of special note. When a fingernail was pulled along the narrow strips which accompanied each card, it acutally "talked" like a crude phonograph recording.

The Edgar Bergen Charlie McCarthy Dancer manufactured by the Marks Brothers Company of Boston is worthy of mention for two reasons. First, the toy is an interesting character variation on a much earlier folk-type toy design. Secondly, the manufacturing company, Marks Brothers, is the very same company that manufactured many of the most beautiful of all Disney character paper items.

The large advertising page in Plate 153 shows Charlie's association with Chase and Sandborn as both a sponsor and as an agent for his premiums. This ad is promoting the Charlie McCarthy paper puppet which is pictured in Volume I of *Character Toys*.

From Charlie McCarthy and Mortimer, we move from radio to television and from two puppets to four others. Howdy Doody and his "Doodyville" gang are often remembered as some of the most famous characters of early television. The toys associated with Bob Smith's fun characters are extremely colorful and playfully innocent. In Plates 155 and 156, we meet the toy versions of the original marionettes: Howdy Doody, Mr. Bluster, Princess Summer-Fall Winter-Spring and Clarabell the Clown. These wooden folks represent the very best in televi-

sion for children when the medium itself was very young. The colors on the Howdy Doody toys are so wonderful that it is an absolute shame that kids couldn't see the actual show in such brilliant color. But since the televisions were black and white then, at least the toys let the buying public know what Howdy Doody was really supposed to look like "in person."

One of the rarest of all the marionettes associated with the televison show is the Flub-a-Dub puppet shown in Plate 160. More common, but just as wonderful in design and color, is the "Howdy Doody Color TV Time Picture Set" shown in Plate 169. Single framed copies of these prints are not very rare, but a packaged, complete set as shown is becoming increasingly hard to find. The Howdy Doody character watch in its mint condition is also worthy of special attention.

After Howdy Doody and all of his gang were turned into not only a successful television program but also a marketing bonanza, it was clear to see that more programming for children and more toy marketing geared toward the television audience were soon to follow. Consider the representation of early shows found in Plates 184 through 186 with the Phil Silvers Sgt. Bilko Game, the J. Fred Muggs chimp pulltoy inspired by the little fellow who appeared on NBC's young "Today" show, and the "Groucho Goggles" inspired by "You Bet Your Life."

Obviously, the Warner Brothers Studio cartoon characters did their best to upstage their Disney rivals over the years, and in association with this, they were marketed into a limited number of toy designs over the years. Their appearance in the toy market never matched anything near that of the Disney characters, yet their items are very collectible today, especially among general comic character collectors who want to collect every character. The three Plates of Warner Brothers toys (187, 188 and 189) include a pair of Elmer Fudd and Porky Pig metal planters, a Bugs Bunny character alarm clock and a boxed Porky Pig wrist watch. These toys appear in this chapter because their characters have become standardly accepted as television stars and not "movie stars" (since Warner Brothers cartoons seldom, if ever, appear in movie theaters anymore.)

Finally, our chapter section on early television collectibles is rounded out by such interesting collectibles as a "Leave It to Beaver Treasure Board" (Plate 190), a "Jackie Gleason Bus Driver's Outfit" (Plate 191), Shari Lewis' "Lamb Chop" puppet doll (Plate 194) and an "I Dream of Jeannie Barbara Eden Doll" (Plate 195) which brings us up to 1966. There are also examples of Fred Flintstone and his friends in Plates 196 and 197, and our chapter concludes with the popular "Munsters" from the mid-1960's.

The toys associated with both radio and television represent a unique sample of how our society entertains itself. The characters represented in this chapter were all created to entertain us, and in turn, their character-inspired toys were also designed to give us long hours of playful joy. Radio and television are simply two stepping stones in the technology of our popular culture. Who knows what future medium lies out there just waiting to burst forth with its own array of new and entertaining characters? Whatever is invented or what form that new medium will take, there is no doubt that it will eventually inspire even more wonderful toys.

PLATE 94
AN ASSORTMENT OF LITTLE ORPHAN AN-
NIE BISQUE CHARACTER FIGURES, circa
1930
Item A: SANDY, 2″ tall.
Item B: ANNIE nodder, 3½″ tall.
Item C: DADDY WARBUCKS nodder, 3½″ tall.
Item D: TINY ANNIE, 1½″.
Item E: TINY SANDY, 1″.
Item F: ANNIE, 3″ tall.
Item G: SANDY 2½″ tall.

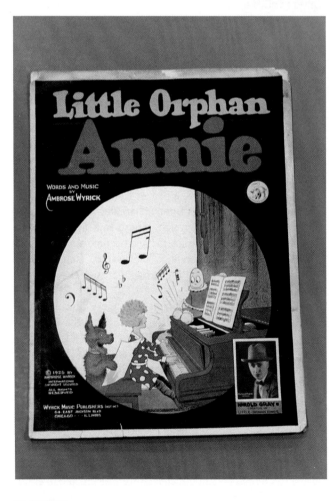

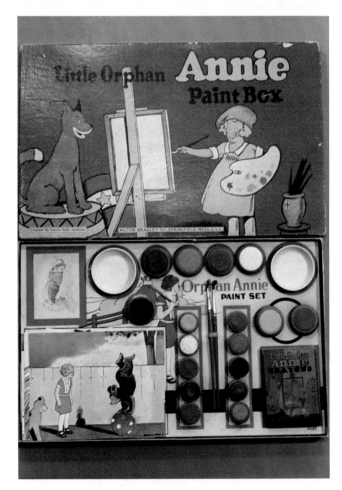

PLATE 95
"LITTLE ORPHAN ANNIE", WORDS AND MUSIC by Ambrose
Wyrick Music Publishers. The piece is copyright 1925 and shows a
wonderful early illustration of Annie playing the piano while Sandy
sings. Note Annie's early polka-dot dress and Sandy's early, sharper
features.

PLATE 96
LITTLE ORPHAN ANNIE PAINT BOX was manufactured by the
Milton Bradley Company of Springfield, Massachusetts and was licensed by Famous Artists Syndicate. This beautiful set still has its paints
intact and untouched along with the two paint mixing pots, original
brushes, paint cards and crayons.

PLATE 97
LITTLE ORPHAN ANNIE WOODEN PULL
TOY manufactured by the Trixytoy Company
of Boston, Massachusetts. This particular toy
is 13″ long and is designed as Sandy pulling Annie along on the front of a cart. All designs are
painted directly onto the surface of the wood.
Note the hole on the front of Sandy's leg which
was used to attach the pull-string.

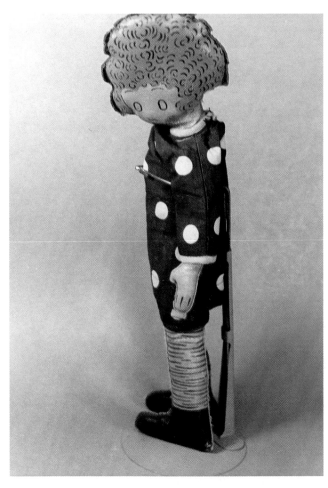

PLATE 98
VERY EARLY OILCLOTH LITTLE ORPHAN ANNIE DOLL, circa
1926 depicting Annie when she appeared in her color comic strip wearing a blue and white polka-dot dress. The doll is all oilcloth construction with a cotton dress. It measures 15″ tall.

PLATE 99
LITTLE ORPHAN ANNIE AND SANDY DOLLS:
Item A: SANDY oilcloth stuffed doll, 8″ tall, circa 1930.
Item B: ORPHAN ANNIE oilcloth stuffed doll, 13″ tall, 1930's.

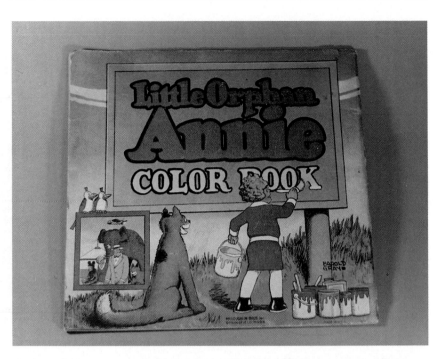

PLATE 100
LITTLE ORPHAN ANNIE COLOR BOOK featuring a very colorful picture of Annie painting the title of the book onto a billboard with Sandy watching. It was published by McLoughlin Brothers of Springfield, Massachusetts and is circa 1930.

PLATE 101
LITTLE ORPHAN ANNIE DOLL shown with its original box. This cute little doll measures 10″ tall and features jointed arms and movable legs. The construction is all of wood composition. The original box has attractive color lithography on all sides. Circa 1930.

PLATE 102
ORPHAN ANNIE WALL POCKET marked on reverse "Licensed by Famous Artists Syndicate · Made In Japan". This piece is 6″ tall and has an opening in the back where it can be mounted on a nail on the wall. Glazed ceramic and lusterware finish make this a nice display piece.

PLATE 103
THE POP-UP LITTLE ORPHAN ANNIE AND JUMBO THE CIRCUS ELEPHANT" published by Pleasure Books of Chicago, Illinois and dated copyright 1935 by Famous Aritsts Syndicate. The book contains a story text and three "pop-up" pictures. It measures 8" x 9".

PLATE 104
THE POP-UP LITTLE ORPHAN ANNIE BOOK. An example picture showing Annie, Sandy, and Jumbo the elephant in a circus scene. Three such scenes are featured in the pop-up book.

PLATE 105
Item A: ORPHAN ANNIE WATCH—A GUARANTEED AMERICAN WATCH FOR THE AMERICAN GIRL, manufactured by the New Haven Clock and Watch Company. This example shows both the original box and the watch on its display card inside. The box measures 7" long and the watch face is 1" long.
Item B: LITTLE ORPHAN ANNIE RUMMY CARDS published by Whitman and copyright 1935 by Harold Gray. The cards contained within are all full-color.

PLATE 106
LITTLE ORPHAN ANNIE ALL WOODEN
CHARACTER PULL TOYS were manufactured
by Trixytoy of Boston, Massachusetts. Usually
pull toys of the 1930's to the 1940's featured
designs printed onto paper labels which were
then glued to the wood. These toys, however,
have designs painted directly on the wood.
Item A: YELLOW TOY is 8" long
Item B: WHITE TOY is 8" long.

PLATE 107
LITTLE ORPHAN ANNIE WHITE AND
YELLOW LUSTERWARE TEA SET PIECES.
Although not a complete set, these circa 1930
pieces show the style of the Orphan Annie line
of the ceramic lusterware set circa 1930 to the
1940's. Probably Japanese in manufacture, even
partial examples of these sets are hard to find.

PLATE 108
A VAST ASSORTMENT OF BIG LITTLE
BOOKS featuring Little Orphan Annie as the
subject. This is only a small sampling of the
many different Little Orphan Annie titles
published by Whitman into the Big Little Books
line. Collectors should demand high quality in
books such as these because damaged examples
are not rare and are almost worthless. All were
published from the late 1930's and on into the
1940's.

PLATE 109
A RARE 1930's LITTLE ORPHAN ANNIE
CHARACTER DECORATED TABLE CLOTH.
This tablecloth is large enough to cover a normal sized kitchen table and probably came with a party set. The cloth itself is paper and it is decorated all around with both facial pictures of many of the characters who appeared in the comic strip and also actual comic strip frames in black, red and orange.

PLATE 110
LITTLE ORPHAN ANNIE KNITTING OUTFIT
is circa 1930 and pictures Annie on the box lid sitting on a box and trying to pull a tangled mess of yarn from Sandy. This beautiful set was manufactured by the J. Pressman Company of New York City and the box measures 14″ x 11½″.

PLATE 111
INSIDE OF KNITTING OUTFIT shown in Plate 110 showing the cleverly designed Little Orphan Annie Knitting Spools formed in the figure of Annie. The bright and colorful set is marked as number 6850 and still contains all original yarn as well as two knitting needles. A fantastic set!

PLATE 112
LITTLE ORPHAN ANNIE TEA SET marked
as "Made In Germany" and circa 1930. The
teapot measures 4″ tall, the creamer is 2½″,
the cups are 3″ in diameter, the plates are 4½″
in diameter and the saucers are 4″ in diameter.
Each bears a colorful picture of Annie as its
decoration.

PLATE 113
Item A: ORPHAN ANNIE DOLL made of oilcloth, dressed in red dress
and marked "Orphan Annie by Harold Gray" on reverse, 10″ tall.
Item B: SANDY TIN TOY is 8″ long and features forward action when
the tail is pushed down. It is marked "SANDY" on the collar.

PLATE 114
LITTLE ORPHAN ANNIE CRAYON SET packaged in a sturdy red
leather-grained cardboard box. The set was manufactured by the
Milton Bradley Company of Springfield, Massachusetts in the 1930's
and it measures 10″ x 14″. The card at lower left in the box is an
example card, all the others had to be colored by the child who owned the set.

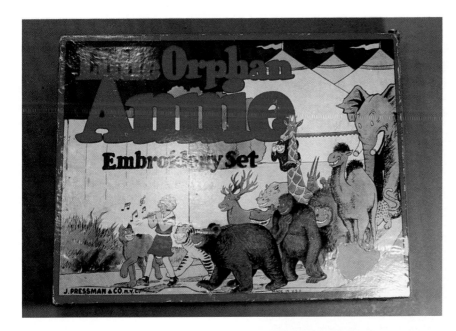

PLATE 115
LITTLE ORPHAN ANNIE EMBROIDERY SET
is circa 1930 and was manufactured by J.
Pressman and Company of New York City. This
gigantic box features a wonderful picture of Annie and Sandy leading a happy parade of circus
animals down the street. The embroidery set inside was unique and functional, but the collector's value of this toy is in its large size and colorful box. It is 18″ x 13½″.

PLATE 116
Item A: LITTLE ORPHAN ANNIE KNITTING
OUTFIT was manufactured by the J. Pressman
Company of New York City and is circa 1930.
This set was marked as number 6830.
Item B: LITTLE ORPHAN ANNIE MOC-
CASINS SHOEBOX which originally held a
child's pair of shoes. It was a character promo-
tion box for the Midwest Slipper Manufactur-
ing of Chicago, Illinois. The box measures 8″x
5½″x 3″.

PLATE 117
LITTLE ORPHAN ANNIE HANKIE HOLDER
in its original box. The holder is marked "Little Orphan Annie Hankies" and would have
been used to hold neatly folded hankies in a
child's purse or chest of drawers. Both the box
and the holder are colorfully decorated and they
measure 8″ square. Circa date is early 1930's.

PLATE 118
LITTLE ORPHAN ANNIE COLORING
BOOKS:
*Item A: LITTLE ORPHAN ANNIE CRAYON
AND COLORING BOOK* published by
McLoughlin Brothers of Springfield, Mass. It is
dated copyright 1933.
*Item B: LITTLE ORPHAN ANNIE COLORING
BOOK JUNIOR COMMANDOS* is published by
the Saafield Publishing Company and
copyrighted 1943. This large book measures
11½" x 15".

PLATE 119
ASSORTED ORPHAN ANNIE ITEMS:
Item A: BEAD GAME TOY, 1930's 3½" x 5".
Item B: EMBROIDERY SPOOL, 1930's. It is
4" long.
Item C: ORPHAN ANNIE DIME REGISTER
BANK, marked 1936, 3" tall.
Item D: NAPKIN RING marked "World's Fair
- 1933, Chicago Century of Progress 1833-1933
on reverse of ring.

PLATE 120
*Item A: THE STORY OF LITTLE ORPHAN
ANNIE, THE BIG BIG BOOK* published by
Whitman and dated 1934. This large book con-
tains 316 pages of stories and pictures.
*Item B: THE GREAT BIG LITTLE ORPHAN
ANNIE PAINT & CRAYON BOOK* was
published by McLoughlin Brothers and is dated
1935. The cover of this paint book is extreme-
ly colorful and measures 13" x 10".

PLATE 121
LITTLE ORPHAN ANNIE CRAYONS marked
"Famous Artists Syndicate" and manufactured
by the Milton Bradley Company. The box is
numbered 8442 and it measures 4" x 8". Made
in U.S.A., it is a very desirable set because of
the beautiful box lid.

PLATE 122
Item A: LITTLE ORPHAN ANNIE JACK SET
is mounted on a colorful card and marked
"Made in U.S.A." in lower right corner. The
card measures 5" x 7".
Item B: LITTLE ORPHAN ANNIE WALL
POCKET is glazed ceramic and measures 5" tall
with a lusterware finish. On the reverse is a
molded-in hole for wall mounting.

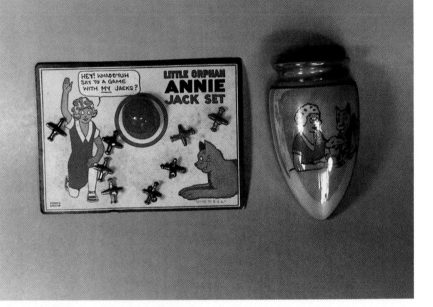

PLATE 123
THREE DIFFERENT ORPHAN ANNIE
CHARACTER WOOD FIGURES, each with
"Made in U.S.A." marked on feet. All are
jointed and strung together with elastic cord.
Item A: SANDY is 3½" tall.
Item B: ANNIE is 5" tall.
Item C: SANDY is 4" tall.
The Sandy figures are both marked "SANDY"
on their sides.

PLATE 124
LITTLE ORPHAN ANNIE BOXED BISQUE
CHARACTER SET. Made in Japan and
marked "copyright Famous Artists Syndicate".
This standard line of bisques contains the
figures of Annie, Daddy Warbucks, a 1930's
radio figure, and a small not-to-scale Sandy.
These Japanese bisques were produced in a host
of different comic characters but they are rare
today when found in the original box.

PLATE 125
LITTLE ORPHAN ANNIE CELLULOID DOLL manufactured in the
1930's, probably in Japan. This cute little doll is 7½″ tall and she
wears a paper belt with the name "LITTLE ORPHAN ANNIE" printed
on it. A rare celluloid piece!

PLATE 126
LITTLE ORPHAN ANNIE BUBBLE SET was manufactured by the
J. Pressman & Company of New York City in the 1930's and it
measures 8″ x 11″. The set is marked as number 025 and features
a spectacular picture of Annie and Sandy in a sky of bubbles with
a castle appearing in one of the bubbles.

PLATE 127
Item A: JUNIOR COMMANDOS LITTLE OR-PHAN ANNIE'S COLORING BOOK measures 11″ x 15″ and features a colorful scene of Annie painting a portrait of a beaming Sandy. Copyright date is 1943.
Item B: THE GREAT BIG LITTLE ORPHAN ANNIE PAINT & CRAYON BOOK, circa 1930 is unusual because of its brunette Annie pictured on the cover.

PLATE 128
AN ASSORTMENT OF LITTLE ORPHAN ANNIE HARDCOVER BOOKS published by Cupples and Leon Publishers during the 1930's. The books display colorful covers and contain text and black and white illustrations. The price listed in the price guide is the average value for books by this publisher in this style.

PLATE 129
LITTLE ORPHAN TRAVEL GAME manufactured by Milton Bradley Company is 13½″ x 7½″ and is marked as model number 4523. Beautiful color lithography is displayed on both the box lid and the game board.

PLATE 130
LITTLE ORPHAN ANNIE CHARACTER STOVE made of metal actually functions with a little hot-plate unit built right in! The stove has four gold finish and color tin plates attached to each of the compartment doors and the back of the burner unit. All doors actually open and the stove heats up very quickly when it is plugged in. Oddly enough, there was no switch on these models. The only way they could be controlled was by plugging or unplugging them. This aqua color is one of the more rare colors.

PLATE 131
LITTLE ORPHAN ANNIE LITTLE LIBRARY MINIATURE SET OF BOOKS circa 1930 and similar to the Mickey Mouse miniature library set. The set included six titles and a cardboard slip-cover case. The books feature colorful little covers and pulp-type story format inside. Individual copies of these are not so rare. Mint condition sets with the original case are very rare.

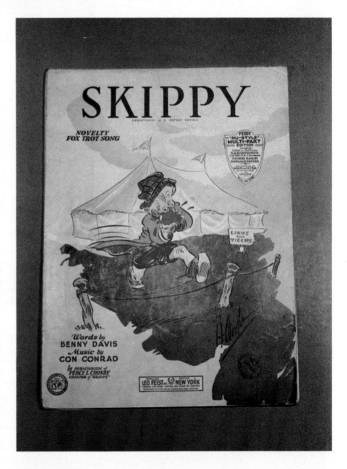

PLATE 132
"SKIPPY" CHARACTER SHEET MUSIC based upon the popular Percy Crosby character. Published by the Leo Feist Music Company, Inc. of New York.

PLATE 133
MORTIMER SNERD CRAZY CAR is one of the most desirable of all Edgar Bergen character wind-ups. The tin toy features very bright and colorful lithography and fun random action when it is wound. This is the companion toy to the Charlie McCarthy Benzine Buggy. The wind-up was manufactured by Louis Marx Toys of New York and is dated copyright 1939 by Edgar Bergen.

PLATE 134
CHARLIE McCARTHY DOLL by Effanbee shown in original black cut-away "tails." This very attractive doll moves its mouth when a string in the rear is pulled. He stands 17″ tall and still has the original "Charlie" button on his satin lapel.

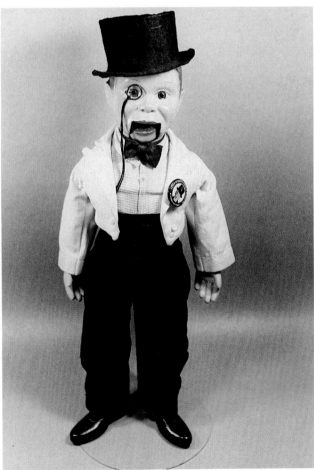

PLATE 135
CHARLIE McCARTHY DOLL dressed in original waistcoat COSTUME with movable mouth and original Charlie button on the lapel. This doll could also be used as a small ventriloquist's puppet by pulling the mouth string in the rear of its neck. Manufactured by Effanbee, 17″ tall. (Felt top hat shown is a replacement.)

PLATE 136
Item A: EDGAR BERGEN'S CHARLIE McCARTHY MEETS WALT DISNEY'S SNOW WHITE, circa 1930. A crossover collectible book desired by both Disneyana fans and McCarthy buffs alike. It features a very colorful cover.
Item B: TIME MAGAZINE featuring Bergen and Charlie McCarthy on the cover.

PLATE 137
LOBBY CARD picturing Charlie McCarthy and Edgar Bergen in the movie "Here We Go Again" released and copyright 1942 by R.K.O. Pictures. It measures the usual 11″ x 14″ dimensions of a standard lobby card. Lobby cards make excellent background displays and are valuable bits of movie memorabilia.

PLATE 138
EDGAR BERGEN'S CHARLIE McCARTHY PICTURE PUZZLES boxed as two in a set. The puzzles are circa 1938, and one is shown along with the original box in this photo plate. The colors are extremely vivid as was the case with most color lithography on paper during that period.

PLATE 139
Item A: EDGAR BERGEN'S CHARLIE McCARTHY GAME OF TOPPER Number 2903 and manufactured by Whitman Publishing Company. The game is marked "c. 1938 McCarthy, Inc." The box measures 9" long.
Item B: CHARLIE McCARTHY GLASS signed "Charlie McCarthy" measures 4½" tall.

PLATE 140
CHARLIE McCARTHY CHARACTER TALKING CARDS. Each of the cards pictured contains a "talking card" strip which when pulled along a fingernail allows the recipient to "hear" Charlie's voice.
Item A: RED CARD, left, is circa 1939.
Item B: GREY CARD, center, is circa 1938.
Item C: RED CARD, right, is circa 1939.

PLATE 141
Item A: CHARLIE McCARTHY MAZUMA PLAY MONEY is 9¼" long and was manufactured by Bronson Specialties.
Item B: MORTIMER SNERD TEETH mounted on a bright card measuring 3½" x 5½". The card is marked "c. Edgar Bergen, 1940."
Item C: CHARLIE McCARTHY VALENTINE bears no marking as far as copyright, but is an excellent likeness of him in western garb.

PLATE 142
Item A: A DAY WITH CHARLIE McCARTHY and EDGAR BERGEN CHARACTER BOOK which included instructions for the budding young ventriloquist, circa 1930.
Item B: CHARLIE McCARTHY COWBOY DETECTIVE COMIC BOOK published by Dell containing stories centered upon Charlie as the key character.

PLATE 143
Item A: CHARLIE McCARTHY SCRAP BOOK marked "Creator, Edgar Bergen" on cover and circa 1930. The scrap book features a dark green cover with the figures done in tan, white and black.
Item B: CHARLIE McCARTHY PROMOTIONAL POSTER for STAMS vitamins picturing Charlie at the NBC microphone, circa 1930.

PLATE 144
THREE MOVIE, LITERARY, AND FAN MAGAZINES featuring Charlie McCarthy on the cover.
Item A: LITERARY DIGEST circa 1938.
Item B: MOVIE LIFE MAGAZINE featuring Carol Lombard and Charlie on the cover.
Item C: 1000 NEW JOKES FAN BOOK marked as a "Winter Edition" circa 1930 featuring Charlie McCarthy on the cover.

PLATE 145
Item A: CHARLIE McCARTHY FAN CARD picturing Charlie and Mortimer is circa 1930 and was personalized with the child's name in the balloon of Mortimer's dialogue. It measures 8″ x 10″ and bears a printed-on Bergen autograph.
Item B: CHARLIE McCARTHY PREMIUM PUNCH-OUT FIGURE reads "Charlie McCarthy appearing with Edgar Bergen in Universal Pictures".

PLATE 146
Item A: CHARLIE MCCARTHY . . .SO HELP ME MR. BERGEN, book published by Grosset and Dunlap and coyright McCarthy, Inc. 1938. The book contains black and white drawings and photos.
Item B: CHARLIE McCARTHY IRON-ON STENCIL, circa 1930 was a premium for Nabisco and is very rare when found on original tissue, in unused condition.

PLATE 147
CHARLIE McCARTHY DANCER TOY manufactured by the Marks Brothers Company of Boston, Massachusetts. This is not to be confused with the Louis Marx Company which produced fine tin toys. This toy features fine action when the doll is held on the end of a stick and made to dance like a puppet on the wooden board. Circa 1930's.

PLATE 148
Item A: EDGAR BERGEN AND CHARLIE McCARTHY FLYING HATS GAME copyright 1938 by McCarthy, Inc. and manufactured by Whitman. The game worked along the same lines as a tiddley-winks game.
Item B: MORTIMER SNERD PUPPET manufactured by the Hollywood Magic Manufacturing Company. The original box is shown with this soft rubber puppet and the set included a "ventriloquial booklet" packed inside.

PLATE 149
Item A: EDGAR BERGEN ARCADE CARD, postcard size, marked "Edgar Bergen, N.B.C."
Item B: CHARLIE McCARTHY BIRTHDAY CARD, dated 1938 and published by White and Wyckoff Manufacturing Co.
Item C: CHARLIE McCARTHY AND EDGAR BERGEN ARCADE CARD also marked "N.B.C." pictures both of the pair in top hats.
Item D: BOOK MATCHES SET featuring Charlie McCarthy and Edgar Bergen in the Tournament of Roses Parade, 1957 on CBS TV and offered by the Quaker Oats Company.

PLATE 150
Item A: CHARLIE McCARTHY PENCIL SHARPENER, red, 2″ tall and marked "C.Mc. Inc."
Item B: CHARLIE PINBACK CELLULOID BUTTON, ¾″.
Item C: RARE CHARLIE AND EDGAR COLOR MOVIE SLIDE, 4½″ x 3½″.
Item D: CHARLIE FIGURAL PIN, 1½″, 1930's.
Item E: CHARLIE McCARTHY RING, circa 1950.
Item F: CHARLIE McCARTHY PENCIL SHARPENER, orange, celluloid, 1¼″ diameter.

PLATE 151
EDGAR BERGEN'S CHARLIE McCARTHY
QUESTION AND ANSWER GAME, circa 1930,
features a very bright box lid picturing Charlie
wearing his beret. The cards inside and as pictured contain a picture of Bergen asking a question on the blue side and show Charlie with the
answer on the white reverse side.

PLATE 152
CHARLIE McCARTHY PUT AND TAKE BINGO GAME manufactured by the Whitman Publishing Company and dated copyright 1938
by McCarthy Incorporated. The game box measures 9″ x 15″.

PLATE 153
CHARLIE McCARTHY CHASE AND SANBORN COFFEE
PREMIUM TOY OFFER AND AD, circa 1937 and published by Standard Brands. This ad depicts the much-sought after cardboard Charlie
premium puppet. In the lower right is the order blank for the puppet.

PLATE 154
ORIGINAL BOXES FOR THE HOWDY
DOODY CHARACTER MARIONETTES shown
in this chapter. All are marked "c. Kagran" and
are brightly colored in red, blue, and yellow.

PLATE 155
HOWDY DOODY CHARACTER MARIONETTES
Item A: Mr. BLUSTER PUPPET with composition hands, head, and
feet is 15″ tall.
Item B: HOWDY DOODY PUPPET with composition head is 16″ tall.

PLATE 156
HOWDY DOODY CHARACTER MARIONETTES
Item A: PRINCESS SUMMER FALL - WINTER SPRING PUPPET
with a composition head is 14″ tall.
Item B: CLARABELL THE CLOWN PUPPET FIGURE has composi-
tion hands, head, and feet. It measures 15″ tall.

PLATE 157
Item A: FLUB-A-DUB PLASTIC CHARACTER FIGURE with original box, 3½" tall.
Item B: HOWDY DOODY MAGIC PUZZLE BALL, box is 8" tall and marked "c. Kagran".
Item C: HOWDY DOODY RUBBER BALL, 4½" in diameter with picture of Clarabell on one side and Howdy Doody on the other.

PLATE 158
ASSORTED HOWDY DOODY CRAFT KITS
Item A: HOWDY DOODY AND CLARABELL PUPPET MITTEN KIT, copyright Kagran Corporation.
Item B: HOWDY DOODY MAKE IT YOURSELF BEE-NEE KIT, copyright Kagran with box measuring 4½" x 6".
Item C: HOWDY DOODY AND CLARABELL SLIPPER SOCK KIT by Connecticut Leather Company, box measures 9" tall.

PLATE 159
HOWDY DOODY IN ADVERTISING
Item A: ROYAL JELLOW PUDDING BOXES originally 9¢ each, copyright Kagran.
Item B: PALMOLIVE SOAP PREMIUM CARD, 7" tall and marked "copyright Bob Smith".
Item C: HOWDY DOODY ADHESIVE BANDAGE STRIPS, copyright Kagran Corporation 6½" x 4".
Item D: HOWDY DOODY FROSTY SNOW SPRAY, 12.5 oz, can, 7½" tall, manufactured by the U.S. Packaging Corporation of Bridgeport, Connecticut.

PLATE 160
Item A: FLUB-A-DUB SCOPE DOODLE - A
HOWDY DOODY CHARACTER PUPPET is
marked copyright Kagran and manufactured by
Peter Puppet Playthings. The box is 5½″ tall.
Item B: FLUB-A-DUB MARIONETTE is 11″
tall and is the most unusual of all the Howdy
Doody character marionettes. This is also the
rarest of all the Doodyville character
marionettes.

PLATE 161
HOWDY DOODY'S ELECTRIC CARNIVAL
GAME - ANOTHER WIRY DAN ELECTRIC
GAME is copyright Harriet Gilmar, Inc. and also
marked "copyright Kagran". The toy was
manufactured in Far Rockaway, New York and
features a very brightly colored electric game
board on which Clarabell's nose lights up. It
measures 13½″ x 8½″.

PLATE 162
HOWDY DOODY WATER RING picturing
Howdy Doody, Clarabell, and Flub-A-Dub. This
bright yellow ring measures 15½″ deflated and
was manufactured by Ideal Novelty and Toy.
Probably circa 1950.

PLATE 163
HOWDY DOODY'S OWN GAME
AMERICA'S TELEVISION FAVORITE is
marked "copyright Bob Smith" and was
manufactured by Parker Brothers, Inc. of Salem,
Massachusetts. This game includes four wooden
balls of assorted colors which are used to bowl
down the target cards of Clarabell, Flub-a-Dub,
Howdy Doody, and Dilly Dally. A colorful, fun
action game.

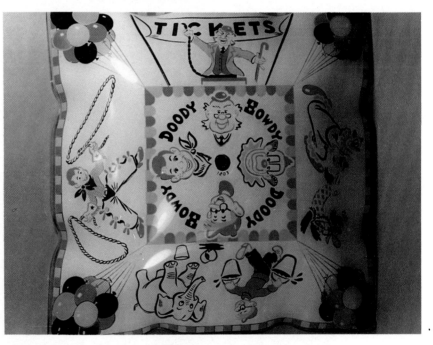

PLATE 164
HOWDY DOODY CHARACTER GLASS
LAMPSHADE for overhead measures 13"
square and is decorated with colorful pictures
of all of the major Howdy Doody characters. The
lampshade is marked as number 1203 at the
center, but it bears no other markings other
than "HOWDY DOODY" and "TICKETS".

PLATE 165
HOWDY DOODY CHILD'S PLACE SETTING
includes a cereal bowl, plate, and cup. The set
is marked "Taylor" and is entirely glazed
ceramic with colorful Howdy Doody character
designs on each.
Item A: CUP, 3" tall.
Item B: BOWL, 5½" x 2¼".
Item C: PLATE, 8½" diameter.

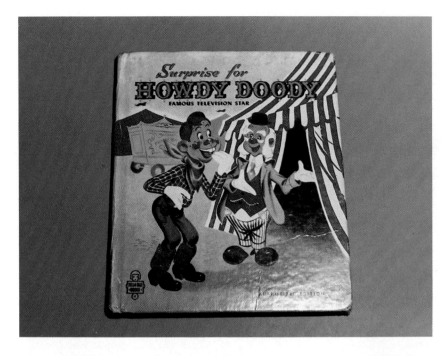

PLATE 166
SURPRISE FOR HOWDY DOODY - FAMOUS TELEVISION STAR small size Whitman "Tell A Tale Book", circa 1950. Filled with full-color illustrations throughout.

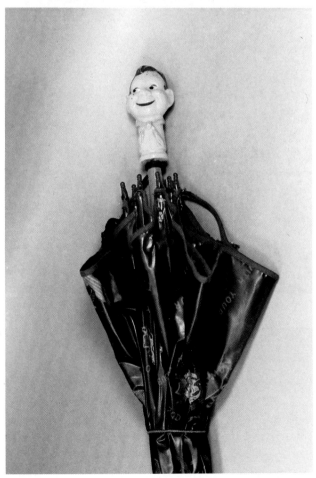

PLATE 167
HOWDY DOODY CHARACTER UMBRELLA is 18″ long and has a wooden handle and plastic character decorated umbrella cover. The handle is formed into the head of Howdy Doody in plastic with a blue scarf tied around his neck.

PLATE 168
HOWDY DOODY CERAMIC CHARACTER BANK is 7″ tall and is marked "c. Bob Smith" on the back. The bank also sports a silver and red label on the back of the pig.

PLATE 169
HOWDY DOODY COLOR TV TIME PICTURE SET in original "television style" picture folder contained eight full-color Doodyville character photos. (Photo shows only five. Price listed in guide is for complete set.) Each picture measures 8″ x 10″ and the set was manufactured by the Donald Art Company of New York. Circa date is 1950's.

PLATE 170
HOWDY DOODY COLORING AND ACTIVITY BOOKS all published by Whitman from 1951 to 1955.
Item A: HOWDY DOODY COLORING BOOK, 8½″ x 11″.
Item B: HOWDY DOODY'S FOLLOW THE DOTS, No. 1410, 8½″ x 11″.
Item C: HOWDY DOODY COLORING BOOK, No. 2018 by Whitman, 8½″ x 11″.

PLATE 171
Item A: HOWDY DOODY TV TIME PICTURE copyright Bob Smith, manufactured by Donald Art Company of New York. The print measures 8″ x 10″.
Item B: HOWDY DOODY ON COVER OF *TV GUIDE* for the period June 25 to July 1, 1954. It is Vol. 2, No. 26.
Item C: HOWDY DOODY TV TIME PICTURE also by the Donald Art Company of New York.

PLATE 172
HOWDY DOODY SAND SET maufactured by Ideal and date copyright 1954 by Kagran Corporation. The height of the display card onto which all of the toys are mounted is 10″ and the large bucket in the center is 6″ tall. This toy is in mint, unused condition. The set contains a bucket, a sand shovel and four character sand molds. All are either plastic or vinyl.

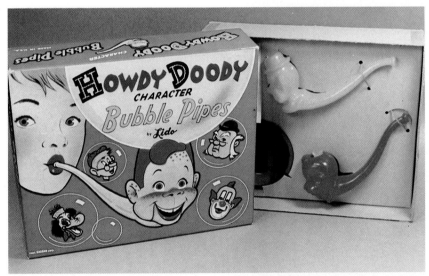

PLATE 173
HOWDY DOODY CHARACTER BUBBLE PIPES by Lido. This set is marked number 777 by the Lido Toy Company of New York and the box measures 8″ x 6½″. Included in the set are two character pipes and one bubble dish.

PLATE 174
HOWDY DOODY UKE manufactured by Emenee is circa 1950. This "uke" is shown with its original box. It is marked "copyright Kagran" and measures 17″ long. The construction is plastic.

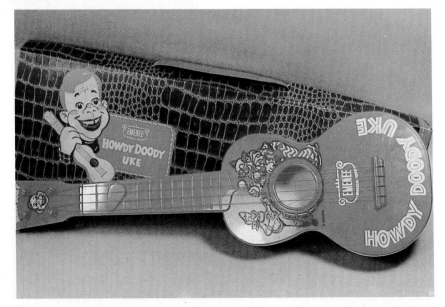

PLATE 175
Item A: HOWDY DOODY COLORING BOOK
marked on cover as "Authorized Edition" and
bearing the style number 2093. Published by
Whitman.
*Item B: TELEVISION'S FAMOUS HOWDY
DOODY COLORING BOOK* copyright Kagran
Corporation marked as Whitman number 2176.

PLATE 176
HOWDY DOODY TRAPEZE TOY is made of tin, plastic and wood
composition. The toy is 9″ wide at the metal base and 12″ tall. On
the base is marked "Made in Western Germany" and "Imported by
Toy Novelty Associates".

PLATE 177
HOWDY DOODY TRAPEZE TOY ORIGINAL BOX for toy shown
in Plate 176.

PLATE 178
Item A: CLARABELL THE CLOWN wooden push-puppet manufactured by Kohner Products and copyright by Kagran. The figure is 6″ tall.
Item B: HOWDY DOODY wooden push-puppet also by Kohner and copyright Bob Smith. Howdy Doody is 5″ tall and he "sings" at a mike marked "NBC."

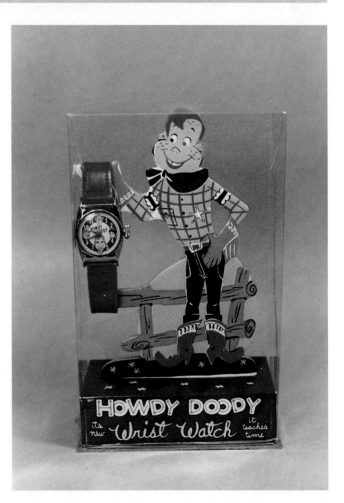

PLATE 179
Item A: HOWDY DOODY BUBBLE BATH 6 oz. container, enough for 50 baths, copyright Kagran and manufactured by Champrel Company of New York. Container is 8″ tall.
Item B: HOWDY DOODY NITE LITE, box 3″ tall, manufactured by Leco Electric Manufacturing Company and made in Japan. Copyright Kagran.

PLATE 180
HOWDY DOODY WRIST WATCH on its original platic-covered cardboard stand. Manufactured by the Ideal Watch Company, Inc., the package stands 7″ tall.

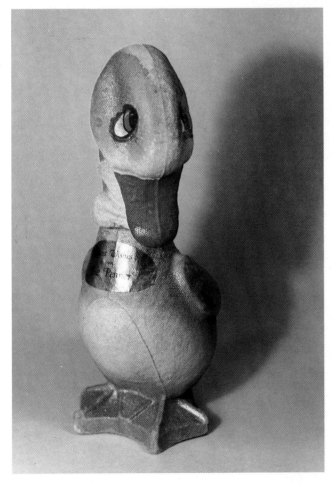

PLATE 181
PUPPET CHARACTER KNOCK-OFF CERAMIC SALT AND PEPPER SHAKERS patterned to look like Charlie McCarthy. These brightly colored shakers are each marked "JAPAN" on the base and are 3″ tall. Each has a cork stopper in the base. The unusual thing about these knock-off (unlicensed and unauthorized) items is that Charlie is pictured wearing glasses. Charlie fans will remember that he always wore only a monocle (one eyepiece).

PLATE 182
JOE PENNER'S DUCK GOO-GOO marked with a label on the front which reads "Best Wishes from Joe Penner". This 9½″ tall, paper composition figure has a removable head and could have served as a candy or treat container.

PLATE 183
AMOS AN' ANDY ASH TRAY is circa 1940 and made out of plaster. The figures stand approximately 8″ tall, and on the front of the base of the ash tray are the words "I'se Regusted." An unusual piece of memorabilia from the radio days.

PLATE 184
GAME FROM "PHIL SILVERS SGT. BILKO
. . .CBS TELEVISION'S YOU'll NEVER GET
RICH" distributed by CBS Television Enter-
prises. A unique and hard-to-find early televi-
sion game. This game was manufactured by
Gardner and Company and is circa early 1950's.
The box measures 13¼" x 20½".

PLATE 185
J. FRED MUGGS TRICYCLE TOY featuring the
chimp from the days of early television was
manufactured by the N.N. Hill Brass Company
of East Hampton, Connecticut. The toy is of
metal and wood with paper label construction.
It measures 9½" tall.

PLATE 186
GROUCHO GOGGLES AND CIGAR SET
manufactured by Eldon, Los Angeles, California. The card to which the toys are attached
measures 7½" x 8½". The set originally sold
for 98¢.

PLATE 187
Item A: ELMER FUDD CAST METAL
CHARACTER PLANTER, (Warner Brothers
cartoon character) marked only as "ELMER"
on the front of the base. Approximately 6″ tall.
Item B: PORKY PIG CHARACTER PLANTER,
patterned after the Warner Brothers cartoon
character, approximately 5″ tall. Cast metal.

PLATE 188
BUGS BUNNY ALARM CLOCK marked
"BUGS BUNNY" and "Ingraham U.S.A."
measures 4½″ high. This is an outstanding
quality character clock with a beautiful face
showing Bugs Bunny munching on a carrot as
he relaxes. Also written around the clock face
are the phrases "5 past, quarter past, half past"
etc. to help a young child tell time. The face
of the clock is also marked "Copyright Warner
Brothers Cartoons, Inc."

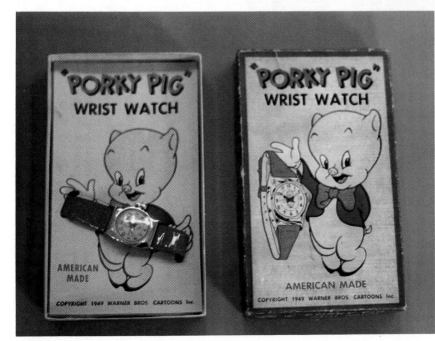

PLATE 189
PORKY PIG WRIST WATCH manufactured by
Ingraham Company and shown with original in-
ner display card and box. Watches in such mint
condition with the box are highly collectible, and
a box in good condition can sometimes add as
much as 50% or more to the value. Marked "c.
Warner Bros. Cartoons" and dated 1949.

PLATE 190
Item A: LEAVE IT TO BEAVER TREASURE
BOARD, a Saalfield super slate. Published by
Saalfield Publishing, 14″ tall.
Item B: LEAVE IT TO BEAVER book,
published by Whitman, 1962.
*Item C: LEAVE IT TO BEAVER COLORING
BOOK*, published by Saalfield Publishing Company, dated copyright 1958.

PLATE 191
JACKIE GLEASON BUS DRIVER'S OUTFIT was manufactured by
Empire Plastics of Pelham Manor, New York. The set includes a bus
driver's hat, bus tickets tokens, ticket puncher, and a working money
changer. It is an interesting early television collectible set marked
"copyright 1956".

PLATE 192
LEAVE IT TO BEAVER MONEY MAKER GAME is copyright 1959
by Gomalco Productions, Inc. and was manufactured by Hassenfeld
Brothers, Inc. The game box measures 8½″ x 17″.

PLATE 193
Item A: TV CLUB SONGS, PAUL WINCHELL AND JERRY MAHONEY manufactured by Decca records, #k164.
Item B: JERRY MAHONEY KEYCHAIN on original card; card is 5″ tall and marked "c. Paul Winchell".
Item C: TV DIGEST with Paul Winchell and Jerry Mahoney on the cover. Issue is for April 5, 1952.

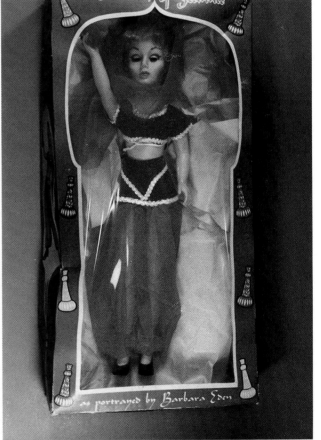

PLATE 194
Item A: AUTOGRAPHED JIMMY NELSON'S FARFEL CHILD'S CERAMIC CUP, 3½″ tall.
Item B: "SHARI LEWIS AND HER PUPPETS" MAGIC SLATE, published by Saalfield Publishing Company 14″ tall.
Item C: SHARI LEWIS'S LAMPCHOP DOLL, 11″ tall, circa 1960's.

PLATE 195
I DREAM OF JEANNIE DOLL "as portrayed by Barbara Eden" stands 19″ tall and the original box measures 23″ in length. Manufactured by the Libby Marjorette Doll Corporation and copyright 1966.

PLATE 196
FRED FLINTSTONE AND DINO THE DINOSAUR BATTERY-OPERATED MECHANICAL TOY FIGURE. Plush, metal, and vinyl construction. Dino measures 22″ from nose to tip of tail. This toy was made in Japan, but is unusually marked Louis Marx and Company. Actually, Line Mar Toys was the Japanese Marx trade name. This bright and authentic looking toy is circa 1960's.

PLATE 197
Item A: FRED FLINTSTONE VINYL SQUEAK TOY, marked "Hanna Barberra Productions" circa 1960, 12″ tall.
Item B: DINOSAUR VINYL SQUEAK TOY, 1960's, Hanna Barberra Productions.
Item C: BARNEY RUBBLE CHARACTER VINYL SQUEAK TOY, copyright Hanna Barberra Productions, 1960. Barney figure is 10″ tall.

PLATE 198
TOYS FROM THE MUNSTERS TV SERIES
Item A: HERMAN MUNSTER TALKING HAND PUPPET by Mattel, dated 1964.
Item B: THE MUNSTERS PAPER DOLLS, #1959 and dated 1966, 9½″ x 12″. Published by Whitman.
Item C: MUNSTERS THEATRE GUM BOX & WRAPPERS, by Leaf, copyright 1964.

Disney Comic Character Collectibles

Mickey Mouse is THE comic and movie character phenomenon of this century. No other character has such universal recognition and appeal to all ages. He is the comic character superstar who was responsible for producing the revenues that have allowed the Walt Disney Studios to grow to what they have become today. Mickey Mouse met many rivals throughout his earlier film career, but none could ever match up to the standard that Walt Disney set for him. He is the symbol for much of what the Disney organization has stood for over the years: family entertainment, sharp and colorful animation images, clever marketing, and a continual positive outlook.

From his first appearance in "Steamboat Willie" in 1928, Mickey Mouse grabbed hold of his audience's imagination and never let go. The first Mickey films seem crude and unfinished by todays animation standards, but they were an important beginning. Walt Disney must certainly have had an organization which kept his dreams and future plans in respective priori-

ty, and the early Mickey Mouse films were simply a foundation, a stepping stone.

Late 1920's Mickey Mouse items are very hard to find. Since we are dealing with only the last two years of the decade, Mickey and Walt had hardly had time to get the marketing ball rolling. A few items have surfaced over the years, and many of these are unlicensed foreign designs. It wasn't until the entrance of a man by the name of Kay Kamen into the life of the Disneys that character merchandising for Mickey Mouse became what it should be. The early 1930's Mickey Mouse collectibles are primary targets for today's serious and advanced Mickey Mouse collector. They first seek out Mickey Mouse examples which have a very ratty-looking Mickey likeness on them. It didn't take the studio long to realize that Mickey needed a bit of refreshment. Very early in the 1930's, the ratty smile and many of his rodent-like characteristics were softened to become a smoother, more marketable comic film character.

It is the Mickey Mouse of the mid to late 1930's that we have all come to love. He is usually dressed in red pants with oversized buttons on the front, large yellow shoes, a more rounded black and white face with big saucer-shaped ears and eyes drawn in a style that has commonly been described as the "pie-eyed Mickey." The name is derived from the fact that the eyes look like oval, black pies with one wedge missing out of each. Later in the 1930's, the pied eyes begin to vanish and they were drawn as solid black circles. This was only the beginning in a gradual evolution toward a cuter and more humanized Mickey Mouse of the 1940's that sometimes makes 1930's Mickey devotees cringe with abrasive disgust.

The very earliest Mickey items are often marked only "Walt Disney" or "Walter E. Disney." Most of these Mickey items pre-date those with either "Walt Disney Enterprises" or "Walt Disney Productions." Generally, "Enterprises" items are from the mid 1930's up through 1939 when the marketing of Disney characters and the copyrights shifted back to just "Walt Disney Productions."

So much has been written about all of the early Walt Disney characters in the past few years that its hard to find any book or price guide on antique and collectible toys that doesn't say at least something about them. The characters presented in the pictorial pages of this chapter are the superstars of the Disney marketing organization. Snow White, Pinocchio and Bambi, among others, will be discussed in the chapter dealing with the Disney feature films. This chapter will discuss only those characters who appeared in either Disney comic films or serialized comic strips.

When mentioning early Mickey, it is impossible to overlook Donald Duck. Although he didn't make his appearance onto the scene until 1935, he is still extremely collectible. Early Donald Duck has his own visual clue to collectors. The Donald of the later 1930's looks very much like the Donald that we know today, but the early Disney duck items present him with the appearance more as would befit a duck. His hands are missing and in their place are feathers or wings. His sailor suit is often presented in a lighter than navy blue. But, most obvious is his bill. In the earliest Donald Duck designs, the bill is usually long, and he sometimes looks a little more like a goose than he does a duck. It's this Donald that devoted collectors are usually "duck hunting" for.

Some early Disney characters made their successful appearance into the films and books of the 1930's and then sort of slipped into oblivion. Horace Horsecollar and Clarabelle the Cow are the two most obvious characters missing from the late 1930's and early 1940's Disney character lists. Evidently, as the success of Walt Disney's feature films began to build momentum, the studio trimmed back its list of stock characters and chose to promote Donald Duck and Mickey Mouse (along with Minnie and Pluto) as its true superstars. Goofy, as we know him today, hasn't changed much in form over the years. Originally introduced in early films and printed matter as "Dippy the Goof," his name was later shortened to simply "Goofy."

It is interesting to note the way the Disney cast of characters complimented one another. There was the very wild and volatile Donald Duck who could explode in anger and complete frustration without a moment's notice. Then there was Mickey Mouse, the straight man to many of Donald's antics

and foibles. But old Mickey was not without his own weaknesses. Enter one perky, starched-skirted little Minnie Mouse and Mickey could be quite easily reduced to bumbling and showing off. The two famous mice made an interesting romantic pair, and being female, Minnie made hundreds of new toys possible which could be geared toward the little-girls-only market. Finally, what group could be complete without America's favorite friend (and Mickey's best one) Pluto the Pup? Over the years, serious Disneyana collectors seem to have focused mainly on early Mickey and Minnie Mouse toys combined with those of Donald Duck. Pluto and Goofy toys are anxiously sought by collectors, but the wealth of merchandise produced in the 1930's was geared toward the studio's three biggest stars: Mickey, Minnie and Donald. Collectors simply have to pick up the few 1930's toy examples of Pluto and Goofy whenever they can.

Two later comic character creations of the Walt Disney Studio are presented at the very end of this chapter's photo section. Uncle Scrooge, Donald Duck's miserly old uncle, was not as popular in Disney films as he was a comic book subject. Consequently, his name is more synonymous with comic books than it is with films. Another character, Professor Ludwig Von Drake, actually made his debut as a regular on the popular television program "Walt Disney's Wonderful World of Color" and because he was actually the educational "authority" on many of the subjects presented, he will remain a popular Disney character of the 1960's. Obviously, his toys do not command the high prices of 1930's characters, but, for the money, his toys are worthy collectibles.

The pictorial section on Disney Comic Characters opens with a rare and unusual toy. Shown with its original box in Plate 199, the Mickey Mouse Piano by the Marks Brothers Company of Boston is a real collectors' prize. (There's an interesting story about this actual piano mentioned in the Collector's Resource Chapter.) The piano has mechanical figures of Mickey and Minnie Mouse which dance on top of it every time a note is struck. Their arms move up and down and their legs swing back and forth. Aside from this interesting action of the toy, the fact that it actually is musical makes it even more desirable as a collectible. Finally, the bright paint finish and the colorful paper label lithography make this toy an exceptional item.

The Mickey Mouse/Santa Lionel handcar is also an unusual piece. According to most dealers and collectors, this is the hardest of the popular Disney character wind-up hand cars to find. The Santa car features a fine likeness of the old chap, but the real collecting power of this toy lies in one of the items peeking out of the back of his pack. Sticking out of the bag is a cute Mickey Mouse figure, and therein lies the reason for its Disneyana appeal. (Plate 201)

The same Marks Brothers Company that manufactured the piano mentioned above was also responsible for bringing to the market many wonderful boxed games and paper lithographed toys. The Mickey Mouse Scatter Ball Game pictured in Plates 202 and 203 is a clear example of the quality product offered by this company. Both the box and the game itself are lithographed in beautiful full color and these make excellent display items among collections.

The giant 9″ celluloid wind-up Mickey Mouse made in

Japan and pictured in Plate 204 is also a very rare Mickey Mouse toy. It is not only collectible for its extremely large size and celluloid construction, it is also a wind-up toy! The Ohio Art Company of Bryan, Ohio, was responsible for creating some of the most attractive comic character tin-lithographed pieces produced in this century. The graphics are always action-oriented on the Mickey Mouse and Donald Duck pieces and the finishes are bright and rugged. The long-spouted Mickey watering can pictured in Plate 205 is a more unusual design, and the sand pails and buckets pictured in Plates 232A, 233, 239, 267, 275, 284 and 312 all attest to the fact that Ohio Art brought forth many wonderful Disney character toy designs. The bucket shown in Plate 267 is a rare design and the pail pictured in Plate 312 is unusual because of the rounded metal base attached to the bottom of it. There are enough available designs still surfacing at shows and flea markets that a Disneyana collector could specialize only in Ohio Art tin-lithographed toys if that was his choice. The company also manufactured sand and snow shovels and several other designs of watering cans (Plates 251, 285 and 302.)

Two versions of Mickey Mouse projectors appear in this chapter. The first is the "Movie Jecktor" pictured in Plate 210A. This projector produces an animated image by the use of two alternating projection lenses. A more sophisticated version of the same toy is the "Mickey Mouse Talkie Jecktor" pictured in Plate 255 which added the inclusion of a phonograph turntable and amplification horn. Both versions are identified by wonderfully colorful Mickey decals on the sides.

The little Mickey Mouse figure shown in Plate 212 is a rare and interesting piece. Designed in heavy metal, the painted figure holds a small umbrella which is marked on the underside, "Germany." Such examples of Mickey from the early 1930's are today very desired by collectors. Other rare Disney collectibles marketed with a likeness of Mickey Mouse are the celluloid "Mickey Mouse Rolatoy" pictured in Plate 214A and the Mickey saxophone made in Czechoslovakia featuring a full-color decal of Mickey Mouse on the bell of the instrument. (Plate 215).

Many unique bisque figure designs are shown in the pages of this chapter. Two very desirable large bisque figures are the Mickey and Minnie Mouse matching toothbrush holders with jointed arms pictured in Plates 218 and 219. Both of these 5″ tall figures have indentations in one foot where the toothbrush could rest, and the handle of the brush could then rest inside the figure's looped arm. The noses on these figures are almost triangular, and they appear to be early designs. Both figures have paper labels which read "Walter E. Disney" on their bases. Two other bisque toothbrush holder figures, also in a standing pose, are pictured in Plate 220. Note that these figures have taller, leaner looking bodies and more rounded noses, but their method for holding a toothbrush in the looped arm is the same.

The spring-legged Mickey Mouse ashtray shown in Plate 222 is an oddity with no markings except for "Made in Japan." Mickey is presented as playing a tiny little violin, but the unusual thing about the ashtray's design are the spring-like legs. It is the first of this kind that the author has seen.

Plate 223 pictures a colorful boxed set of printing stamps manufactured by Fulton Faultless Educational Toys in the 1930's. Pictured in Plates 224 and 225 is the popular "Mickey Mouse Coming Home Game" which came in two parts. The board came separately, and the game tokens, dice, dice cup and instructions were all contained in a small cardboard box with an extremely colorful paper label on top. This attractive early Disney game was manufactured by the Marks Brothers Company of Boston.

Two fine Patriot China pieces manufactured by the Salem China Company are shown in Plate 229. The plate features a bright picture of Mickey and Pluto on the front, and the child's cup features a large picture of Pluto on the front and a smaller likeness of Mickey Mouse on the reverse. Early Disney china pieces are extremely popular with Disney collectors because they are rarely found in unbroken, collectible condition.

Several very collectible Disney books are pictured in this chapter. One of the rarest is *Walt Disney's Donald Duck* shown in Plate 231. This was the first Donald Duck title ever published and its attractive linen-like paper stock and fantastic color illustrations make it a book that is at the top of the "want list" for many Disneyana collectors. The die-cut Mickey Mouse book titled *A New Mickey Mouse Book To Color* published by Saalfield in 1937 is another fine example of paper Disneyana. The *Mickey Mouse Stories* book pictured in Plate 228 and the *Mickey Mouse and Donald Duck and All Their Pals* over-sized book pictured in Plate 230 are also popular items among collectors.

The Mickey Mouse and Pluto blue lusterware ashtray shown in Plate 244 is a quality collectible partly because of the excellent likenesses of the two characters and partly because of the fine, large imprinting on the back which reads simply "Walt E. Disney." The two versions of early Mickey Mouse banks pictured in Plate 253 are sought after by both Disneyana collectors and those who collect still banks. Mickey Mouse items such as these are often prized subjects for general line toy collectors.

The original 1930's Post Toasties boxes pictured in Plate 259 are a real rarity. No one is really quite sure just why such items survived. Regardless of their secret of survival, they are perfect examples of where all those little cardboard figures that continually "pop up" at flea markets came from (see Plate 263). The Mickey Mouse bow and arrow set pictured in Plate 266 is another display miracle because the toy has never been removed from the original packaging card. It is a mystery how such a fun-looking toy could remain untouched for over half a century.

Sometimes, in regard to toy production materials, it seems that some designers must have been permanently "out to lunch." The paper drum head picturing Mickey Mouse holding his ears as Donald Duck beats a drum in Plate 270 is wonderfully colorful and most attractive. But, it too seems miraculous when one considers the sort of beating that such a toy must have taken. Imagine! A paper drum head for a child's toy drum. Such a design certainly would not last long today.

The Donald Duck Lionel Hand Car pictured in Plate 283 is one of the most desired of all Donald Duck toys, and today it commands a hefty price in the collector's marketplace. Its design is superb with excellent details and coloring. Another interesting Donald toy is the Fisher-Price pull toy pictured in Plate 287 which depicts a long-billed Donald Duck quacking happily as he is pulled along. In Plate 288, a very rare celluloid wind-up long-billed Donald makes its appearance.

The two Line Mar Donald Duck wind-up toys photographed in Plate 289 are excellent examples of the color tin lithography found on many tin Donald toys. The drummer toy is shown with its bright and colorful original box. One of the rarest of the later Line Mar toys is that which is called "Walt Disney's Rocking Chair" and it is designed as a Donald Duck figure sitting in a Dumbo-shaped rocker pulled by Pluto. The toy is a true triple collectible because it ties in three popular Walt Disney characters. When Pluto and the string connected to the chair are pulled, the toy is wound and it begins its rocking action.

The Donald Duck night light in Plate 291 is a tiny but pleasing Disney collectible. Aside from the fact that the toy actually works as a battery-powered light, it has a colorful die-cut figure of Donald Duck on one side and a beautifully lithographed tin battery tube which also supports the little light bulb.

A rare and exquisite long-billed Donald Duck planter is pictured in Plate 292. This piece out-does all of the other Disney character planters because of its sharp and simple design combined with its brilliant, bright colors. This example looks to be a brand new item; it is hard to believe that such an item could be at least fifty years old!

The Donald Duck character lamp pictured in Plate 296 is yet another fine example of quality "duck memorabilia." The glazed ceramic Donald figure is attached to the base and he is presented with a rather angry and exasperated expression. The lamp shade shown is original. A later collectible version of Donald, but one that is extremely sought by collectors is the Lars of Italy Donald Duck doll shown in Plate 303. The quality of dolls manufactured by this company was consistently excellent, so the few examples that can be found of these are prized among serious collectors. This is one toy where recent age makes no difference!

Mickey Mouse, Minnie Mouse, Donald Duck, Pluto, Goofy, Uncle Scrooge and Ludwig have been the main subjects of the photographs accompanying this chapter. All of these characters contributed, in one way or another, to helping make Walt Disney and his studio successful. It is appropriate that the toys remain today among collections of people who once loved them all in the past and seek to continually remember them in the present.

Two nationally organized fan clubs are strictly devoted to the subject of Disneyana and Disney film fan collector interests. The addresses of both are printed here as a service to all those persons who find Mickey Mouse and his friends to be something a little more than simply children's cartoon characters. (Both organizations charge an annual membership fee.)

The Mouse Club
Kim & Julie McKuen
2056 Cirone Way
San Jose, CA 95124

National Fantasy Fan Club For Disneyana Collectors
P.O. Box 19212
Irvine, CA 92713

To close, the author is reminded of a picture of a thoughtful Walt Disney standing in an interior doorway of his early studio as the sun beams in through a side window. As the sunlight enters the doorway, it casts a shadow of Mickey Mouse on the wall created by the studio's sign outside. It's an old 1930's photograph, but it is my favorite. Like many of us who have known hard-working fathers who could never completely leave their work behind, Mickey's shadow beckons to Walt, and he seems to understand. Like Henry Higgins who made a fair lady out of a street urchin in Shaw's immortal play *Pygmalion*, Walt Disney took the likeness of a lowly rodent and built an entertainment empire out of him.

Such a teacher and such a creator of happiness as Walt Disney will not soon be found again.

PLATE 199
MICKEY MOUSE PIANO manufactured by the Marks Brothers Company of Boston, Massachusetts. This is probably the rarest of all Disney toys pictured in this book and it is in near mint condition. Shown with its original box, this is an extremely desired toy among Disney character collectors. It is marked "c. Walt Disney Enterprises" and it measures 10¼" x 9" wide. When the notes are played on the piano, Mickey and Minnie dance above and wiggle their arms.

PLATE 200
DISNEY LEAD CHARACTERS probably made from the mold of a 1930's Disney character lead-mold set. All three characters are solid lead and measure 2½" tall. Probably circa 1930, but some of these have been found that were recently made by persons who own the 1930's mold sets.

PLATE 201
LIONEL SANTA AND MICKEY MOUSE HANDCAR. This is the rare one. Of the three big Disney collectibles by Lionel in regard to their handcar line, this one is the hardest to find. Mickey and Minnie Mouse are the most common, followed by Donald Duck's version. The Santa handcar with Mickey Mouse in the sack on his back is a very hard-to-find piece. It is marked "c. Walt Disney" and "No. 1105 Lionel Corp." The handcar measures 10" x 7".

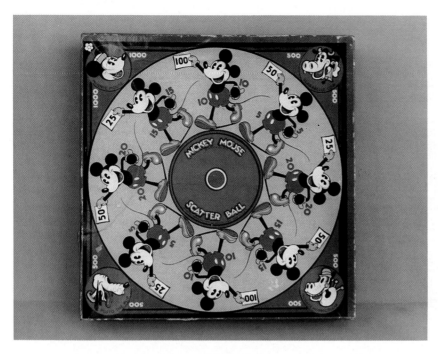

PLATE 202
MICKEY MOUSE SCATTER BALL GAME manufactured in the 1930's by the Marks Brothers Company of Boston, Massachusetts. This picture shows the box lid of this wonderfully colorful set. Box measures 12" square.

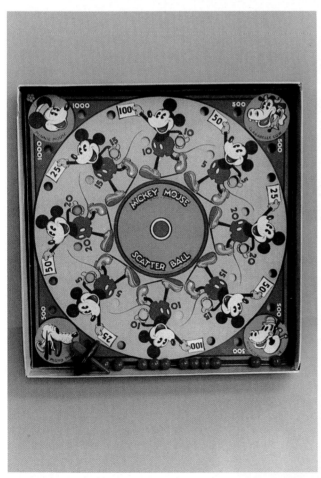

PLATE 203
MICKEY MOUSE SCATTER BALL GAME by Marks Brothers Company of Boston. This plate shows the inside of the box which included a very colorful spinner board, red wooden balls, and a green and red spinner. This is a superb set!

PLATE 204
MICKEY MOUSE GIANT CELLULOID WIND-UP TOY. This toy is an example of Japanese toymaking at its best. This very tall Mickey stands 9" to the tops of his ears and is marked "Walt Disney" and "Japan" on his back. The body is entirely celluloid and contained within is an action wind-up mechanism. Circa 1930.

PLATE 205
MICKEY MOUSE TIN LITHOGRAPHED LONG SPOUT WATERING CAN manufactured by the Ohio Art Company of Bryan, Ohio. The lithograph design shows Mickey on the front quite frustrated by a rooster that is pecking away the seeds from his garden. It is marked "c. Walt Disney" and measures 6″ tall.

PLATE 206
MICKEY MOUSE AND MINNIE MOUSE CERAMIC LUSTERWARE TEA SET. This attractive set has pieces marked "c. Walt E. Disney Made in Japan" and is circa 1930. The teapot in the center stands 3½″ tall, the saucers are 3½″ in diameter, and the cups are 2″ across. Collectors often try to piece together such a set. It is rare to find one all together at once.

PLATE 207
MICKEY AND MINNIE MOUSE CHARACTER SWEEPER is a brightly decorated tin lithographed child's toy with "Mickey Mouse" printed on both sides and a cute picture of Mickey and Minnie on the top. The sweeper head itself measures 4″ x 7″. It is marked "c. Walt Disney" and is circa 1930.

PLATE 208
MICKEY MOUSE PENCIL BOX manufactured by Dixon and marked "c. Walt Disney" and identified as model number 2745. The red/orange/and black box measures 6½" x 11" and contained school supplies. Circa 1930.

PLATE 209
GIANT MICKEY MOUSE WASTE BASKET from the 1930's measures a full 10" tall and shows all of the early Disney characters standing on an island. Missing from the scene is Donald Duck, so it is safe to assume that the toy was manufactured prior to 1935. The front is mainly a tan color, but oddly enough, the back side of the can was done in light green.

PLATE 210
Item A: MICKEY MOUSE MOVIE JECKTOR from the 1930's is marked "c. Walt Disney Enterprises" and has a bright Mickey label on its top. The projector showed rolled-up paper movie rolls. It is 10" tall.
Item B: MICKEY MOUSE SAND SIFTER marked "c. Walt Disney Enterprises" is 2" tall and 8" in diameter. It was manufactured by Ohio Art in the 1930's.

PLATE 211
MICKEY MOUSE SAFETY BLOCKS manufactured by the Halsam Company and shown in the original box. On the box lid are the markings "c. W.D.E." for Walt Disney Enterprises. The set is circa 1930 and the box lid is a beautiful design. Although the boxed sets of these as shown are seldom found, individual blocks from these sets often turn up at flea markets.

PLATE 212
RARE AND EARLY MICKEY MOUSE FIGURE, which stands approximately 4″ tall and is of all-lead construction, a highly desirable piece. He is painted over the metal with enamel and is identified by Walt Disney markings. Also, on the underside of the umbrella is hand painted "Germany."

PLATE 213
Item A: "MICKEY MOUSE AND PLUTO" Big Little Books, copyright 1936, Walt Disney Enterprises.
Item B: "MICKEY MOUSE BY WALT DISNEY" Better Little Books, circa 1938 by Walt Disney Enterprises.

PLATE 214
Item A: MICKEY MOUSE ROLATOY early
baby roll toy constructed entirely of celluloid.
Why these toys seldom survived is quite obvious. One step on it or once the baby rolled
onto it - that was it! The toy has a rattle in it
and displays three fun pictures of Mickey Mouse
at play with his nephews. It measures 3½" long
and is marked "c. Walt Disney Enterprises".
Item B: GOOFY CHARACTER BISQUE marked "THE GOOF" (his earlier Disney name) on
his back. This Japanese bisque figure stands
3½" tall and is also marked "Walt Disney."

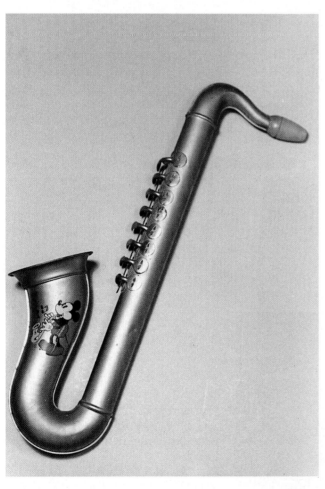

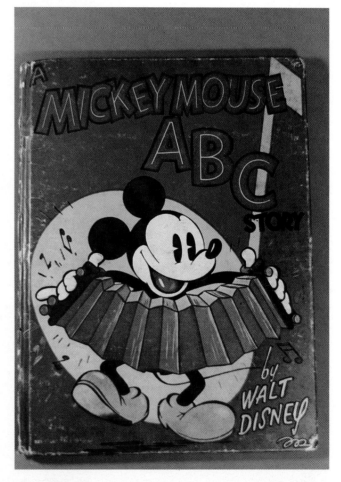

PLATE 215
MICKEY MOUSE SAXOPHONE made entirely out of tin was manufactured in Czechoslovakia by Haro. This unusual piece measures 16"
tall and actually plays a full octave of notes. Pictured on the bell of
the instrument is Mickey Mouse playing his own sax. The piece is
marked "c. W.D."

PLATE 216
A MICKEY MOUSE ABC STORY BY WALT DISNEY is book number
921 published by Whitman and copyright 1936 by Walt Disney Enterprises. Inside are character alphabet pages and the music to a song.
This brightly colored book measures 7" x 9¼". Inside are illustrations in black and red.

PLATE 217
MICKEY AND MINNIE MOUSE CHARACTER
BISQUE FIGURES, made in Japan in the 1930's
each stand 4½″ tall. Mickey holds a cane and
Minnie holds an umbrella. Both pieces are
marked ''c. Walt E. Disney'' which attests to
their early design.

PLATE 218
MICKEY MOUSE LARGE BISQUE TOOTHBRUSH HOLDER
FIGURE made in Japan and marked on his back and on a sticker
beneath his feet ''c. Walter E. Disney''. This 5″ figure also sports
a movable, jointed arm. These larger bisque figures are becoming increasingly hard for new collectors to find.

PLATE 219
MINNIE MOUSE LARGE BISQUE TOOTHBRUSH HOLDER
FIGURE, made in Japan, with similar markings to those on the figure
in Plate 218. She also stands 5″ tall and has a jointed arm. The
toothbrush would have been put in the loop of Minnie's arm and rested
in an indentation on her left foot.

PLATE 220
Item A: MINNIE MOUSE CHARACTER BISQUE TOOTHBRUSH HOLDER. She stands 5″ tall and is marked "c. Walt E. Disney" on reverse. The toothbrush would fit through her "looped" arm and rest in an indentation on her foot.
Item B: MICKEY MOUSE CHARACTER BISQUE TOOTHBRUSH HOLDER has same markings as Item A and is also 5″ tall. These are rare.

PLATE 221
MICKEY AND MINNIE MOUSE CHARACTER BISQUES, made in Japan. These 1930's bisque figures are each 2½″ tall and marked "c. Walt E. Disney" on the reverse.

PLATE 222
MICKEY MOUSE ASHTRAY WITH SPRING-LEGGED FIGURE is an unusual Mickey piece. The Mickey Mouse figure is playing a violin and stands 5″ tall. The base is marked only "Made in Japan." No Disney markings are visible. With only the slightest of motion applied to it, Mickey starts wobbling back and forth on his spring legs.

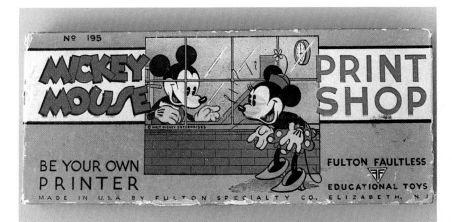

PLATE 223
MICKEY MOUSE PRINT SHOP manufactured by Fulton Faultless Educational Toys of Elizabeth, New Jersey. This company made a host of Disney character printing sets, and this is one of the smallest ones. The box measures 3½" x 8½" and contained rubber stamps and pad.

PLATE 224
MICKEY MOUSE COMING HOME GAME manufactured by the Marks Brothers Company of Boston, Massachusetts. The game set is marked "c. Walt E. Disney" and is a beautiful early set. Shown in this plate is the separate box which held all of the game pieces including dice, dice cup, wooden tokens and instructions. The box measures 3¼" x 5".

PLATE 225
MICKEY MOUSE COMING HOME GAME BOARD for the Marks Brothers set is pre-1935 because of the absence of Donald Duck on the game board. It is extremely colorful and vividly graphic. The game board measures 17" square.

PLATE 226
MICKEY MOUSE PENCIL CASE manufactured by Dixon as model number 2917 is marked "c. Walt Disney Enterprises" and is a late 1930's set. Pictured with the pencil box is a Mickey Mouse character ruler which was included inside.

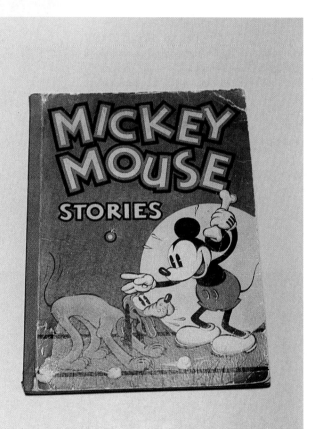

PLATE 227
A NEW MICKEY MOUSE BOOK TO COLOR, large Mickey coloring book published by the Saalfield Publishing Company and copyright 1937 by Walt Disney Enterprises. The book measures 10½" x 17". Note the unusual die-cut design at the top.

PLATE 228
MICKEY MOUSE STORIES Book No. 2 published by David McKay and copyright 1934 by Walt Disney. This book is not illustrated with picture drawings; its illustrations are actually film clips from the very early Mickey Mouse cartoons. All pictures are black and white. The book measures 6½" x 8½".

PLATE 229
Item A: MICKEY MOUSE AND PLUTO THE PUP CHILD'S DINNER PLATE manufactured by the Patriot China line of the Salem China Company. The plate is brightly glazed and then attractively trimmed with a red rim. The piece is signed ''Walt Disney'' with the likeness of his signature. It is 7″ in diameter.
Item B: PLUTO THE PUP MATCHING PATRIOT CHINA cup for the Mickey and Pluto plate. It is 4″ tall and also has a small picture of Mickey on the back.

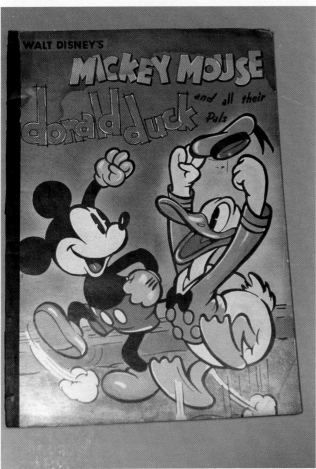

PLATE 230
WALT DISNEY'S MICKEY MOUSE AND DONALD DUCK AND ALL THEIR PALS BOOK published by Whitman Publishing and copyright 1937 by Walt Disney Enterprises. This book is not a coloring book; it is a large storybook with text and pictures inside and measures 11″ x 15″.

PLATE 231
WALT DISNEY'S DONALD DUCK book published in 1935 and coyright by Walt Disney Enterprises. This was the first Donald Duck book ever published and it is anxiously sought by collectors today. It measures 9½″ x 13″ and has 14 exquisitely colorful pages. It is printed on linen-like paper.

PLATE 232
Item A: DONALD DUCK TIN PAIL showing an angry Donald trying to direct traffic at a light while his nephews speed by him. The pail is 5″ tall and is marked "1938 Walt Disney Enterprises." By Ohio Art.

Item B: DONLD DUCK YELLOW PAIL measuring 4½″ tall shows Donald leading a parade of various Disney characters. This pail has written on it "By permission of Walt Disney Mickey Mouse, LTD."It is also marked as "Happynak Seaside pail number 7". English origin.

PLATE 233
DONALD DUCK, MICKEY MOUSE, AND PLUTO tin lithographed pail manufactured by the Ohio Art Company. This pail measures 5″ tall (not including the handle) and is marked "c. Walt Disney Enterprises." Minnie Mouse is pictured in the rear of the rowboat in which they are all riding.

PLATE 234
MICKEY MOUSE CHARACTER DRUM measures 11″ in diameter and 5″ high. The heads are paper reinforced with a fabric mesh and the body of the drum is colorfully lithographed tin. It is circa 1930 and pictures nearly all of the popular Disney comic characters of the day parading around the sides. A pristine mint example of a toy that is usually found in used condition!

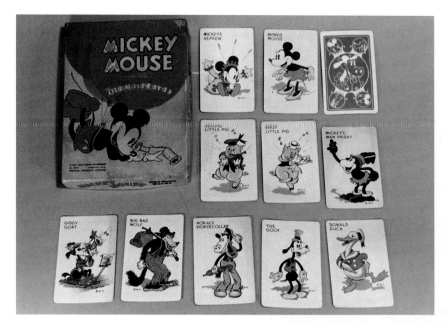

PLATE 235
MICKEY MOUSE OLD MAID CARDS as shown were published by Whitman and are marked "c. 1937 W.D. Ent." for Walt Disney Enterprises. This set was number 3067 and the box measures 5″ x 6½″. The box lid features a colorful picture of Mickey floating in the sky attached to balloons while looking through a telescope. Notice the early Disney characters on the cards including Giddy Goat, The Goof, and Horace Horsecollar. Also note the long bill of Donald Duck.

PLATE 236
EARLY MICKEY MOUSE AND CHARACTERS PUZZLE is copyright 1933 and measures 8″ x 10″. Because of their standard size frame measurement, many collectors like to frame and display these.

PLATE 237
PAIR OF MATCHING MINNIE AND MICKEY MOUSE NURSERY PICTURES, circa 1940. Both pictures measure 8″ x 10″ and have matching frames. Some versions of these pictures have flocked or glittered surfaces. A few versions were designed with luminous paint to glow in the dark.

PLATE 238
Item A: MICKEY MOUSE DRUMMER BISQUE
FIGURE, 3½" tall marked "Walt E. Disney".
Item B: MICKEY MOUSE CHILD'S CLOTHES
BRUSH marked "c. W.D.E." has a wooden body
with bristles and a tin-plate trim over the top
with a laquered red and black Mickey Mouse
figure.
Item C: MICKEY MOUSE SOLDIER FIGURE
from a Marks Brothers Target Set. He is 6" tall.

PLATE 239
MICKEY MOUSE ISLANDER TIN SAND PAIL manufactured by the
Ohio Art Company and marked "c. Walt Disney Enterprises." The
pail is shown with its original companion shovel (not character
decorated). The pail is 4¼" tall and the shovel is 7" long.

PLATE 240
MICKEY MOUSE CELLULOID WIND-UP TOY, made in Japan,
stands 7" tall and features fine action. When wound, Mickey circles
about and the umbrella above spins. Note: The celluloid umbrella is
a replacement on this toy.

PLATE 241
Item A: MICKEY MOUSE TEAPOT from a
1930's lusterware tea set. The front shows
Mickey serving Minnie a meal. The piece is 3½"
tall and is marked "Copyright Walt E. Disney"
on the base.
Item B: MICKEY MOUSE BEETLE - WARE
CUP, circa 1930, also stands 3½" tall. White
is one of the most unusual colors of Beetleware
since it was usually produced in red, blue, and
yellow.

PLATE 242
Item A: MICKEY MOUSE 1930's POSTCARD
with the caption reading "Looking forward to
seeing you" along the base. Extremely bright
colors!
Item B: MICKEY MOUSE BIRTHDAY CARD
picturing Mickey as a magician doing a card
trick on the front. Designed for a child's seventh
birthday, the card is in the shape of the number
seven. Circa 1930.

PLATE 243
MICKEY MOUSE CHARACTER LUSTER-
WARE ASHTRAY has only the markings
"Made In Japan" on the base. This character
ashtray may possibly have been unauthorized,
but it is identical in style to several other versions which *did* bear Disney markings. The
ashtray is glazed ceramic and measures 3" tall
and 5" across the base.

PLATE 244
MICKEY MOUSE AND PLUTO LUSTERWARE-TYPE ASHTRAY. Mickey is playing what appears to be a mandolin in this version. The figures are colorful and very brightly glazed. It is 4″ wide and 3″ tall. Marked on the underside of the base is "Made in Japan" and on the rear of the ashtray is "c. Walt E. Disney."

PLATE 245
WALT DISNEY CHARACTER CHILD'S TEA SET PIECES manufactured by the Salem China Company under the brand name "Patriot China." All pieces are circa 1930.
Item A: MICKEY MOUSE CUP, 2″ tall glazed china.
Item B: PLUTO CREAM PITCHER, 2½″ tall, glazed china.
Item C: MINNIE MOUSE 2″ tall ceramic china cup.

PLATE 246
Item A: MICKEY MOUSE CINE ART FILMS, 8 mm film box containing Mickey Mouse film. Cine Art boxes are marked "Walt Disney Productions."
Item B: MICKEY MOUSE FILMS, 8 mm box, earlier than Item A is marked "Walt Disney Enterprises."
Item C: INGERSOLL MICKEY MOUSE POCKET WATCH, 2″ in diameter has the unusual black ebony-like body. It is marked "W.D. Ent."
Item D: MICKEY MOUSE CLUB MEMBER CARD from J.C. Penny for the year 1932-1933. Early and rare paper piece. The tag is 3½″ long.

PLATE 247
CENTERFOLD POP-UP PAGE FROM *THE MICKEY MOUSE POP-UP* BOOK shown in Plate 248.

PLATE 248
THE POP-UP MICKEY MOUSE BOOK published by Blue Ribbon Books, Inc. of New York. The book is copyright 1933 by Walt Disney Enterprises. Inside are three Mickey Mouse character pop-up scenes. (The center pop-up is shown in Plate 247.)

PLATE 249
MINNIE MOUSE HAND-CUT PLYWOOD DOORSTOP FIGURE stands 11″ tall and has been done with precision and neatness. Although this piece may have been a kit, collectors will often run on to such "folk-art" pieces. Depending upon their neatness, rarity, and apparent age, some items can make quality additions to private collections.

PLATE 250
MICKEY MOUSE MECHANICAL RACING
CAR (400 Series) is shown here with its original
and brightly colored box. These cars came in
several numbers and styles, so it is possible for
collectors to piece together complete sets. The
car measures 4″ long with a tiny tin figure of
Mickey in the driver's seat. The car is a tin wind-
up with the hole for the key just behind the front
left wheel.

PLATE 251
MICKEY MOUSE OHIO ART WATERING
CAN from the 1930's is 5″ tall and is decorated
with very colorful tin lithography. Mickey is
shown on the front watering his flower garden.

PLATE 252
MICKEY MOUSE SOAP shown with its original
box is marked "Copyright Walt Disney Enterprises". The box itself is very attractive with a
full-color picture of Mickey on a background of
bubbles. This set was manufactured by the
Lightfoot Schultz Company of New York. The
soap was made by Castile Soap. Mickey stands
4½″ tall and the globe is 2½″.

PLATE 253
Item A: MICKEY MOUSE DIME REGISTER BANK is dated 1939 and copyright "Walt Disney Productions". This is one of the harder-to-find character dime banks. It measures 2½" across.
Item B: MICKEY MOUSE BANK produced in a book design of leatherette and brass-plate metal. It is marked "c. Walt Disney" and stands 4¼" tall.

PLATE 254
MICKEY MOUSE ALARM CLOCK manufactured by Ingersoll and marked "made in U.S.A." on the face. The clock measures 4½" tall and is a very popular display item among Disneyana collectors. The alarm set mechanism on the reverse is styled in French.

PLATE 255
MICKEY MOUSE TALKIE JECKTOR FILM AND RECORD SET. The projector mechanism for this set is similar to the Movie Jecktor shown in Plate 210, but this toy goes far beyond that. In addition to the projector, this toy featured sound that would accompany the films. The record turntable and sound mechanism were attached to the top and back, with full-color Mickey Mouse decals on all sides. Pictured here are also the sound horn and needle mechanism, record, and original movie films in their boxes. What a set!

PLATE 256
Item A: MINNIE MOUSE HULA DANCER CHARACTER VALENTINE, copyright 1939 by Walt Disney Productions. The card is mechanical and bends at the waist.
Item B: MICKEY AND MINNIE MOUSE PARTY HORN by the Marks Brothers Company of Boston. The horn is marked "c. Walt E. Disney" and is early 1930's. It stands 6½" tall.

PLATE 257
MICKEY MOUSE, DONALD DUCK, AND ELMER THE ELEPHANT TEA SET. Manufactured in glazed ceramic china, the set was made in Japan. The dishes are 4" in diameter, the cups are 2½" across, and the teapot is 5" tall. No Disney copyright markings.

PLATE 258
Item A: MICKEY MOUSE HANDKERCHIEF with stitched-on character design, circa 1930 showing Mickey in striped pants.
Item B: MICKEY MOUSE IN GIANT LAND - 12 COLOURED LANTERN SLIDE PICTURES marked as "Copyright Walt Disney's Mickey Mouse, LTD." These were English slides packed as two slide strips to a box.
Item C: MICKEY MOUSE IN PIGMYLAND SLIDE SET with same identifications as in Item B.

PLATE 259
POST TOASTIES CORN FLAKE BOXES
shown in their original 1930's condition. These
boxes not only pictured a fine likeness of Mickey
Mouse on the front of the box; they also featured
great cut-out figures on the back that could be
saved and collected. The cut-outs alone (even
without the boxes) are very collectible today.

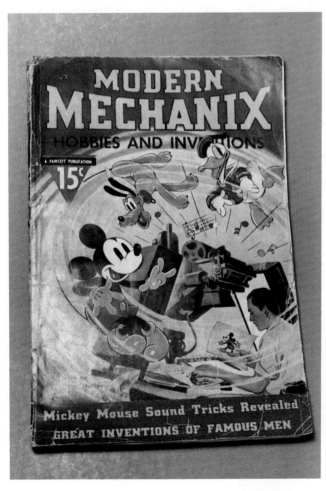

PLATE 260
MODERN MECHANIX ISSUE, circa 1930 featuring Mickey Mouse,
Donald Duck, and Pluto on the cover along with a Disney artist
photographing several Mickey Mouse cels.

PLATE 261
Item A: MICKEY MOUSE ICE CREAM CONE PREMIUM FIGURES
featuring figures of Mickey Mouse, Clarabelle the Cow, Minnie Mouse,
Pluto, and a Disney cat. The Mickey figure holds an ice cream cone.
The set was probably designed to be displayed as a hanging mobile.
Item B: (top right of display) MICKEY MOUSE DENTIST'S APPOINT-
MENT REMINDER CARD, circa 1930. "c.W.D. Ent."
Item C: (lower left) MICKEY MOUSE PREMIUM BREAD CARD #9,
"c. Walt Disney".

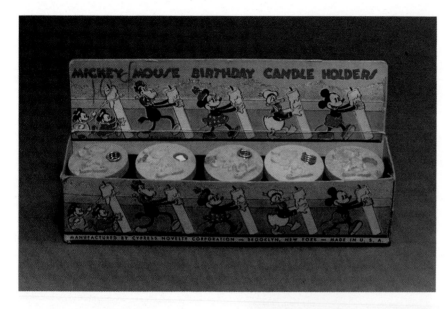

PLATE 262
MICKEY MOUSE BIRTHDAY CANDLE HOLDERS manufactured by the Cypress Novelty Company of Brooklyn, New York are copyright Walt Disney Enterprises and packaged in a colorful Disney character box. Each holder is 1″ in diameter and the box is 6″ long.

PLATE 263
DISPLAY SET OF POST TOASTIES MICKEY MOUSE AND DISNEY CHARACTER CUT-OUTS. This display shows the tremendous variety in theme and design of the many cut-outs that were printed on the back of the cereal boxes. Most range from 3″ to 5″ tall.

PLATE 264
Item A: DONALD DUCK PAINT BOX, probably circa 1930 measures 8″ long.
Item B: MICKEY AND MINNIE MOUSE BREAD CARD PREMIUM for Maier's Bread, "c. Walt Disney Enterprises."
Item C: MICKEY MOUSE AND MINNIE MOUSE STATIONARY, circa 1930.

PLATE 265
MICKEY MOUSE CHARACTER TRIVET or hotplate is circa 1930 and made of cast iron. This unusual and functional kitchen piece measures 5½″ in diameter.

PLATE 266
MICKEY MOUSE BOW AND ARROW SET, circa 1938 is in mint condition here and shown on its original display card. The set was manufactured by the Rollin Wilson Company of Memphis, Tennessee.

PLATE 267
MICKEY MOUSE AS A GONDOLIER TIN PAIL manufactured by the Ohio Art Company. This colorful pail is 6″ tall and pictures Mickey Mouse and Minnie riding a boat on a Venician canal. It is a strikingly designed pail, and is one of the more unusual Ohio Art versions.

PLATE 268
Item A: MICKEY MOUSE MAGIC SLATE, 2½"
x 4" is marked "c. W.D. ENT" and is circa
1930.
Item B: MICKEY MOUSE MOVIE JECKTOR
ROLLS in original boxes.
Item C: DONALD DUCK CELLULOID PENCIL
SHARPENER, 1" tall picturing a long-billed
early Donald Duck decal on the front.

PLATE 269
MICKEY MOUSE CELLULOID FIGURE made in Japan and marked
"MICKEY MOUSE" on his belly. This jointed-arm figure measures
5" tall and features Mickey with a very wide ear-to-ear grin. Celluloid
doll figures this size are very hard to find.

PLATE 270
MICKEY MOUSE AND DONALD DUCK CHILD'S TIN AND PAPER
TOY DRUM. The drum measures 6½" in diameter and 4" deep. The
drum head on top is paper and the drum head on the bottom is paper
with a reinforcing net mesh. The body of the drum is a lightweight
wood and the head frames are tin. An unusual, late 1930's piece.

PLATE 271
MICKEY MOUSE SKI JUMP TARGET SET manufactured by the American Toy Works Company and circa 1930. The object of the set was to knock off the characters one at a time and cause the others to ski on down the slope. The set came with a colorful box and a dart gun with darts. The target board measures 13″ x 19″.

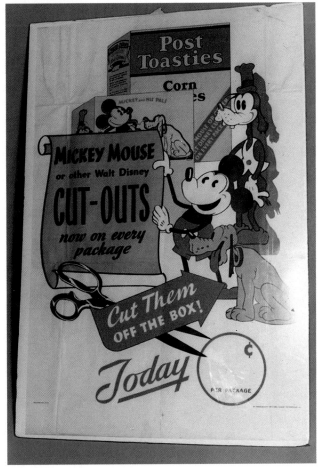

PLATE 272
MICKEY AND MINNIE MOUSE BLUE LUSTERWARE WALL POCKET showing Minnie carrying an umbrella and Mickey playing a horn. This piece measures approximately 5½″ tall and is marked "Copyright by Walt E. Disney Made in Japan" on reverse. Circa 1930.

PLATE 273
MICKEY MOUSE DISPLAY AD promoting Post Toasties and the Mickey Mouse cut-outs on the back. This large poster is circa 1930 and is copyright Walt Disney Enterprises. It would have been used as an in-store display.

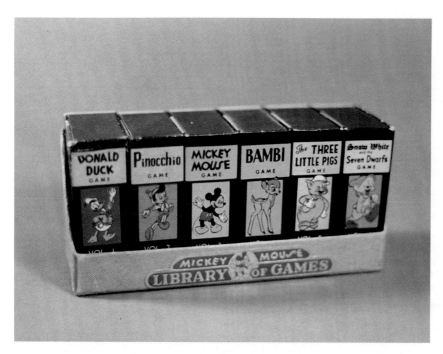

PLATE 274
MICKEY MOUSE LIBRARY OF GAMES, circa 1940's featured six different card games all based upon Disney characters. Collectors should be on guard against buying individual miniature card boxes from this game since they were reproduced into the 1970's. However, the "Library of Games" box has not been reproduced.

PLATE 275
MICKEY MOUSE PAIL manufactured by the Ohio Art Company of Bryan, Ohio and showing Mickey being pulled on roller skates by a running, energetic Pluto. This brightly colored tin lithograph pail is only 3½" tall. It is marked "c. Walt Disney" on the reverse.

PLATE 276
MICKEY MOUSE CHARACTER CHALKBOARD manufactured by the Richmond School Furniture Company of Muncie, Indiana and circa 1930. The blackboard is copyright 1934 by Walt Disney. Its overall measurements are 20" x 42". The author notes that this company manufactured several styles of school blackboards in both green and red. All are decorated with fine likenesses of 1930's Disney characters.

PLATE 277
MICKEY MOUSE DRUMMER PULL TOY with mechanical action measures 9″ tall and is circa 1940's. Pull toys have grown in popularity in recent years because of their fine graphic design and their lower prices when compared to the skyrocketing economics of collecting tin wind-up comic characters.

PLATE 278
MICKEY MOUSE TOOL CHEST, circa 1936 has two bright Mickey, Donald, and Pluto decals on it. The chest is of all metal construction and measures 4″ x 18″. A printed-on ruler also decorates the top. The chest is copyright Walt Disney Enterprises.

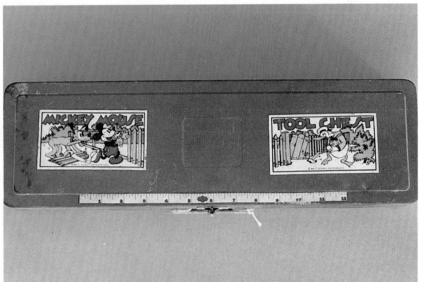

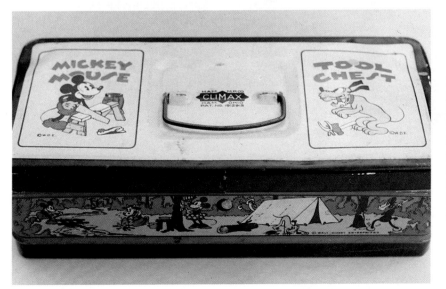

PLATE 279
MICKEY MOUSE TOOL CHEST manufactured by the Climax Manufacturing Company of Hamilton, Ohio. Pictured on the top are large likenesses of Mickey Mouse and Pluto. Pictured all around the edge of the tool chest are scenes of the Disney characters at work. The tin lithography is beautiful on this piece, especially on the scenes around the edges. Approximately 12″ long.

PLATE 280
DISNEY CHARACTER LITES manufactured by Diamond Brite and circa 1950 to 1960 shown in their original box. The box is decorated with the Mickey Mouse Club logo and it measures 5½" x 10¼".

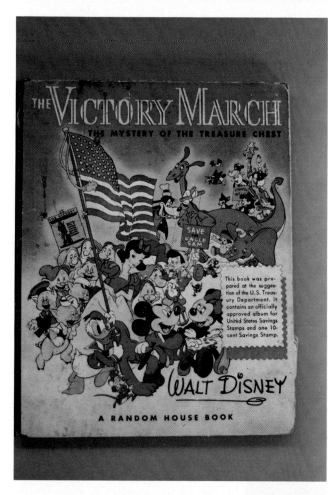

PLATE 281
THE VICTORY MARCH - THE MYSTERY OF THE TREASURE CHEST BOOK published by Random House Books and copyright 1942 by Walt Disney Productions. The overall measurements of the book are 8" x 10". Several mechanical action features of the book can be found inside.

PLATE 282
MICKEY AND MINNIE MOUSE GIANT TIN SAND PAIL, manufactured by the Ohio Art Company. This large pail measures 8" tall to the rim and pictures Mickey and Minnie in a scene in front of their house. This is one of the largest Ohio Art sand pails ever produced. This piece is marked "c. 1938 Walt Disney Ent."

PLATE 283
LIONEL DONALD DUCK RAIL CAR manufactured by the Lionel Corporation of New York. This is the companion car to the Mickey and Minnie Mouse handcar that was so popular in the 1930's. The original box shown here illustrated the toy itself. The design of Donald on the toy is his earlier long-billed version, and Pluto emerges from his little dog house. The toy came with a circle of track packed into the box. It utilized a wind-up mechanism. This is one of the most desired items of the 1930's by Disney collectors.

PLATE 284
Item A: HARD-RUBBER DONALD DUCK TOY manufactured by the Seiberling Latex Products Company of Akron, Ohio in the 1930's. The style is most unique in that Donald is painted all white on top of his solid rubber body. Even his sailor suit is all white. He has a jointed head and stands approximately 5″ tall.
Item B: DONALD DUCK TIN SAND PAIL WITH SHOVEL with Donald as the captain of a pirate ship, manufactured by the Ohio Art Company. Sand shovel is original. 1930's set copyright Walt Disney Enterprises. The pail is 4½″ tall.

PLATE 285
DONALD DUCK WATERING CAN manufactured by the Ohio Art Company of Bryan, Ohio and marked near base "c. 1938 W. D. Ent." for Walt Disney Enterprises. This shows one of the more unusual designs manufactured by the company picturing Donald Duck leaping off a crate and in mid-air about to land on the back of a young donkey. The brightly lithographed tin watering can measures 6″ tall to top of handle.

PLATE 286
DONALD DUCK PURITY MAID BREAD
LOAF WRAPPER, circa 1940 to 1950. Collectors new to character collectibles often wonder where such oddities can be found. Who on earth saves old bread wrappers? Actually, most of those that have survived were never used and found in warehouses or factories. The one shown here is wrapped over cardboard. It has probably never even been NEAR bread.

PLATE 287
WOODEN DONALD DUCK PULL TOY from the 1930's picturing Donald with a very long bill. When pulled along, the toy rocks up and down on wheels with axles set off center so that he jerks a bit and his wings flap up and down. Note, when Donald's arms are depicted as wings and not hands, he is generally an earlier version.

PLATE 288
DONALD DUCK WIND-UP CELLULOID TOY with metal mechanism which, when wound, causes his head to nod up and down. Because this is an extremely fragile piece, it is hard to find a working, undamaged example of this toy. The long-billed Donald dates this as a mid-1930's item. He stands 6″ tall on his metal base.

PLATE 289
Item A: WIND-UP DONALD DUCK TIN TOY showing Donald with an umbrella. This 5″ toy was manufactured by Line Mar and is marked "c. Walt Disney Productions".
Item B: MECHANICAL DONALD DUCK DRUMMER TIN WIND-UP TOY manufactured by Line Mar and marked "c. Walt Disney Prod." This wind-up toy is 6″ tall and is shown with its attractive original box.

PLATE 290
WALT DISNEY'S ROCKING CHAIR DONALD DUCK AND PLUTO ACTION TOY manufactured by Line Mar and copyright Walt Disney Productions. The chair is designed as Dumbo and a jointed Donald figure sits on it. When the Pluto figure (attached to the front of the toy by a cord) is pulled, the rocking mechanism is wound and the action begins. It is a bright, unusual Line Mar toy.

PLATE 291
DONALD DUCK NITE LIGHT stands 4″ tall and is marked "1938 W.D.ENT" on the lower edge of the standing Donald figure. The cylinder which holds the light and the battery inside is circled by a tin lithograph design with Donald and Mickey Mouse pictured.

PLATE 292
DONALD DUCK CERAMIC PLANTER. This very beautiful rare planter depicts Donald in his early style with a winking eye. The planter compartment is hidden in the rear of the fence behind Donald. The figure measures 6″ tall and is brightly colored and attractively glazed. This is one of the more rare Donald ceramic items.

PLATE 293
Item A: DONALD DUCK NAPKIN RING, celluloid, is marked "c. W.D. Ent" and is circa 1930. The ring is 3″ tall with decals of Donald on the front and back.
Item B: DONALD DUCK CELLULOID PENCIL SHARPENER stands 1½″ tall with a decal of Donald Duck in a light blue sailor suit on it. The piece is marked "c. W.D. Ent" and is circa 1930.

PLATE 294
DONALD DUCK TEA TRAY is copyright 1939 by Walt Disney Productions and measures 5″ x 7″. The tray was manufactured by the Ohio Art Company of Bryan, Ohio. The tray pictures Donald holding two overloaded trays of food and beverages.

PLATE 295
DONALD DUCK PAINT BOX, metal, measures
4″ x 10″ and pictures Mickey, Donald, Pluto,
and an early Daisy (or Donna) Duck. Circa 1940.

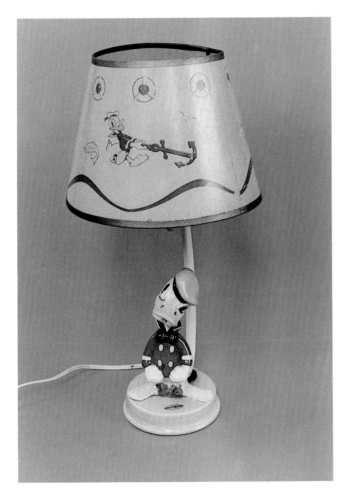

PLATE 296
DONALD DUCK CHARACTER LAMP manufactured by the Railley
Corporation of Cleveland, Ohio. This most attractive lamp measures
17″ to the top of the original shade. The base and Donald figure are
highly glazed ceramic.

PLATE 297
DONALD DUCK CLOTH DOLL by Knickerbocker and circa 1930's
stands 12″ tall and depicts Donald dressed in his standard sailor suit.
This doll shows the early design of Donald with his long bill. The
doll is of all-fabric construction with felt and trim additions.

PLATE 298
DONALD DUCK CHOO-CHOO WOODEN
PULL TOY manufactured by Fisher-Price toys
and circa 1940. Earlier Fisher Price toys are the
ones most desired by today's collectors, but the
market for later comic character toys by the
company is growing. When this toy is pulled
along, the clapper hits the bell on the front of
the train.

PLATE 299
DONALD DUCK CAMERA is pictured here
with its original box. This camera required 127
film and takes 12 pictures. It is marked
"copyright Walt Disney Productions" and was
manufactured by the Herbert George Company.
Colorful Disney comic character artwork
decorates all sides of the box.

PLATE 300
DONALD DUCK WIND-UP CAR, circa 1950 is
of all metal construction including the Donald
figure. The toy measures 7" x 4½" tall. Mickey
and Minnie Mouse (1950's version) are pictured
on the hood of the car and Donald is pictured
on the trunk.

PLATE 301
Item A: DONALD DUCK PLASTIC WIND-UP TOY manufactured by Marx. When wound, Donald spins his tail and wiggles about. He is 7″ tall.
Item B: GOOFY PLASTIC WIND-UP TOY manufactured by Marx. When wound, Goofy spins his tail that has a squirrel attached to it, 8½″ tall.

PLATE 302
DONALD DUCK SHOVEL manufactured by the Ohio Art Company measures approximately 6″ x 7″ on the shovel scoop itself with a much longer handle. The shovel is dated "copyright 1939, W.D.P." It pictures Donald Duck testing out the water for his nephews.

PLATE 303
DONALD DUCK DOLL manufactured by Lars of Italy. This doll is circa 1960 and is an example of the very finest in workmanship. Dolls of Disney characters manufactured by this company are extremely "hot" among collectors because each one has the beauty of a true museum piece! Although they are 30 years newer than many prime collectibles, they are just as desired.

PLATE 304
WALT DISNEY'S OWN GAME · DONALD DUCK'S PARTY GAME FOR YOUNG FOLKS" was manufactured by Parker Brothers of Salem, Massachusetts and is dated "c. 1938 Walt Disney Enterprises". The game board for this game is pictured in Plate 305.

PLATE 305
GAME BOARD FOR "DONALD DUCK · A PARTY GAME" also showing game spinner and tokens.

PLATE 306
DONALD DUCK PLUSH DOLL, probably circa 1930's. This version of Donald Duck presents him with an unusual, awkward - looking appearance. The doll has glass-type eyes and is constructed of stuffed felt and plush. It stands 12″ tall.

PLATE 307
DISNEYLAND MELODY PLAYER manufactured by the J. Chein Company and copyright Walt Disney Productions. This brightly colored hurdy-gurdy style musical player is 7″ tall and is decorated on all sides with Disney characters.

PLATE 308
DONALD DUCK CERAMIC FIGURE BY LEEDS CHINA measures 7″ tall and is marked "c. Walt Disney, DONALD DUCK". Although such figures are not rare and were produced in great numbers, collectors value them today because of their great variety in styles and attractive pastel color finishes under the ceramic glaze.

PLATE 309
DONALD DUCK PILLOW CASE is all fabric with fringe and features a great likeness of Donald on the tapestry-like top. Circa 1939.

PLATE 310
DONALD DUCK AND HIS NEPHEWS HARD PLASTIC WIND-UP TOY was probably manufactured in the 1950's by Marx, but no visible markings are apparent. When wound, the 4″ tall Donald pulls the train-like cart of his three nephews behind him. The toy is 10″ long.

PLATE 311
DONALD DUCK ALL RUBBER HOT WATER BOTTLE, date and manufacturer uncertain. The stopper for this actual hot water bottle is disguised in Donald's hat. Probably circa 1940 to 1950.

PLATE 312
OHIO ART PAIL. Donald Duck, Pluto, Goofy, and Mickey Mouse's nephews are all pictured at the beach on this pail marked "c. Walt Disney Enterprises." It stands 6″ tall and has the unusual addition of a beveled base. It appears that Goofy is trying to drown Pluto in the water. Donald seems much amused by this.

PLATE 313
WALT DISNEY'S DONALD THE SKIER
GIANT PLASTIC TOY by the Louis Marx Company. Complete with poles and mechanical action, Donald actually can ski along on little wheels built into his base. Pictured here with his original box.

PLATE 314
Item A: DONALD DUCK ON A MOTORCYCLE small friction toy manufactured by Line Mar Toys and approximately 4″ long.
Item B: GOOFY WIND-UP TIN TOY manufactured by Line Mar and copyright Walt Disney Productions. He stands approximately 6″ tall.

PLATE 315
Item A: DONALD DUCK FRUIT JUICE CAN, 7″ tall.
Item B: DONALD DUCK BALL manufactured by the Sun Rubber Company, 5″ in diameter.
Item C: DONALD DUCK REGISTER BANK, copyright Walt Disney Productions.
Item D: DONALD DUCK POP CORN CAN with bright paper label, 5″ tall.

PLATE 316
Item A: PLUTO THE PUP BISQUE FIGURE, made in Japan and circa 1930. He measures 3″ tall and is marked on the back "PLUTO THE PUP, c. Walt E. Disney."
Item B: PLUTO AND PUPPY MECHANICAL VALENTINE, 4½″ tall, and marked with a copyright date of 1939 by Walt Disney Productions.

PLATE 317
Item A: SCHUCO DONALD DUCK WIND-UP TOY manufactured by the famous German Company in the 1960's. This toy is shown with its original box, but it should not be confused with the earlier 1930's version. The box and duck are 6″ tall.
Item B: PLUTO CHARACTER LANTERN by Line Mar is marked "c. Walt Disney Productions" and stands 7″ tall. The batteries for this toy are stored in its base.

PLATE 318
PLUTO THE PUP STUFFED CHILD'S TOY made of a plush or velvet material. This piece is probably circa 1930 or early 1940 and is approximately 12″ tall. Pluto wears a thin collar and sits with floppy ears and turned-up nose. His head was designed with a rather severe point on top. Nose and mouth features are stitched on. It is a quality stuffed collectible.

PLATE 319
PLUTO PLASTIC FRICTION TOY manufactured by Marx. Pluto is posed here in a sniffing posture. The toy measures 6″ long and 4½″ tall. It is marked "c. W.D.P." near the base.

PLATE 320
LARGE PLUTO MECHANICAL TOY manufactured by Louis Marx Brothers toys. This toy is constructed of all hard plastic.

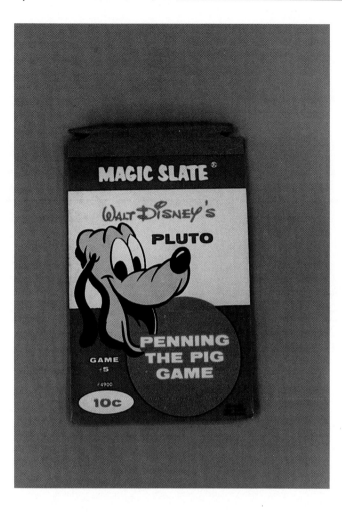

PLATE 321
PLUTO MAGIC SLATE is circa 1950 to 1960 and originally sold for 10c. The slate is marked "copyright Walt Disney Productions" and it measures 3½" x 5".

PLATE 322
DISNEYLAND EXPRESS WIND-UP CHILD'S TRAIN SET. This metal set features brightly lightographed designs on the track surface, two tunnels, and three railcars. The engine is plastic and contains the wind-up mechanism. The set was manufactured by the Louis Marx Company and the track board measures 13" x 22".

PLATE 323
WALT DISNEY'S MICKEY MOUSE METEOR CHILD'S METAL TRAIN SET. Shown here are the five cars that were included. The engine measures 10″ long and the caboose is 7½″ long. The train is circa 1950 and was manufactured by Marx. The engine was powered by a key-wound spring mechanism with an on/off switch on top of the engine. All cars and the engine feature lively lithographed graphics.

PLATE 324
MOUSKETEER TELEVISION, this large and unusual toy simulates a real television by means of large paper picture rolls which could be loaded inside by lifting up the top. All around the outside of this metal toy are brightly lithographed Disney character designs including children dressed as Mouseketeers.

PLATE 325
Item A: LUDWIG VON DRAKE GO CART TOY, manufactured by Marx and dated "copyright 1961 by Walt Disney Productions", is 6" long and utilizes a friction motor. The toy is of all-metal construction except for a vinyl head.
Item B: PROFESSOR LUDWIG VON DRAKE WIND-UP TOY manufactured by Line Mar Toys and dated c. 1961. Walt Disney Productions. The toy has an off/on switch on the reverse and stands 6" tall.

PLATE 326
LUDWIG VON DRAKE CHILD'S CHALKBOARD, Disney's television professor character. This piece was manufactured by Diamond H. Brand Toys and is copyright Walt Disney Productions, 1961. It measures 23" x 16".

PLATE 327
UNCLE SCROOGE'S BANK WITH DONALD DUCK'S NEPHEWS is a hard vinyl bank manufactured in the 1960's with the character inspired by Disney's popular comic book character of that decade.

Hollywood Personality Collectibles

How America loves the movies! Since its very earliest days, Hollywood has stood as a mecca for lovers of the silver screen. As with all forms of the mass media, when success is sweetest, soon follow the toys. Over the years, an interesting assortment of collectibles based upon Hollywood's screen characters has helped to fill this country's toy shelves.

Hollywood personality collectibles have not been associated with all stars. As with animation studio licensing, Hollywood stars have salable rights either owned by the studios or their personal legal agents. Few stars, if any, refused the lucrative financial opportunity of having their likenesses reproduced into toys. It was certainly good business and usually tremendous publicity.

Obviously, not all stars or starlets made their way into toys. Some characters simply had no appeal to children since their movies were adult oriented. Generally, it was the comedians and child stars whose likenesses adapted well to mass produced toys. The early movie funny men were hilarious in their antics, and their humorous appeal made for some crazy toys. Kids could share a bit of Hollywood every time they played with the Ed Wynn whistling fire chief siren or wound up their Harold Lloyd mechanical tin walking figure.

The Harold Lloyd tin lithographed sparkler is another example of an early Hollywood character toy pictured in this chapter. Such items are highly collectible not only to character

toy buffs; they are also sought frequently by collectors of movie memorabilia. While many of our toys from today and the past are a reflection of our popular culture, toys based upon movie stars go one step further. They are actually a tangible link with the history of one of America's most unique industries and as such they are themselves history. Hollywood personalities have a double value in the toy marketplace because they are popular to both toy enthusiasts and film memorabilia fans.

Character collectors who enjoy the early days of Hollywood memories often choose to focus on a specific period of films. Some collectors may choose only characters associated with the silent days of film. Others may focus only on one character throughout their career. Still other collectors of Hollywood character toys choose to focus upon only one type of collectible, such as the dolls of Hollywood or paper dolls.

In doing the photography for the radio and television chapter of this book, this author stumbled onto a nice surprise. With camera and equipment all set up to do dozens of frames devoted to Howdy Doody (that's what the husband collects) I was surprised to find that the wife's passion is Hollywood character paper dolls. Most of those pictured in this chapter come from that collection. She has chosen to take a small slice of Hollywood character toy production and exhaust it. As a result, the paper doll collection tells a colorful, visual story of the development of film starlets.

Paper dolls devoted to the popularity of Rhonda Fleming, Betty Grable, Gloria Jean, Claudette Colbert, Jane Powell and Shirley Temple are all pictured in this chapter. Paper dolls are popular among collectors for many reasons. First, they are normally strongly graphic, visual and easy to display. Secondly, they usually are devoted to the Hollywood star at a time when they are at their prime, the peak of their career. Finally, because of the "Dress-up" nature of paper dolls themselves, they give us insight not only into the Hollywood character; they also do a good job of reminding us about the styles of film costuming popular during a given period.

Other paper memorabilia to be discovered in this chapter are examples of a Charlie Chaplin coloring book, Rock Hudson paper dolls, Shirley Temple storybooks and scrapbooks, Movie-land Keeno games and picture cards, an Our Gang storybook and several others. All of these items represent an important moment in the spotlight for each of their subjects.

A very exciting area of collecting Hollywood characters is dolls. What better way was there to meet and greet your favorite child movie star than to take their likeness home with you in the form of a character doll? Most of the attractive Hollywood personality dolls pictured in this chapter have a permanent home today in the Memory Lane Antique Toy and Doll Museum in the Olde Mistick Village section of Mystic, Connecticut. It is an unusual place to meet up with such a fine looking group of Hollywood dolls. Nestled snugly in a small building which appears to be at the heart of a very antique looking shopping village is Violet Meier and her wonderful dolls. The admission charge is so reasonable one wonders how she manages to keep up expenses. And as a part of her warm cast of hundreds and hundreds of dolls, Mrs. Meier has done a remarkable job of helping to preserve the toy past of America's movie idols.

Among the impressive array of ladies and gents that the visitor there can meet are an attractively dressed Deanna Durbin doll (Plate 332), a sweet Sonja Henie doll complete with her ice skating dress and skates (Plate 333), an imposing W.C. Fields ventriloquist's doll manufactured by Effanbee (Plate 338) and an unusual and huggably cute Jackie Cooper character doll, circa 1930's (Plate 339). There are also fine examples of Fanny Brice manufactured by Ideal and pictured in Plate 345, a giant composition Shirely Temple doll also by Ideal pictured in Plate 347 and a Judy Garland doll manufactured by the same company in 1939. Rounding out the doll examples pictured in this chapter are a Jane Withers doll, circa late 1930's and a stunningly beautiful Margaret O'Brien doll, complete with pigtails pictured in Plate 353.

A puzzling dilemma presented itself in the preparation of this chapter. Obviously, collectibles associated with Canada's Dionne Quintuplets are very collectible among today's nostalgia fans. But, where is a well-meaning author supposed to place them? Obviously, they're not western, space, heroes, Disney, Kewpie or comic related, so where do they belong? Because toys devoted to the Dionne Quintuplets did not regard them as characters as much as they did personalities, they should really be classified as personlity collectibles. Since this chapter is the most likely one to deal with personalities both real and created, this is where the Dionnes will appear.

Aside from being a wonderful natural oddity, the news stories associated with the Dionne Quints and their subsequent appearance in books, dolls, toys and a myraid of forms of character marketing made them nothing short of a national obsession. Their toys are unique because they imitate history; they are very collectible because many Americans prize the decade of the 1930's as being a very special time in our past. The Dionnes have come to be as popular a symbol of the 1930's as Shirley Temple or Walt Disney's Mickey Mouse.

Pictured in this chapter is a rare set of large Madame Alexander Dionne Quint dolls, all in mint condition with their original clothes and wrist tags. (These are pictured in Plate 360). Also included here are two 1930's books devoted to the quints and a rare infant set of the Dionnes by Madame Alexander pictured in their wooden baby bed. (see Plate 362).

And what chapter devoted to Hollywood would be complete without a sampling of what Shirley Temple meant to both 1930's children and the toy industry of the day? To say the least, she was THE superstar! Shirley Temple dolls today are most difficult to acquire cheaply because just about every American realizes that they are as good as gold. A Deanna Durbin or a Jane Withers doll might slip right under the nose of an uninformed flea market dealer, but not Shirley! Her own film success and place in history has resulted in her collectors and fans being forced to pay premium prices to add to their collections. The few books and the doll pictured in this chapter are not even the tip of the iceberg when it comes to collectible Shirley Temple memorabilia, but they are presented here to note her importance among the Hollywood characters. She holds a special place in the heart of those who first saw her in the movie theatres, and she has won her way once again into the hearts of baby boom children who grew up with Shirley's movies on Saturday afternoon television.

My wife, Ann, is a born-and-bred Shirley Temple fan. If she hears as much as a line or two being sung on the tube or a cut from a dance number, she will instinctively rush in front of the television and stay there, mesmerized until the clip is over. Shirely Temple still has that hypnotic energy on the screen, even though her movies are now half a century old. Why was she so special? Maybe her success was due to the fact that we just couldn't believe a little child could upstage and out-act all of those talented adults around her. How did she learn all those lines and cute dance steps when she was so very young? Whatever are the answers, her appeal is just a strong today as it was fifty years ago. She sang and danced her way into our hearts and there she will stay. My wife will undoubtedly continue to be a Shirley fan and I will continue to get goosebumps every time I see her and Bill "Bojangles" Robinson do their street dance. To this author, she represents what is best in America, there's no other way to explain it. Her collectibles today are as good as money in the bank.

Our short memory tour of Hollywood has taken us from the days of Charlie Chaplin and Harold Lloyd as the early funny men and brought us around to Shirley Temple. Whether it's "The Little Tramp" or "The Little Princess," we like to remember them all with the toys that they inspired. In many ways, Hollywood of the past touched the child in all of us, and the movie star character collectibles discussed in this chapter are an important link with that past. We will never forget the great stars because we will always cherish their toys!

PLATE 328
Item A: HAROLD LLOYD CELLULOID DOLL marked "Made In Japan" on his back. Arms are strung on elastic to make them movable. 6½".
Item B: JACKIE COOGAN CELLULOID FIGURE bears no markings but is exquisitely painted in white and pink. He stands in a cute arms-folded pose and is 5½" tall.

PLATE 329
Item A: PATHE MOVIE CAMERA, manufactured by Marx is 6" tall.
Item B: HAROLD LLOYD TIN CHARACTER WIND-UP stands 11" tall and rocks back and forth when wound. His top lip also moves up and down to reveal a very toothy smile.
Item C: ED WYNN FIRE CHIEF JOINTED WOOD DOLL, 5" tall and marked "Ed Wynn" on front of his coat.

PLATE 330
HAROLD LLOYD SPARKLER TOY emits light sparks when bottom handle is pushed upwards. No markings to identify this toy, but it measures 5½" long.

PLATE 331
MOVIELAND KEENO GAME manufactured by the Wilder Manufacturing Company and dated copyright 1929. This St. Louis-based company produced several Hollywood-inspired games during this period. The box measures 7¼″ x 8½″ and pictures various caricatures of Hollywood stars, circa 1920.

PLATE 332
DEANNA DURBIN DOLL from Hollywood's golden age of young starlets was manufactured in 1939 by the Ideal Toy and Novelty Company. With jointed arms and legs, and original clothes, she stands a giant 24″ tall.

PLATE 333
SONJA HENIE CHARACTER DOLL manufactured by the Madame Alexander Doll Company, 1939. She is dressed in her original ice-skating costume complete with metal-bladed ice skates. The doll is a petite 13″ tall and is made of wood composition.

PLATE 334
"CHASING CHARLIE"CHARLIE CHAPLIN GAME showing a very distressed Chaplin being chased by a driverless roadster. The game was manufactured by Spears Games of England. The game box measures 10″ x 7¼″.

PLATE 335
Item A: (rear)CHARLIE CHAPLIN GLOVE BOX is marked on inside of lid "c. C.C.A.S. Co." and is made of light wood covered with a textured leather-like fabric. Picture of Charlie is on both top and inside of lid. It measures 10″ tall.
Item B: (foreground) CHAPLIN CANDY CONTAINER distributed by George Borgfeldt & Company, of New York. Glass figure is 4″ tall.

PLATE 336
CHARLIE CHAPLIN COLORING BOOK published in 1941 by the Saalfield Publishing Company of Akron, Ohio. This huge coloring book measures 10½″ x 15¼″.

PLATE 337
CHARLIE CHAPLIN CHARACTER WIND-UP TOY, is of all-metal construction with a pot metal head and lead feet. The painting on the toy is of fine quality and appears to be hand-done. The wind-up action allows the character to shuffle along. This fine Hollywood character-inspired toy measures 8″ tall.

PLATE 338
W.C. FIELDS CHARACTER DOLL marked "THE ORIGINAL W.C. FIELDS - AN EFFANBEE PLAY PRODUCT". This wonderful all-composition ventriloquist's doll stands 18″ tall. An unusual character piece!

PLATE 339
JACKIE COOPER CHARACTER COMPOSITION DOLL, circa 1930 stands 12″ tall and has the cutest of expressions on his face!

PLATE 340

Item A: RUDY VALEE VALENTINE pictures the smiling crooner with his musical megaphone in front of an "ABC" radio microphone. The card is 6″ tall and bears no copyright markings.

Item B: ED WYNN FIRE CHIEF TOY SIREN. When air is blown through the stem end, this fun toy emits a loud whistling sound of a fire truck siren. It is very simple, but an amazing toy. Copyright date is 1935 by Northwestern Products.

PLATE 341

A STORY OF OUR GANG BOOK published by Whitman Publishing Co. of Racine, Wisconsin and dated copyright 1929. This book contains beautiful full-color photos throughout. It measures 6½″ x 9″ in this hard-cover edition.

PLATE 342

MOVIELAND CUT-UPS, a set of boxed puzzles manufactured by the Wilder Manufacturing Company of St. Louis picturing Our Gang on one side and Rin Tin Tin on the reverse. The set is marked "A.J. Saxe" and "c. 1930." The box measures 8″ x 9″.

PLATE 343
MILTON BERLE FUNNY CAR has markings on the side "Oh, Milton, Your Wonderful" and "Whirl with Berle". This 6" long funny action car was manufactured by the Louis Marx Company. The toy is a tin wind-up, but Milton's hat is made of plastic.

PLATE 344
FANNY BRICE BABY SNOOKS CHARACTER Tums premium promoting Brice's radio show on NBC radio every Tuesday night. Copyright date is 1950 and the cardboard figure measures 15" tall.

PLATE 345
FANNY BRICE BABY SNOOKS DOLL manufactured by the Ideal Toy and Novelty Company of New York. This unique character doll stands 12" tall and is made of wood composition.

PLATE 346
Item A: NOW I AM EIGHT by Shirley Temple published by the Saalfield Publishing Company of Akron, Ohio and marked as No. 1766. Circa date 1937. The book contains story and photos. It measures 9½″ x 10″.
Item B: SHIRLEY TEMPLE IN HEIDI - A 20TH CENTURY FOX PRODUC-TION BOOK with text and photos measures 9½″ x 10″ and is dated 1937. This book was also published by Saalfield.

PLATE 347
SHIRLEY TEMPLE DOLL stands a giant 20″ and is circa 1935 but is not wearing her original clothing. The pin on her IS an original Shirley Temple pin. This doll was manufactured by the Ideal Toy and Novelty Company as is marked on the back of her head and also mark-ed on her back "Shirley Temple". Composition.

PLATE 348
SHIRLEY TEMPLE CHRISTMAS BOOK Number 1770 and copyright 1937 by Saalfield Publishing. This very colorful book measures 10″ x 12½″. Contained inside are colored paper dolls, cut-outs, and games. A very desirable book!

PLATE 349
JUDY GARLAND DOLL depicting her as Dorothy in "The Wizard of Oz" complete with blue-bowed pigtails and blue checked gingham dress. This doll was manufactured by Ideal Toy and Novelty and dates at 1939. She stands 18″ tall and is wood composition with jointed legs and arms.

PLATE 350
JANE WITHERS DOLL pictured in a Scottish plaid wool skirt. This doll is circa 1930's and is made of wood composition also with jointed arms and legs. This doll example stands 15″ tall.

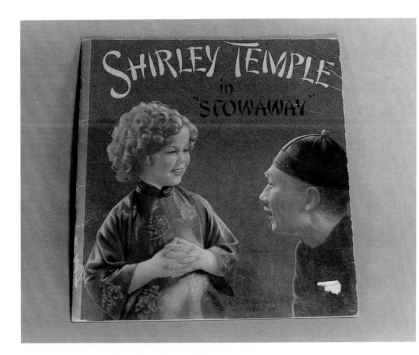

PLATE 351
SHIRLEY TEMPLE IN STOWAWAY, A 20th CENTURY FOX PRODUCTION. This bright red book pictures Shirley on the cover in Chinese garb. The photo and story book was published by Saalfield Publishing Company of Akron, Ohio and is copyright 1937. This book has a very slick, laminated finish. Shirley collectors often try to put together complete sets of the Saalfield movie title books.

PLATE 352
Item A: DR. DEFOE DOLL, (the doctor to the Dionne Quints) by Madame Alexander is all composition and stands 14″ tall.
Item B: NURSE DOLL companion doll to DeFoe, same construction, stands 13″ tall and is also by Alexander.

Plate 353
MARGARET O'BRIEN WOOD COMPOSITION CHARACTER DOLL has jointed legs, arms, and head and measures a large 21″ tall. She has sleepy eyes that close when she reclines.

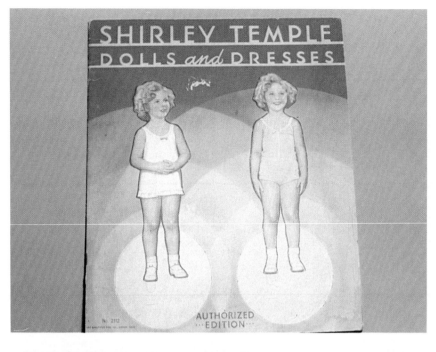

PLATE 354
SHIRLEY TEMPLE DOLLS AND DRESSES
PAPER AND CARDBOARD DOLL CUT-OUT
SET. This set was manufactured by the Saalfield
Publishing Company and is circa 1930. It is
marked as title number 2112.

PLATE 355
SHIRLEY TEMPLE BOXED SET OF BOOKS *5 BOOKS ABOUT ME*
published by Saalfield Publishing. The set is dated copyright 1936.
The box and books measure 7″ x 8″ and each contains a story and
actual photos. Also packed inside the set was a souvenir photo.

PLATE 356
SHIRLEY TEMPLE SCRAPBOOK picturing Shirley peeking out from
inside of a giant scrapbook which sits in front of a jar of paste. This
title was published in 1935 by Saalfield and it measures 12″ x 13″.

PLATE 357
Item A: RHONDA FLEMING PAPER DOLLS AND COLORING BOOK, published by Saalfield Publishing and dated 1954. The book measures 10½" x 14".

Item B: BETTY GRABLE PAPER DOLLS · A LOOK THRU BOOK was published by Merrill Company Publishers and is copyright 1953. This book also measures 10½" x 14".

PLATE 358
Item A: GLORIA JEAN PAPER DOLL CUT-OUTS A NEW UNIVERSAL STAR* BOOK published by Saalfield and copyright 1940. The book measures 11" x 13".

Item B: CLAUDETTE COLBERT PAPER DOLLS · Authorized edition measures 11" x 13" and was published by Saalfield in 1943.

PLATE 359
MOVIE STAR DOLL CUT-OUT BOOKS.
Item A: ROCK HUDSON UNIVERSAL INTERNATIONAL STAR 2 CUT-OUTS BOOK copyright 1957 by Whitman.

Item B: JANE POWELL CUT-OUT DOLLS PAPER DOLLS BOOK copyright 1952 by Loew's Inc. and published by Whitman.

PLATE 360
Items A through E: DIONNE QUIN-TUPLET DOLLS manufactured by the Alexander Doll Company of New York. The set dates at 1937. Each doll measures 12″ tall and is shown with its original wrist tag. Each wears a pin with her name on it. From left to right are: Yvonne, Cecile, Annette, Emilie, and Marie. Price Guide reflects dolls priced individually.

PLATE 361
Item A: DIONNE QUINTUPLETS PICTURE ALBUM THE COM-PLETE STORY OF THEIR FIRST TWO YEARS BOOK published in 1936 by Dell Publishing Company. It contains photos and story.
Item B: SOON WE'LL BE THREE YEARS OLD - THE FIVE DIONNE QUINTUPLETS BOOK, copyright 1936 by the Whitman Publishing Company. Both are fine examples of the media's fascination with the quintuplets.

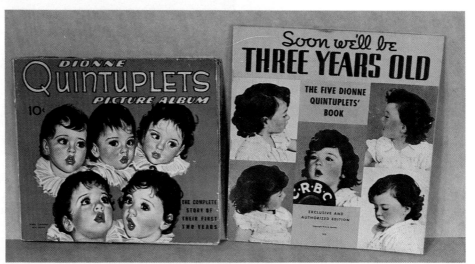

PLATE 362
DIONNE QUINTUPLET SET OF DOLLS by Madame Alexander. Each of the five dolls is made of wood composition and has jointed legs and arms. The dolls are 6″ tall and are shown with their original clothes, bonnets and baby bed with official decals. The set is marked "c. 1936 NEA Services".

Heroes of Earth & Space

We Americans love a winner. Be it in fiction or reality, we all love to cheer for the good guy. It is not surprising that so many toys of the past have taken as their subjects our favorite heroes. This chapter will discuss a unique sampling of character toys and collectibles which were devoted to America's love affair with the good guys.

Popeye opens our discussion because he is probably the most collected character presented in this chapter. One of the reasons for that fact is that he has been around so long. Ask any baby boomer of the 1940's or 1950's if Popeye is a creation of their generation and they will likely answer with an unqualified "yes." Popeye's appeal over the years has been timeless and universal. The plots of his cartoons are all so similar and simple. Popeye gets himself into an awful situation by meeting up with a villian, be it Bluto or Brutus, and then he gets himself out of it by reaching for his trusty can of spinach.

Popeye's career did not begin in the cartoons, however. He first appeared in a comic strip titled the "Thimble Theatre" in 1929. The heroic sailor character was created by Elzie Crisler Segar, who went on to bring us Wimpy, Olive Oyl and a host of others. Because Popeye as a character in both the comic strips and cartoons was always involved with plenty of action, his toys are very action-oriented. The "Dippy Dumper" toys pictured in Plates 363 and 364 are unusual examples of action toys. These wind-up cars have a fun crazy-car type of action, but the figures driving are odd. In Volume I of Character Toys we find an example of these same figures used on a fire engine toy. Here, the boxing gloved figures of Popeye and Bluto each attempt to drive a dump truck. Isn't this a bit odd as far as toy design goes? Yes. Apparently, the Louis Marx Company chose to make a rather generic Dippy Dumper toy a character toy by adding character figures, even if they didn't

exactly match the theme of the toy. Thus, we get drivers wearing boxing gloves even though there is no apparent reason for this. Obviously, because of the addition of these celluloid figures, the toys today are worth far more on the collector's market than they would be if they were sold as just plain, non-character, wind-up dump trucks.

Another interesting Popeye toy pictured in this chapter is the Line Mar Popeye and Bluto boxing toy. The design of this toy is not terribly unique. It is a Japanese imitation of other earlier toys which utilized the same structure, most notably the Ferdinand the Bull and the Matador of the 1930's and the rare Maggie and Jiggs wind-up. But the wonderful action of the toy as it applies to the characters makes it particularly fun to watch. When the toy is wound, the base mechanism jerks back and forth causing the spring arm that joins the two bases to pop up and down. In turn, this makes the two lightweight celluloid figures swing their jointed arms and appear to fight and bob back and forth toward one another. It's a simple design idea, but it works quite well.

Another Popeye item which is popular among today's collectors is the *Pop-up Popeye Book* published by Blue Ribbon Books in 1935. The pop-up illustrations are done in wonderful color, and the book features three of them. Collectors should pay particular attention to the condition of all pop-up figures inside a book before purchasing it. If parts are ripped or torn and the pop-up mechanism no longer works when the book is opened to those pages, the book really has little value. Because pop-up books in the 1930's had a special popularity, they can still be found today. But finding one in unspoiled, collectible condition is another matter. Young hands often liked to play with the pop-up figures and even remove them entirely from the pages of the book, so collectors should inspect pop-up purchases with great scrutiny.

The wood composition Popeye character doll pictured in Plate 371 is a beautiful three-dimensional representation of the salty sailor man. Likewise, celluloid dolls such as the one pictured in Plate 370 are equally true comic renditions of the character. And when it comes to paper memorabilia, boxed games, and play sets, there is an impressive array of Popeye character merchandise available to today's collector because Popeye has never really lost popularity in all of his fifty-seven years.

Chester Gould brought Dick Tracy into the comic strip scene in 1931 and his sharp-jawed detective is still alive and well in syndication. Gould's comic strip was adventurous and followed an interesting episodic story line to continually "hook" the reader into wanting to read the next appearing strip.

The Dick Tracy characters which have appeared in the comic strip over the years are extremely graphic, colorful and memorable. The Dick Tracy playing cards published by Whitman in 1937 are a particularly fine example of the strong characters and bright colors which typically appeared in the Sunday comics. The Dick Tracy Junior Click Gun and the Sparkling Riot Car with siren pictured in Plates 374 and 375 are fine examples of fun detective toys which were marketed in association with the characters created by Gould.

One of this author's favorite Dick Tracy toys pictured in this book is the Dick Tracy Automatic Police Station pictured in Plate 382. This toy has a lot going for it! First, there's a very colorful and graphic box which contains the whole set. Inside, there is a bright and attractively lithographed tin police station with plastic garage doors on the front. Finally, inside there is stationed a colorful tin lithographed Dick Tracy car which can be made to bolt out of the station garage on cue. This toy wraps up great design, great action and durability all into one. It is one of Marx's best Dick Tracy toy designs.

Other earthbound heroic characters who make their debut in this chapter are Milton Caniff's "Terry and the Pirates" which first appeared in 1934 and featured lively action in an adventure comic strip. Although characters from this strip are often overlooked by many comic character collectors because they never attained the superstar status of Dick Tracy or Popeye, they are an important link in the chain of comic strip adventure development. Most of the collectibles marketed in association with this strip were paper items and books. (See Plates 387 and 388.)

Moving from characters here on earth towards outer space, we must set our sights on the planet Krypton. Superman's origin in the movie cartoons and his comic books was that remote planet, but his early roots are attributed to Max Fleischer's studio. The first Superman cartoon appeared in 1941 and his appearance in comic books soon followed. His status as a collectible character is evidenced by the fact that most first issues of Superman comic books today are kept in banks or personal vaults, not on bookshelves. Early Superman comics are the Rolls Royces of the comic book field.

Superman related toys do not command the same prices attributed to his earliest comics, but they do make interesting collectibles. One small wind-up toy is particularly popular among collectors because of its action and design. The Superman tank toy pictured in Plate 391 features a rather flat Superman tin figure which acts as a lever when wound and actually lifts the whole tank up on end! It all sounds ridiculously simple, but this toy manufactured by Marx is a true joy to watch in operation because it shows what Superman was really supposed to be able to do.

In the middle of this chapter is a short segment of pictures devoted to heroic characters who were the subjects of Big Little Books and Better Little Books. Although the popularity of collecting these seems to have dropped off a bit in the past several years, they still remain a fun challenge to collect since so many of them have been published over the years. Heroic characters who appeared as subjects of Big and Better Little books that are pictured in this chapter are Dick Tracy, Terry and the Pirates, Tarzan, Flash Gordon, Jack Armstrong and Buck Rogers. One of the reasons that these characters were so popular as subjects is that their heroic deeds and acts translated well into the short adventure stories that these books required. Some collectors today specialize only in Big Little Books, but many collectors of character merchandise maintain small collections of these as an offshoot of their primary collection.

Buck Rogers has been around since 1929 when his science-fiction storyline was first created by Phil Nowlan. The actual artwork for the strip was penned by Dick Calkins and the two men continued at work on the successful strip into the 1940's. Buck Rogers actually resembles a sort of futuristic Rip Van Winkle. But whereas Washington Irving's character falls asleep one day under a tree and wakes up 20 years later, Calkins' Buck Rogers falls asleep in this century and wakes up 500 years later!

The Tootsietoy Buck Rogers 25th Century cast metal spaceships are popular items among collectors. Not only are these little metal ships brightly painted and attractively boxed; they are also highly collectible because there was a series of them manufactured by the company. (See Plates 404 and 406.)

A contemporary rival to Buck Rogers and his popularity was Flash Gordon, created by Alex Raymond. He is represented in this chapter by the Flash Gordon pencil case in Plate 395 and the collection of Big Little Books devoted to him in Plate 398.

Other heroes who make their appearance in this chapter are Captain Marvel and friends and Captain Video. Although these characters are products of the 1940's and 1950's, they are still quite collectible because they help to "round out" collections of space and super heroes. They have not presently reached the status of Flash Gordon and Buck Rogers among collectors of science fiction memorabilia, but they are on their way.

Finally, because science fiction as a movie subject seems to be enjoying a new renaissance among today's young people with the popularity of *Star Trek* and *Star Wars*, it is quite possible that toys in this category may be the super collectibles of tomorrow. Of course, no one can be certain where today's generation of youth will place their collecting interests in thirty years, but it is a prime possibility that this renewed interest in science fiction subjects will spill over into the space characters of the 1930's and 1940's. If that happens, demand for already rare space collectibles witll greatly increase and prices will soar! Space toys may very well be THE investment for the future!

PLATE 363
POPEYE DIPPY DUMPER TIN WIND-UP
CHARACTER TOY. This toy was manufactured
in the U.S.A. by Marx toys and was one of a
matched set. The other toy features Bluto driving an identical style dump truck. The figure
driving the toy is made of jointed celluloid and
the overall dimensions are 9″ long and 6″ high.
It is a very colorful and rare Popeye character
collectible.

PLATE 364
BLUTO DIPPY DUMPER TIN WIND-UP
CHARACTER TOY manufactured by Marx.
This is another version of the Popeye Dippy
Dumper showing Bluto at the wheel of his own
truck. The toy measures 9″ in length and 6″
tall. Overall construction is of tin and the figure
of Bluto is celluloid.

PLATE 365
POPEYE AND BLUTO BOXING WIND-UP
TOY manufactured by Line Mar Toys. This toy
measures approximately 4″ from the wheelbase
to the top of Popeye. The wind-up mechanism
is mounted under Bluto and the action causes
the pair to bounce and jerk as it moves back
and forth. The celluloid arms of the two figures
also swing with nice action. Tin mechanism and
base, the figures are entirely celluloid.

PLATE 366
WIMPY DIVING OVERBOARD POP-UP IL-
LUSTRATION from Popeye pop-up book pic-
tured in Plate 367.

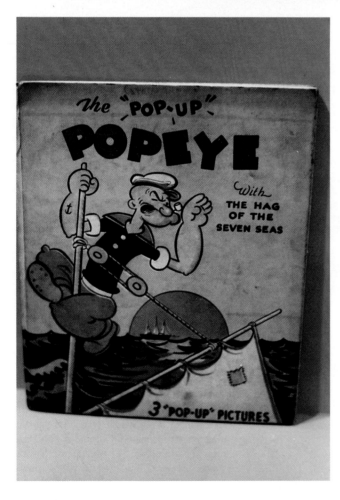

PLATE 367
THE POP-UP POPEYE WITH THE HAG OF THE SEVEN SEAS
BOOK published by the Blue Ribbon Press and coyright 1935 by
E.C.Segar and Pleasure Books, Inc. of Chicago, Illinois. The book
featured three colorful pop-up pictures.

PLATE 368
POPEYE IN ROWBOAT POP-UP ILLUSTRATION from book pictured in Plate 367.

PLATE 369
POPEYE THE SAILOR CHILD'S CHARAC-
TER HAT is made of fabric with a
leatherette/vinyl bill. This bright and attractive
hat measures 8″ from the front of the bill to
the back and has various designs applied. Circa
1940.

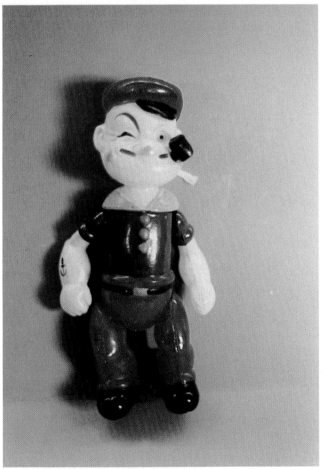

PLATE 370
POPEYE CELLULOID FIGURE with jointed arms. This brightly
painted figure measures 6″ tall and was made in Japan. It is circa 1930.

PLATE 371
POPEYE WOOD COMPOSITION CHARACTER DOLL manufactured
by the J. Chein Company of Harrison, New Jersey. The toy bears a
copyright marking of 1932 by King Features Syndicate. It is 10″ tall
and features beautifully painted details and a jointed wood-composition
body. This is one ALL Popeye collectors want to have!

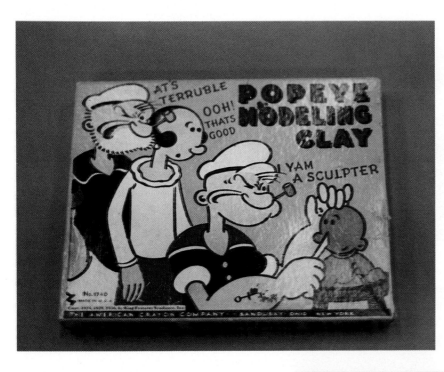

PLATE 372
POPEYE MODELING CLAY manufactured by the American Crayon company marked "copyright 1936". Inside, the set included wood molds and clay. On the box lid, Popeye is attempting a sculpture of Sweet Pea.

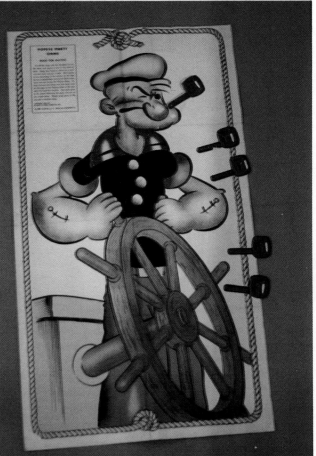

PLATE 373
POPEYE PARTY GAME where the object was to pin the pipe on Popeye much as in "Pin the Tail on the Donkey." The set came boxed (not shown) with a large fold-out game poster and included approximately two dozen red pipes.

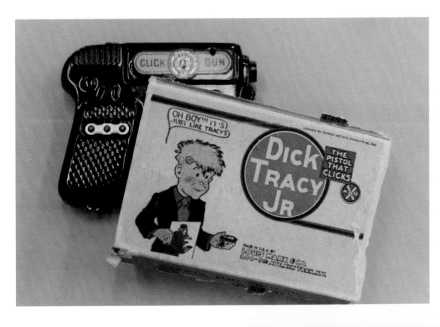

PLATE 374
DICK TRACY JUNIOR CLICK PISTOL billed as "the pistol that clicks" and "It's just like Tracy's" on the colorful box top. This pistol was manufactured by the Louis Marx Company and is copyright by Famous Artists Syndicate. Dick Tracy guns found in original boxes today are very rare.

PLATE 375
DICK TRACY SPARKLING RIOT CAR WITH SIREN was manufactured by the Louis Marx & Company, Inc. of New York. This particular example is marked as "Squad Car No. 1" and is a sky blue color. Dick Tracy and comrades are pictured inside the car. The car measures 6½" long and is shown with its original box.

PLATE 376
DICK TRACY PLAYING CARD GAME. This colorful boxed playing card game measures 6½" tall (box) and features very colorful cards with likenesses of the various Chester Gould characters from the strip. The card game is copyright 1937 by Chester Gould. The set was manufactured by Whitman Publishing Company.

PLATE 377
SPARKLE PLENTY CHRISTMAS
TREE LIGHTS SET manufactured by
Mutual Equipment and Supply Company.
The box measures 6½″ x 18″ and con-
tained a set of normal Christmas lights
(no character decorated plastic globes as
found with some sets). Copyright Famous
Artists Syndicate.

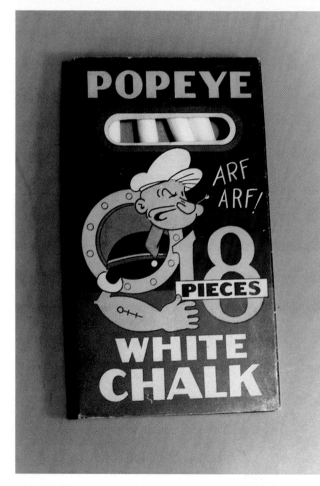

PLATE 378
POPEYE WHITE CHALK manufactured by the American Crayon
Company of Sandusky, Ohio. The box measures 4″ x 7″ and is
copyright 1936 by King Features. The back of the box has a bright
picture of all of Popeye's friends on it.

PLATE 379
DICK TRACY COLORING BOOK published by the Saalfield
Publishing Company of Akron, Ohio. This standard size coloring book
is copyright 1946.

PLATE 380
POPEYE PAINT AND CRAYON SET featuring 96 pages of pictures inside was published by Whitman Publishing Company is copyright 1938. This boxed set measures 15½″ x 9½″.

PLATE 381
POPEYE TANK TOY manufactured by Line Mar Toys and made in Japan. This toy is marked "copyright King Features Syndicate" and measures 4″ tall. It is identical in basic design to the Superman Tank Toy pictured in Plate 391. The mechanical action of this toy allows Popeye to "lift" the army tank.

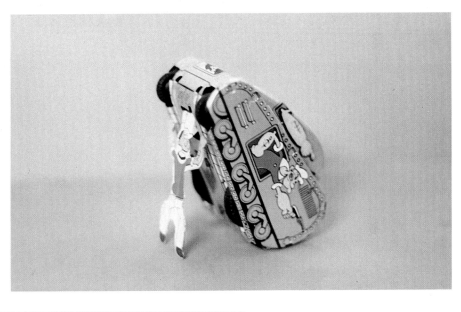

PLATE 382
DICK TRACY POLICE STATION AUTOMATIC. This wind-up toy set features a real functioning doorway on the police garage that allows the wind-up mechanism to propel the squad car out the doors. This very colorful toy features most attractive lithography and a very brightly colored box. Manufactured by Marx, the box itself measures 6″ x 9″ x 3″.

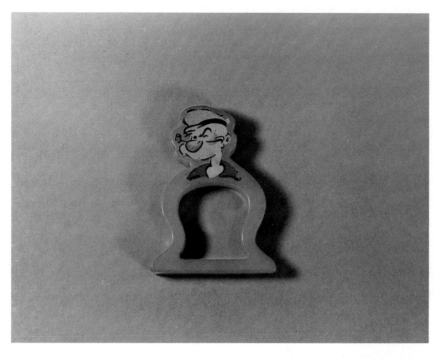

PLATE 383
POPEYE CHARACTER CELLUOID/
BAKELITE NAPKIN RING, 2″ tall features a
nice decal of Popeye on the top. Pencil
sharpeners made of this same material are much
more common, as napkin rings with comic
character decorations are rare.

PLATE 384
POPEYE TELESCOPE manufactured by the United Products Company
measures 8½″ long in its closed position. The telescope actually did
magnify and it came in an attractive box picturing Popeye looking
through his own telescope. The telescope also was decorated with a
colorful decal of Popeye.

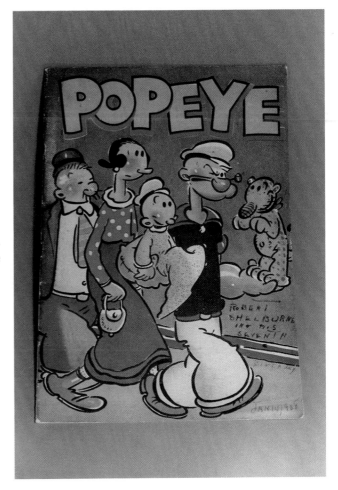

PLATE 385
POPEYE LINEN-LIKE BOOK copyright 1937 by King Features Syndicate and listed as No. 892. The cover shows Popeye holding "The Jeep" in one arm. The book measures 9¼″ x 13″.

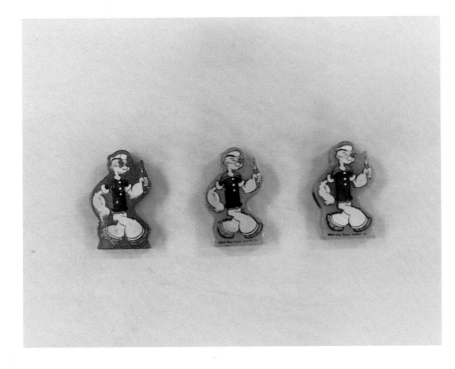

PLATE 386
POPEYE CHARACTER PENCIL SHARPENERS showing three of the different colors these celluloid/bakelite plastic pieces came in. From left are red, amber, and green. Each measures 2″ tall with a decal applied to the front and the design outline somewhat die-cut to the contour of Popeye. All are marked on decal near the base "c. 1929 King Features Syndicate".

PLATE 387
TERRY AND THE PIRATES COLORING BOOK, circa 1940 measures
8½″ x 11″. The cover design on the front and back is identical.

PLATE 388
THE ADVENTURES OF TERRY AND THE PIRATES by Milton
Caniff, The Big Big Book is one of the more rare Terry and the Pirates
items. The book contains 316 pages and measures 7″ x 9½″.

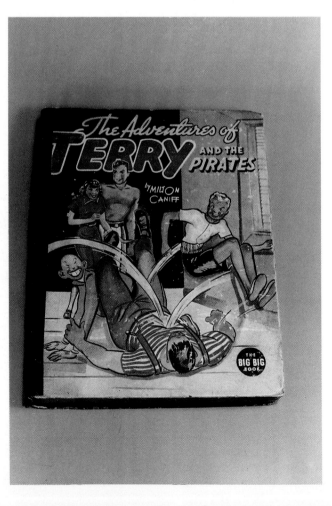

PLATE 389
BATMAN BELT manufactured by the Morris Belt Company of Long Island City, New York and copyright 1966 by National Periodical Publications. Such a toy was manufactured due to the increased popularity of Batman during the 1960's because of the television series.

PLATE 390
BATMAN AND ROBIN BOOKENDS are 7″ tall and are marked with a decal on the base "copyright National Periodical Publications Inc." and are circa 1960. Both figures are extremely colorful and the design of the figures is sharp and attractive.

PLATE 391
SUPERMAN TANK TOY manufctured by Marx. This 4″ tall toy features the fun action of a very "flat" Superman who appears from below the tank and "lifts" it when the toy is wound.

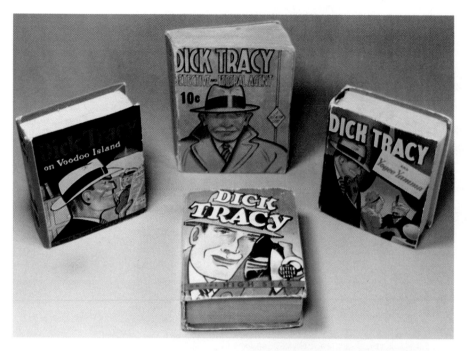

PLATE 392
DICK TRACY BOOKS, all circa 1930 and 1940.
Item A: DICK TRACY ON VOODOO ISLAND.
Item B: DICK TRACY, DETECTIVE AND FEDERAL AGENT (rare and early).
Item C: DICK TRACY ON THE HIGH SEAS.
Item D: DICK TRACY AND YOGEE YAMMA.

PLATE 393
TARZAN BOOKS
Item A: TARZAN AND THE GOLDEN LION - Better Little Books, 1943
Item B: THE BEASTS OF TARZAN - Big Little Book 1937
Item C: TARZAN AND THE LOST EMPIRE - Better Little Book 1948.

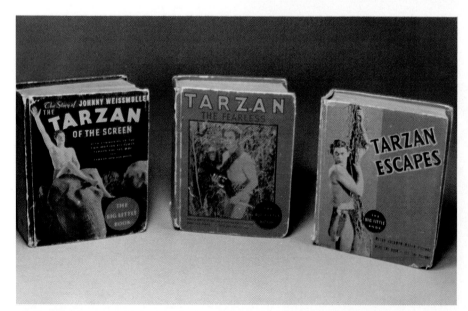

PLATE 394
THREE BIG LITTLE BOOKS BASED UPON TARZAN IN THE MOVIES . . .
Item A: THE STORY OF JOHNNY WEISSMULLER THE TARZAN OF THE SCREEN - Big Little Books, Whitman, 1934.
Item B: TARZAN THE FEARLESS Big Little Book, 1934, showing Buster Crabbe in his rare appearance as Tarzan.
Item C: TARZAN ESCAPES - Big Little Book, copyright 1936 by Edgar Rice Burroughs.

PLATE 395
FLASH GORDON PENCIL CASE manufactured by the Eagle Pencil Company and copyright 1951 by King Features Syndicate. The case measures 4½″ x 8″ and features illustrations identical to those found in Flash Gordon comic strips. Pencil cases were as popular in the 1930's through the 1950's as character inspired school folders are among today's students.

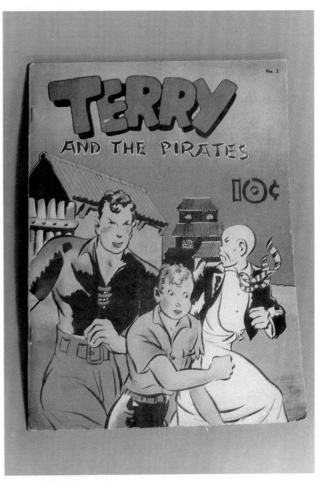

PLATE 396
MARY MARVEL BEAN BAG is marked copyright Fawcett Publications, Inc. and measures 5″ long. It is constructed of a felt-like fabric with a silkscreened or printed design.

PLATE 397
TERRY AND THE PIRATES NO. 2 published by Dell and copyright New York News Syndicate. The book is also marked with a Chicago Tribune copyright of 1937. It measures 8½″ x 11″.

PLATE 398
FLASH GORDON BIG LITTLE AND
BETTER LITTLE BOOKS:
*Item A: FLASH GORDON THE ICE
WORLD OF MONGO* copyright 1942
King Features Syndicate.
*Item B: FLASH GORDON AND THE
PIONEER MEN OF MONGO* copyright
1943 King Features Syndicate.
*Item C: FLASH GORDON AND THE
TOURNAMENTS OF MONGO* copyright
1935 King Features Syndicate.

PLATE 399
ATOMIC DISINTEGRATOR GUN often
associated with and labelled as a Buck
Rogers toy, but actually a space gun
design with no particular series identification. This is one of the most desired of
all space cap guns because of its futuristic
styling. The gun is approximately 7″
long.

PLATE 400
COMIC CHARACTER BIG LITTLE
BOOKS — TERRY AND THE PIRATES
. . .
*Item A: TERRY AND THE PIRATES IN
THE MOUNTAIN STRONGHOLD*
copyright 1941.
*Item B: THE SHADOW AND THE
GHOST MAKERS* copyright 1942 by
Street & Smith publications.
*Item C: TERRY AND THE PIRATES
AND THE GIANT'S VENEGEANCE*
copyright 1939.
Item D: TERRY AND THE PIRATES
The Big Little Book, copyright 1935.

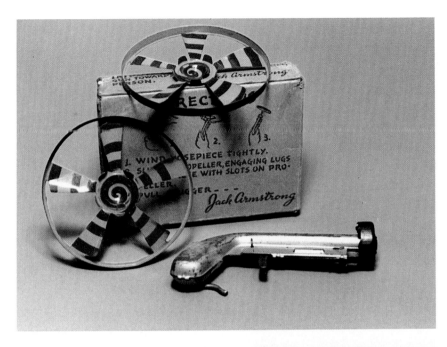

PLATE 401
JACK ARMSTRONG PROPELLER GUN with notes on box telling that it was designed by Jack himself. The tin gun measures approximately 5″ long and shoots tin propellers lithographed with bright red and yellow swirling patterns. The box is signed by Jack Armstrong and most of the writing on the box refers to directions for the toy. It's an interesting Jack Armstrong collectible.

PLATE 402
Item A: JACK ARMSTRONG AND THE IVORY TREASURE Big Little Book, copyright 1937.
Item B: JACK ARMSTRONG ATOMIC BOMB SIGHT, wood construction, measures 2½″ tall, based upon the radio character's show.
Item C: JACK ARMSTRONG AND THE MYSTERY OF THE IRON KEY copyright 1939 A Better Little Book.

PLATE 403
SUPERMAN—THE OFFICIAL COSTUME BY BEN COOPER with Superman stating on the box lid "It looks just like mine"! This circa 1950's set was manufactured by Ben Cooper Costumes and included a pajama-type costume made of a rayon-like fabric with pants and a shirt with the Superman "S" symbol. It also included a tie-around-the-neck red cape!

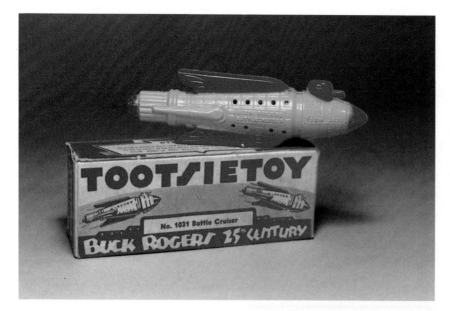

PLATE 404
TOOTSIETOY #1031 BATTLE CRUISER
(from Buck Rogers 25th Century) die-cast metal
toy. This mint condition example shown with
its original box displays both the beauty in
design simplicity and crafty detail. The box art
is attractive and the sturdy little ship measures
5″ long. The toy is copyright 1937 by the John
F. Dille Company.

PLATE 405
*Item A: BUCK ROGERS AND THE
PLANETOID PLOT* copyright 1936 by the John
F. Dille Company and published by Big Little
Books.
*Item B: BUCK ROGERS AND THE 25th CEN-
TURY A.D. DOOM COMET* a Big Little Book
copyright 1935 by the John F. Dille Company.

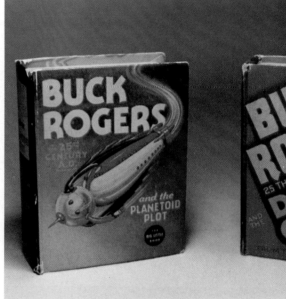

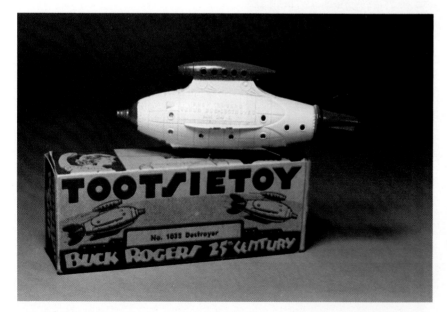

PLATE 406
TOOTSIETOY #1032 BATTLE CRUISER from
Buck Rogers 25th Century is also dated 1937
with a copyright by the John F. Dille Company.
The toy has an interesting airship or dirigible
similarity as would be the case of the day. It
measures 5″ in length and is also shown with
its original box. Note the identical design of the
ship on the box lid.

PLATE 407
SET OF THREE CAPTAIN MARVEL AND
CAPTAIN MARVEL SERIES CHARACTER
BOOKLETS published by Fawcett Publications
and designed in small pamphlet form. These
books are more rare than Big Little Books
because of their unusual size approximately 4″
x 5″ and they are circa 1940's.

PLATE 408
CAPTAIN MARVEL TIE CLIP is copyright
1946 by Fawcett Publications and measures
2½″ long. The Captain Marvel container card
for the clip is 4″ long.

PLATE 409
CAPTAIN VIDEO GAME manufactured by the
Milton Bradley Company of Springfield,
Massachusetts. The game box measures 10″ x
19″.

PLATE 410
A SAMPLE POP-UP PAGE LAYOUT FOR THE BUCK ROGERS IN THE 25TH CENTURY POP-UP BOOK pictured in Plate 411. This book is copyright 1935 by the Bluebird Press Books Company of Chicago, Illinois.

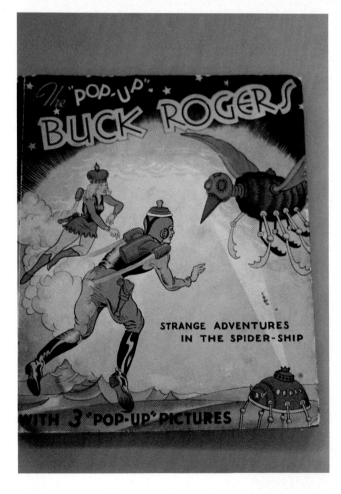

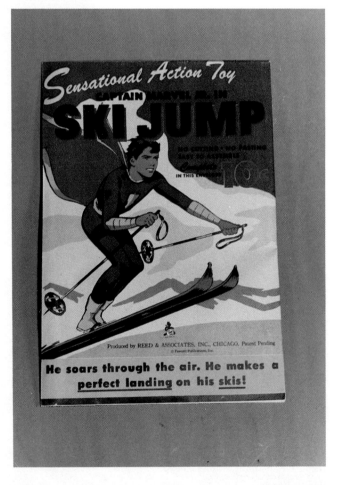

PLATE 411
BUCK ROGERS IN THE 25TH CENTURY POP-UP BOOK is a very desirable paper item among space collectors. This particular book was published by Bluebird Press Books, Inc. and is marked "copyright 1935". It features a wonderful Buck Rogers scene on the cover and contains magnificent pop-up scenes on the inside.

PLATE 412
CAPTAIN MARVEL SKI JUMP PLAY SET was published by Reed and Associates and copyright Fawcett Publications of Chicago. The punch-out and put-together set measures 10" x 7" in the envelope.

Disney Feature Film Collectibles

Over the years, the Walt Disney Studios have become just as famous for their feature films as they have for being the birthplace of Mickey Mouse. Walt Disney had the right idea in the 1930's when he set his sights for the future on moving from short cartoon subjects to the full-length animated feature. It was quite an undertaking for the studio because no one was quite sure if the public even wanted a full-length cartoon feature. It had never been done before. But, *Snow White and the Seven Dwarfs* opened to the public with all the glitter and glamour that any regular film could ever muster, and it has remained a beacon of quality and perfection among animators today.

Snow White was THE classic animated cartoon. Because

of the success over the years in all of its re-releases, it has become the standard among all animated film studios. It is the one that all other imitators are compared to. If *Snow White and the Seven Dwarfs* had any equal rival, it was probably Disney's second major work, *Pinocchio*. Some critics of film even claim that it was his very best work. When *Snow White* opened in 1937, Disney's Studio had been able to spend most of the decade planning and preparing for it. *Pinocchio* opened to theaters in 1939, just two years later, and it is amazing that the studio was able to produce such a quality product in two short years.

But, *Snow White* and *Pinocchio* weren't really the true beginning of feature films at Walt Disney Productions. Long before *Snow White* opened to movie theaters, Disney was testing his art in little segments released to the public under the general title of *Silly Symphonies*. The *Silly Symphonies* were a product of the mid-1930's when Mickey Mouse's success as a film star had begun to bring in ample revenues to enable the studio to branch out. Mickey Mouse cartoons were still being used in theaters as lead-in movies or "fillers" between double features, and Walt Disney desired a film usage which was more substantial. Granted, it wasn't until the gala opening of *Snow White and the Seven Dwarfs* that Walt was able to enjoy seeing one of his films billed with feature film status, but the *Silly Symphonies* film series helped to close the gap between the cartoon and feature film.

These short film subjects in the *Silly Symphonies* series came to be known as "featurettes." They included such titles as "Ferdinand the Bull," "The Ugly Duckling," "Flowers and Trees," (the first full-color cartoon), and of course, one of Disney's early film hits, "The Three Little Pigs."

Disneyana collectors today like to collect toys and merchandise associated with the *Silly Symphonies* because they represent an historic, transitional period in the Walt Disney Studio's development. Probably the most marketed in regard to toys was Disney's "The Three Little Pigs." It was a wonderfully colorful and fun film which was highly popularized by its famous song "Who's Afraid of the Big Bad Wolf?" Many of the toys inspired by the film often have those lyrics from the song printed on the toy itself somewhere. The beautiful Ohio Art tea set pictured in Plate 413 is an example of this. The words "Who's Afraid of the Big Bad Wolf" are printed around the edges of all of the plates and saucers in the set, and the same lyrics are printed across the top of the tea tray.

Another interesting collectible from "The Three Little Pigs" is the bisque character toothbrush holder pictured in Plate 414. This design in bisque is rather an oddity. Usually, the three pigs were all represented as musical, so they are often found playing musical instruments (See figures in Plate 417). However, looks can be misleading. In this toothbrush holder, it appears that what we have is a musical combo of one pig with a fife, one with a violin and the third seated pig playing the piano. That's certainly what it LOOKS like. But the joke is on the collector. Actually, upon very close inspection, what the seated pig is sitting at is a pile of bricks and while the other two pigs play, he appears to be busy building. He even has a trowel in his hand, but nine out of ten collectors who actually own this toy would say that he's playing the piano.

The Ohio Art Three Little Pigs pail pictured in Plate 415 also has the words "Who's Afraid of the Big Bad Wolf" printed across the top as a part of its lithography. (A larger, similar pail is also pictured in plate 416.)

The "Three Little Pigs" ashtray pictured in Plate 419 has a lusterware-type finish. This piece brings up an interesting point for discussion. Disney characters were often produced into ashtrays, but why were clean-cut children's characters used as such? Generally, this was a popular trend of the 1930's. Most popular comic strip characters of the day often made their way into ashtray designs, so the Disney characters were not to be outdone. Evidently, cartoon fans of Disney films thought there was something humorous about grinding out the butts in front of pert little children's characters. It all seems a bit odd to

this author, but the ashtray designs of the 1930's, particularly with Disney characters, are highly desirable collectibles today.

Moving from the "The Three Little Pigs" we meet up with one very friendly and lovable bull. The film, "Ferdinand The Bull" was released in 1938 and it won an Academy Award for the Disney Studio. Ferdinand's story is a simple one. He is a kind bull who does not want to fight. But, "the plot thickens" in the film when Ferdinand gets stung by a bee just at the same moment that scouts for the bullfight are looking around his pasture for the fiercest of bulls. When he finally gets into the arena, his true nature eventually comes to the surface. As a result, the many Ferdinand toys produced during the late 1930's picture the bull with flowers in his mouth and a bee either attached to or painted upon his rear quarters.

And then, of course, there is Snow White. Her likeness, along with that of the dwarfs, has been produced into nearly every product imaginable. The items shown in this volume combined with those pictured in the first volume of *Character Toys* only scratch the surface of Snow White character items which have been produced over the years. The target game pictured in Plates 425 and 426 is a beautiful example of a paper collectible. The set is constructed of cardboard covered with lithographed paper, and the colors are vivid! The object of this game was to shoot the individual dwarfs who rested on a sliding wood track, and as each one was bumped off by the dart gun, the others would slide on down the incline. This fine set was manufactured by the American Toy Works Company of New York.

The Dopey item in Plate 430 is a fine example of a quality character doll. He was manufactured by the Ideal Toy and Novelty Company in the late 1930's and is pictured with his original box. His head is composition, the clothes are soft wool felt, and his hands and body are made of a stuffed cotton or linen.

One of this author's favorite Snow White sets pictured in this chapter are those figures appearing in Plate 431. The items are match or toothpick holders which were manufactured by S. Maw and Sons, Limited of England. Each figure has printed on its base the words "Genuine Foreign Copyright" and they all have exquisite paint detailing. The ceramic figures have an attractive glaze, and their design and quality rivals the standards set by the American Pottery Company for ceramic pieces almost a decade later.

The Madame Alexander Snow White and the Dwarfs marionette dolls pictured in Plates 435 and 436 are prized among today's collectors. Complete sets are rarely found, and most collectors try to acquire them individually, one by one. The detail and costuming are of the fine quality usually associated with the Alexander Doll Company. Each of the puppets has a composition head, hands and feet with a wood and cloth body.

Another company which produced quality Snow White items during the 1930's was LaMode Studios of New York. This company manufactured beautiful bookends (Plate 437), character lamps (Plate 439) and character night lights. All items manufactured by this company have a sculptured clay-like finish and each bears a detailed label on the felt bottom of the figure identifying it as LaMode Studios "Modeware" with additional Disney copyright information.

The Milton Bradley Snow White And The Seven Dwarfs game pictured in Plate 440 has a wonderfully colorful box lid, with the game board and pieces inside being a little less than spectacular. A rare set of English movie lantern (or projector) slides appears in Plate 445. The complete set features a total of six different full-color slides contained within very colorful and attractive packaging.

The Dopey ceramic figure pictured in Plate 447 is an example of the fine quality and devotion to detail evident in nearly all figures manufactured by the American Pottery Company in the 1940's. The paint is bright, the colors are vivid and the glaze is lusterous. These are the figures that Disneyana collectors are crazy about, particularly on the west coast. Another highly desirable toy pictured in this chapter is the Snow White and the Dwarfs pull toy pictured in Plate 452. This toy was manufactured by the N.N. Hill Brass Company in the 1930's and it features a bell-ringing mechanism just beneath the Snow White figure. Toys manufactured by this fine company are sturdy and colorful. They are also much more rare than similar toys which were manufactured by Fisher-Price.

The napkin rings and pencil sharpeners pictured in Plate 456 are good examples of celluloid Snow White collectibles. The material of these is often called "Bakelite" among collectors to help distinguish it from the hollow and brittle celluloid toys imported from Japan in the 1930's. The napkin rings are more rare than the pencil sharpeners. Still another Snow White item worthy of special note is the fine tapestry-type rug pictured in Plate 458. The colors are deep and rich, and the plush-like pile gives it a lavish and luxurious look. The scene pictured shows Snow White, with all of the Dwarfs, standing in a typical pose in front of the cottage.

The musical-posed Snow White and the Seven Dwarfs bisque set is a rare one (pictured in Plate 459). It is hard to find even individual one-piece examples of this set. Most of the bisque sets sold in the 1930's represent the dwarfs simply in standing poses. This set is unusual because of the addition of musical instruments for each character. A boxed set such as the one pictured in this chapter is a real rarity.

The English Snow White card game pictured in Plate 461 is an example of very fine print and design quality. All of the cards in the set are fantastically colorful, bright and charming. The miniature bisque Snow White character figures shown in Plate 462 still stand on top of their 50-year-old cornstarch candy!

And we cannot move away from discussion of Snow White collectibles without mentioning original Disney Studio Art. Ever since the studio's inception, a tremendous supply of animation drawings and celluloids has remained following the completion of a production. Much of the wonderful original Disney art of the 1930's was destroyed by the studio simply because there was not a proper place to store literally millions of sheets of drawings and celluloid paintings. Thus, when 1930's examples do surface, it is because they were of the select few that were chosen to be sold to the public. The best of these were distributed by Courvosier Galleries and all celluloids from this company have an authentication sticker on the back which states that the item is a piece of original Disney art which was actually used in the filming of a production. Theoretically, no two pieces of animation art are ever alike because each single drawing or painted celluloid sheet usually represents one frame of film from the original movie.

The original Grumpy celluloid pictured in Plate 464 was actually a small part of Disney's *Snow White and the Seven Dwarfs*. Such items have begun to skyrocket in recent years, especially celluloids with original backgrounds or multi-character set up scenes. Reports of rare animation paintings selling for several thousands of dollars are not uncommon today.

From *Snow White and the Seven Dwarfs*, we progress to Walt Disney's second great feature-length movie, *Pinocchio*. When the film was released in 1939, it was just around the time that Disney toys began to take on a new copyright status. After *Pinocchio*, Disney toys took on the copyright markings of Walt Disney Productions. Prior to that time and for most of the mid-1930's, toys were often marked "Copyright Walt Disney Enterprises." Pinocchio toys appeared right at the turning point, so some of the early Pinocchio toys, games and books are marked "Enterprises" while others are marked "Walt Disney Productions."

One of the most interesting book designs of Walt Disney's *Pinocchio* is pictured in Plate 474. This is the die-cut Pinocchio picture book which contains wonderful full-color illustrations of all of the characters from the film. Since every page in the book is die-cut with the outline of Gepetto, it makes for an interesting book design. The story book pictured in Plate 473 also contains many brilliant full-color illustrations taken from the movie.

The Pinocchio Express wooden pull toy pictured in Plate 476 is an unusual wooden toy design. It is much more rare than other Fisher-Price toys associated with the film, and the condition of the toy pictured is superb. As Pinocchio is pulled along, his legs move with pleasing action to give the appearance that he is riding a unicycle.

The two Jiminy Cricket pieces pictured in Plate 477 are also worthy of mention here. The smaller item is a wood composition figure of Jiminy manufactured by Multi-Products Company of Chicago. Several other pieces from this set were pictured in Volume One, and the large-style, 5″ Jiminy figure is one of the harder examples to find. Also pictured in this Plate is the Jiminy Cricket wood composition character bank manufactured by the Crown Toy and Novelty Company. The figure is hollow and has a metal trap door built into the base.

The Knickerbocker Jiminy Cricket doll pictured in Plate 479 is one of the rarest of all Jiminy dolls. Shown with its original wrist tag, this doll presents Jiminy in a very cricket-like design. He is less personified here than in other doll designs, so he appears to be much more of an insect with very skinny legs and an abdomen divided into sections.

Two other Pinocchio inspired items are the Figaro the Cat ceramic figure manufactured by Gepetto Pottery and the unusual Pinocchio and Figaro statue produced by the same manufacturer. Both items are from the 1940's and they are examples of fine quality ceramic pieces. The largest Pinocchio doll manufactured by the Ideal Toy Company is shown in Plate 486. This very large doll stands 20″ tall and is one of the "nearest-to-life-size" examples of Disney's Pinocchio ever produced. At least two other sizes of composition and wood Pinocchio dolls were manufactured by Ideal, but this one is the granddaddy of them all!

"When You Wish Upon A Star" has been a musical trademark of the Disney organization over the years. The song comes from *Pinocchio*, and it is obvious that its popularity has helped keep the interest alive in the little puppet character. Whether the recent release of the full-length version of the film into over-the-counter video film sales will increase or decrease his popularity remains to be seen. Regardless of any short-term fluctuations in his popularity, Pinocchio represents all that is best in the art of Walt Disney Studios. The animation of the film was superb, the backgrounds masterful and the development of characters from Figaro the Cat and Cleo the Goldfish to Monstro the Whale was sheer perfection. Pinocchio should remain popular among today's Disneyana and general toy collectors alike because he is the symbol of a true film classic.

Later Disney features also were inspiration for fine character merchandise. The Steiff Bambi dolls pictured in Plate 488 and 490 give evidence to that. The release of *Bambi* by Walt Disney Productions in 1942 proved that the studio now had the perfect formula for animation success, and the movie reels were rolling! The American Pottery figures pictured in Plate 491 are especially popular among today's collectors because of their consistent quality of detail and design. The beautiful Bambi milk pitcher pictured in Plate 492 is yet another example of the many fine products manufactured by the American Pottery Company in the 1940's. The pitcher pictures four characters from the film: young Bambi, Thumper, Flower, and the Owl.

Disney's later releases of feature films such as *Dumbo, Peter Pan* and *Cinderella* all inspired a wealth of character merchandise, but only a few items from these film titles have been shown. There is a degree of collector interest in ALL of the Disney feature film titles, but generally the primary focus

of interest and enthusiasm among collectors is upon the films of the 1930's and early 1940's. It is still too early to analyze collector trends among collectibles from the films of the late 1950's and early 1960's. Some collectors believe that the Disney films of the 1950's are good, but the toys associated with them are not as interesting as those from the first two decades of the studio's productions. This is obviously a very subjective issue, but the toy marketplace has generally reinforced that fact. The early Disney film characters are the ones in most demand and least supply, so their prices often soar. Pricing for items of the 1950's and 1960's is often very erratic because many collectors are just not sure what they are worth now, or what they will be worth in the future.

To many, the collecting of Disneyana is an irresistible obsession. There is so much out there that can still be collected because fantastic amounts of Disney merchandise were marketed over the years. So, the hunt goes on and the collecting momentum never relents. The field of Disneyana collecting is highly recognized in the antiques and collectibles world. That presents a special challenge for the devoted Disney collector to be well informed, constantly on the lookout, and aware of current collecting trends.

With Disneyland in Anaheim, California and Walt Disney World in Florida – the vacation mecca of the world – the Disney characters will live on in the hearts of successive generations of children. What the future generations will choose to collect remains to be seen, but it is difficult to envision a time when the characters from Walt Disney's most popular classics, *Snow White, Pinocchio* and *Bambi* will not be collected.

It is this author's belief that the memories of these fine films will be cherished and evidenced through wonderful collections of toys in the decades to come. Walt Disney was a dreamer for all Americans, and most of us still share the dream.

PLATE 413
WHO'S AFRAID OF THE BIG BAD WOLF -
THE THREE LITTLE PIGS TEA SET
manufactured in the 1930's by the Ohio Art
Company of Bryan, Ohio. All pieces are
beautifully lithographed in fantastic color with
very graphic designs. The cups measure 1½"
tall and the large serving tray measures 5" x 7".

PLATE 414
THE THREE LITTLE PIGS BISQUE
TOOTHBRUSH HOLDER, made in Japan,
stands 3½" tall, has an interesting design in that
two of the pigs are musical and the seated pig
appears to be playing the piano. Upon closer
inspection, he actually is working at a pile of
bricks shaped like a piano. Circa 1930 and marked "c. Walt Disney".

PLATE 415
WHO'S AFRAID OF THE BIG BAD WOLF -
THE THREE LITTLE PIGS TIN TOY SAND
PAIL manufactured by Ohio Art and circa
1930's. This colorful pail pictures the wolf at
the pig's window and stands 4½" tall.

PLATE 416
Item A: GAME BOARD for 1930's version of Who's Afraid of the Big Bad Wolf Three Little Pigs game. The board measures 17″ square and features nice, colorful designs.
Item B: THE THREE LITTLE PIGS TIN SAND PAIL by Ohio Art shows the pigs playing musical instruments in front of their houses. Circa 1930's and approximately 7″ tall.

PLATE 417
BISQUE CHARACTER SET OF DISNEY'S THREE LITTLE PIGS, made in Japan, each of these little pigs is marked "c. Walt Disney" and stands 3½″ tall.

PLATE 418
SET OF FOUR POST TOASTIES CEREAL BOX CUT-OUTS from the 1930's. This set features one of the largest of all the cut-out figures in the form of the Big Bad Wolf. He stands approximately 6″ tall.

PLATE 419
THE THREE LITTLE PIGS CHARACTER
ASHTRAY. This is one of several lusterware
ashtray designs which were popular during the
1930's and marketed as a tie-in to Disney films.
This particular example measures 3″ tall and
4½″ across the front. Marked on the base is
"made in Japan" and "S73" as a model number.
Also marked on the bottom is "c. Walt Disney."

PLATE 420
THE THREE LITTLE PIGS TIN LITHOGRAPHED PAIL by the Ohio
Art Company stands 7″ tall and is unusual because it pictured Little
Red Riding Hood (Disney version) with the Three Little Pigs. Circa
1930.

PLATE 421
FERDINAND THE BULL CHALK STATUE stands 10″ tall and has
the name "Ferdinand" molded into the front of the base. Probably
a carnival piece.

PLATE 422
FERDINAND THE BULL MOVIE
THEATRE LOBBY CARD from an
early release of the film has bright col-
or graphics showing the angry
matador as Ferdinand sniffs at
flowers. The card measures 11″ x 14″
which is the standard lobby card size.

PLATE 423
FERDINAND THE BULL WALKING BULL
STATUE made of chalk or plaster. He is approximately 10″ long and is one of the more rarely
seen Ferdinand chalk piece designs.

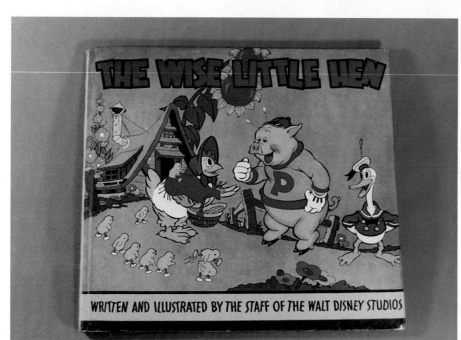

PLATE 424
THE WISE LITTLE HEN HARD-
COVER BOOK based upon the first
film in which Donald Duck appeared.
Donald appears in several of the very
nice full-color illustrations inside.
Copyright Walt Disney Enterprises
and circa 1935.

PLATE 425
BOX FOR WALT DISNEY'S SNOW WHITE
AND THE SEVEN DWARFS TARGET GAME
showing the Prince, Snow White, and all the
Dwarfs as targets on the box lid. The box
measures 19½″ x 13½″ and represents a
wonderfully colorful design. Circa 1938, the set
was manufactured by the American Toy Works
of New York.

PLATE 426
TARGET GAME SET pictured in Plate 425.
The original set included a plastic dart gun
which could be used to knock off the targets.
When one dwarf was struck by the dart, the
others would slide down the wooden slide to fill
in the remaining space until, eventually, all were
gone. The set also includes two wooden braces
to make the target stand up (not pictured here).
The "Grumpy" target pictured here is a
replacement.

PLATE 427
SET OF FOUR SNOW WHITE AND THE
SEVEN DWARFS CUT-OUTS FROM THE
POST TOASTIES BOX SERIES. All of the
figures in this set have hinged folds to make the
characters stand up.

PLATE 428
Item A: GRUMPY BISQUE DWARF marked on reverse "Walt Disney" is one of the largest bisque dwarfs ever produced, 5″ tall.
Item B: BASHFUL BISQUE DWARF with same markings as Item A, 5″ tall.
Each of these dwarfs had their name molded into the front of their hat.

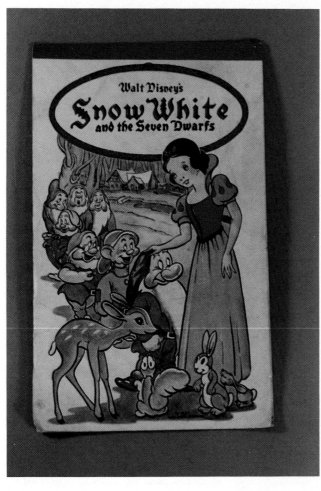

PLATE 429
WALT DISNEY'S SNOW WHITE AND THE SEVEN DWARFS CHILD'S WRITING TABLET with a beautiful paper cover. This tablet is marked "c. 1937 Walt Disney Enterprises" and pictures Snow White with all the dwarfs and several woods animals. It measures 5″ x 8″.

PLATE 430
DOPEY DOLL pictured here with original box was manufactured by the Ideal Toy and Novelty Company. He stands 12″ tall and has a cloth body with a composition head. He also still wears his original tag with pictures of Snow White and all the dwarfs. The toy is copyright 1937 by Walt Disney Enterprises. WHAT A GUY!

PLATE 431
SNOW WHITE, DOC, AND DOPEY GLAZED CERAMIC TOOTHPICK HOLDERS manufactured in England by S. Maw & Sons, Limited and circa 1938. These figures all have printed on their base "Genuine Foreign Copyright".
Item A: DOC CERAMIC FIGURE, 4″ tall.
Item B: SNOW WHITE CERAMIC FIGURE, 6″ tall.
Item C: DOPEY CERAMIC FIGURE, 4″ tall.
All of the figures have a compartment in the back for toothpicks.

PLATE 432
SNOW WHITE AND THE SEVEN DWARFS MOVIE THEATRE LOBBY CARD from the 1951 re-release of the film. This lobby card measures 11″ x 14″ and pictures all of the dwarfs at the foot of Snow White's bed. This lobby card is copyright 1951 R.K.O. Radio Pictures.

PLATE 433
WALT DISNEY'S SNOW WHITE AND THE SEVEN DWARFS LOBBY CARD also from the 1951 re-release of the film with the same markings of identification as in Plate 432. This card pictures Snow White and the Seven Dwarfs happily making music. Movie lobby cards from the 1930's through the 1950's have a duller paper finish than those produced today. However, the size has not changed. Standard size is still 11″ x 14″.

PLATE 434
SNOW WHITE AND FOUR OF THE DWARFS MINIATURE BISQUE SET. This is one of the smallest Japanese bisque sets ever produced. The dwarfs all measure 2″ and the Snow White figure measures 2½″. Many of these tiny bisque figures were used as favors on candy sold in the 1930's.

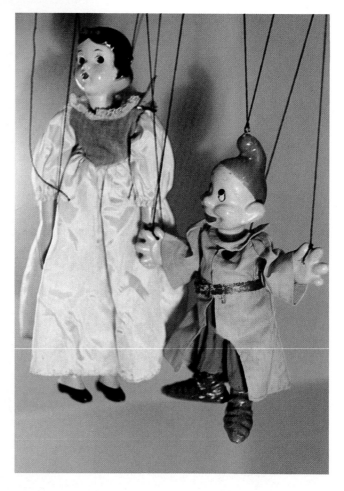

PLATE 435
HAPPY THE DWARF MARIONETTE DOLL manufactured by the Madame Alexander Doll Company and circa 1938. He measures 9″ tall and has a composition head, hands and feet.

PLATE 436
Item A: SNOW WHITE MARIONETTE DOLL manufactured by Madame Alexander Doll Company in the 1930's. She measures 12½″ tall and wears a velvet and satin dress (original). Her head, arms, and legs are all composition.
Item B: DOPEY MARIONETTE DOLL manufactured by Madame Alexander is 9″ tall and circa 1938. His head, feet, and hands are all composition.

PLATE 437
GRUMPY BOOKENDS inspired by Walt Disney's Snow White and the Seven Dwarfs. Each of these matching figures stands 7″ tall and has a label on the base which reads "Walt Disney Enterprises c. 1938 Manufactured by La Mode Studios Modeware, 109 West 26th St., New York". This company made glazed plaster and composition figures to be used for bookends, lamps and night lights.

PLATE 438
DOPEY DOLL made of velvet-like fabric with very large, oversize ears, has an oil-cloth painted on face. He stands approximately 12″ tall and is circa 1938. The manufacturer of this doll is unknown.

PLATE 439
SNOW WHITE LAMP stands 14″ to the top of the shade and was manufactured by La Mode Studios of New York. All pieces made by this company are easily identified by a sticker on their base which reads with all of the information quoted in the description for Plate 437.

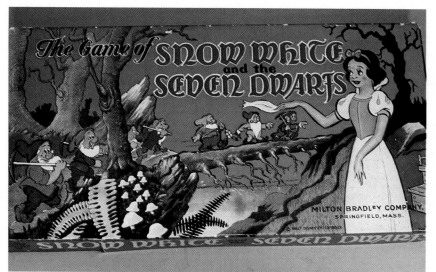

PLATE 440
THE GAME OF SNOW WHITE AND THE
SEVEN DWARFS manufactured by the Milton
Bradley Company of Springfield, Massachusetts
and copyright Walt Disney Enterprises. This
game is circa 1938.

PLATE 441
SNOW WHITE AND DOC GLAZED
CHINA PLATTER with two small
holes for handles measures 6″ across
and is marked on the back "c. 1937
W.D. Ent Made in Japan". The
figures were applied on top of the
glaze, not under it, so examples of
these are often found very chipped
and worn in the area of the decal
figures.

PLATE 442
SNOW WHITE AND THE SEVEN DWARFS
SCHOOL BAG is circa 1937 and measures 11″
tall without the handle. Silk-screened on the
front is the standard 1930's Snow White and
the Seven Dwarfs logo.

PLATE 443
Item A: THE STORY OF SNOW WHITE from
a series titled "The Seven Dwarf Books"
published by Whitman, 1938 Walt Disney
Enterprises.
Item B: THE STORY OF BASHFUL from the
same series as Item A copyright Walt Disney
Enterprises and published by Whitman.

PLATE 444
Item A: THE STORY OF SNEEZY from the
Seven Dwarfs series published by Whitman and
circa 1938.
Item B: THE STORY OF DOPEY from the same
series as item A and also published by Whitman.

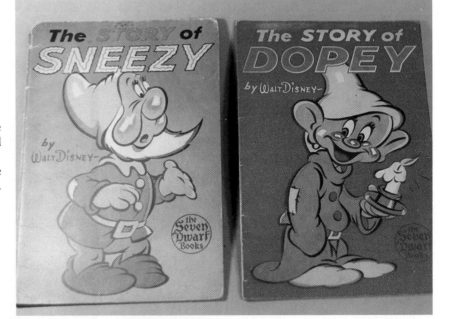

PLATE 445
WALT DISNEY'S SNOW WHITE AND THE
SEVEN DWARFS FULL COLOUR LANTERN
SLIDES, made in England and copyright Walt
Disney's Mickey Mouse, LTD. This beautiful set
featured a total of six color lantern slides packed two to a box, and all of the three individual
slide boxes fit neatly into the one outer box picturing Snow White and all of the dwarfs. Circa
1938.

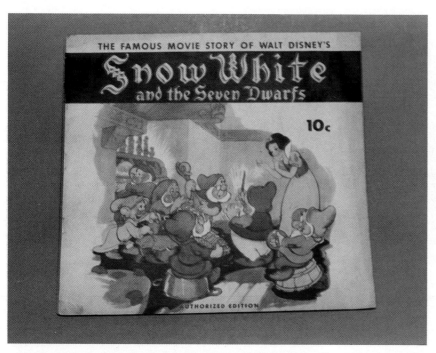

PLATE 446
*THE FAMOUS MOVIE STORY OF SNOW WHITE AND THE SEVEN DWARFS-*AUTHORIZED EDITION published by K.K. Publications and copyright 1938 by Walt Disney Enterprises. The book measures 9¼″ x 10″ and contains 15 pages of full color and black and white illustrations.

PLATE 447
DOPEY GLAZED CERAMIC FIGURE manufactured by the American Pottery Company and circa 1940. The figure stands 5½″ tall. Although these figures were produced generally a decade later than the most desirable Snow White collectibles, today's Disneyana collectors are wild about figures by this company because of their extremely high quality. The greatest action in selling and trading of these seems to be on the West Coast.

PLATE 448
SNOW WHITE AND FERDINAND THE BULL 1930's POSTAL CARDS. Regulation post card size, each of these has superb coloring.
Item A: SNOW WHITE AND THE PRINCE.
Item B: SNOW WHITE ON HER BALCONY.
Item C: FERDINAND THE BULL WITH HIS MOTHER.

PLATE 449
SNOW WHITE AND THE SEVEN DWARFS
MECHANICAL VALENTINE picturing all of
the dwarfs peering in the doorway. Copyright
1938 by Walt Disney Enterprises. Dopey's head
moves in and out of the doorway.

PLATE 450
DOPEY CHARACTER DOLL manufactured by the Knickerbocker
Toy Company and circa 1938. This doll is shown with original velvet
clothes and composition head, arms, body, and feet. His arms are
jointed and he is 9″ tall.

PLATE 451
SNOW WHITE AND THE SEVEN DWARFS TEA SET showing the
original colorful box and the plain aluminum tea set and ''rustproof''
dishes that it contained. These pieces inside are all bright aluminum
and also included is a rolling pin.

PLATE 452
SNOW WHITE AND THE DWARFS PULL TOY manufactured by the N.N. Hill Brass Company. The toy measures approximately 13″ long and has a bell-ringing mechanism located beneath the wooden Snow White figure. The toy is of wood and metal construction with lithograph paper labels applied to the wood.

PLATE 453
GRUMPY COMPOSITION DOLL manufactured by the Knickerbocker Toy Company in the 1930's. He stands 9″ tall and is dressed in original velvet clothes. (The beard is a replacement.)

PLATE 454
GRUMPY GLAZED CLAY FIGURE is circa 1930's but has no visible markings except for the words "MADE IN NORWAY" printed on the bottom of his feet. The figure stands 5½″ tall.

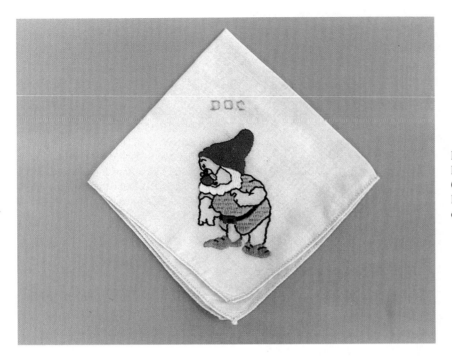

PLATE 455
DOC THE DWARF CHARACTER HANDKER-
CHIEF with embroidery-like sewn-on features.
Linen fabric with the character's likeness sewn
on and the name "DOC" above. Circa 1938.

PLATE 456
SNOW WHITE AND THE SEVEN DWARFS
CELLULOID PENCIL SHARPENERS AND
NAPKIN RINGS manufactured by Plastic
Novelties of New York in the late 1930's.
Item A: SNOW WHITE PENCIL
SHARPENER, "c. W.D. Ent." 2" tall.
Items B & C: SNOW WHITE AND THE
SEVEN DWARFS NAPKIN RINGS, 2½" tall.
Item D: DOPEY PENCIL SHARPENER, "c.
W.D. Ent." 2" tall.

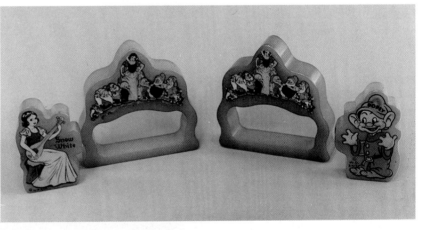

PLATE 457
GLAZED CERAMIC CHILD'S DIVIDED
PLATE picturing Happy, Bashful, and Doc.
Manufactured by Wadeheath of England, this
plate measures 8½" in diameter.

PLATE 458
SNOW WHITE AND THE SEVEN DWARFS TAPESTRY RUG has a velvet-like surface and measures 22″ x 36″. It is trimmed around the edges with a blue fringe (not shown in photo). Circa 1938.

PLATE 459
SNOW WHITE AND THE SEVEN DWARFS BISQUE SET shown in its original box. This set was distributed by the George Borgfeldt Company of New York and was made in Japan. Shown is the colorful box lid and the set of musical dwarfs that it contains. The dwarfs measure 3″ tall and Snow White is 4″. This set is much more rare showing the dwarfs playing musical instruments than the standard non-musical type.

PLATE 460
Item A: DOPEY CERAMIC CHARACTER PLATE, 3″ in diameter.
Item B: DOPEY LEAD-CAST FIGURE manufactured by Lincoln Logs and circa 1938. The figure is 3″ tall.
Item C: DOPEY CERAMIC CHARACTER PLATE, 2½″ in diameter.

PLATE 461
SNOW WHITE AND THE SEVEN DWARFS
CARD GAME published by Castell Brothers,
Ltd. of London in the late 1930's. The card box
measures 2½" x 4" and contains an exquisite-
ly colorful set of English character cards.

PLATE 462
Item A: SNOW WHITE BISQUE FIGURE
mounted on top of its original candy package.
Circa 1938 and 3½" tall.
Item B: GRUMPY BISQUE CHARACTER
FIGURE on top of his original candy package.
Also circa 1938, 3" tall.

PLATE 463
Item A: SNOW WHITE AND THE SEVEN
DWARFS TIN PAIL manufactured by the Ohio
Art Company and dated "c. 1938 Walt Disney
Enterprises". It is 4½" tall and pictures Snow
White seated in the grass with all the dwarfs
around her.
Item B: DOPEY GLAZED CERAMIC CHILD'S
EGG CUP, circa 1938 and 3" tall.

PLATE 464
ORIGINAL GRUMPY CEL from the motion picture "Snow White And The Seven Dwarfs" prepared and matted by Courvosier Galleries and circa 1938. A cel is an actual piece of hand-painted Disney art used in the production of one frame of film in the motion picture. This cel bears a paper label on the back which states that it was actually used in the Walt Disney production of Snow White and the Seven Dwarfs. Stamped into the matt in relief are the initials "c.W.D.E." Such examples of Disney Studio art are extremely valued by collectors today.

PLATE 465
SNOW WHITE AND THE SEVEN DWARF CHARACTER GLASSES are each 5″ tall and decorated with one of the dwarf characters. Both are marked "c. W.D."
Item A: BASHFUL CHARACTER GLASS.
Item B: HAPPY CHARACTER GLASS.

PLATE 466
"PEPSODENT'S MOVING PICTURE MACHINE" is an interesting advertising premium of the 1930's. The piece is copyright 1938 Walt Disney Enterprises and features two sets of moving pictures. One set of moving pictures shows Snow White and the Seven Dwarfs in motion. When the motion crank is turned in reverse, a series of Mickey Mouse and Donald Duck figures can be seen through the viewer. All-cardboard and paper construction.

PLATE 467
THREE-PIECE CERAMIC TEA SET manufactured in the 1930's depicting Walt Disney characters. The plate is 3″ across with the figure and name of "BASHFUL" written on it. The matching saucer and teacup accompany it.

PLATE 468
WALT DISNEY'S SNOW WHITE AND THE SEVEN DWARFS 96 PAGE STORY BOOK published by Whitman and copyright 1938 by Walt Disney Enterprises. The book measures 9″ x 12″.

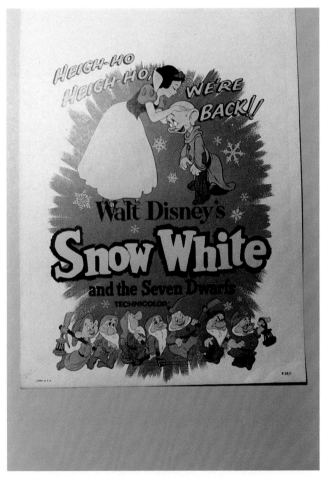

PLATE 469
WALT DISNEY'S SNOW WHITE AND THE SEVEN DWARFS MOVIE THEATRE INSERT CARD from the 1958 re-release of the film. This insert card measures 14″ x 22″ and makes an excellent background display for Snow White collectibles. Copyright Walt Disney Productions.

PLATE 470
SET OF THREE ART-DECO FRAMED DWARF PICTURES from Disney's version of Snow White and the Seven Dwarfs, circa 1938. All three pictures are marked "c. W.D.Ent" near the base and each has the name of the dwarf pictured on the bottom. They measure 5″ x 6″.

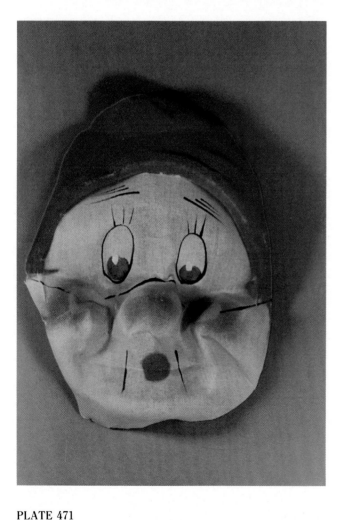

PLATE 471
DOC MASK made of stiff heavily starched cloth and circa 1938. Oddly enough, the mask has no visible holes to see through, so the child must have been expected to cut them out.

PLATE 472
Item A: PINOCCHIO CHALK FIGURE, approximately 6″ tall. No identification markings.
Item B: DOPEY CHARACTER CHALK FIGURE, approximately 12″ tall with no visible identification markings. Both items were probably used as carnival prizes. Circa 1938.

PLATE 473
Item A: WALT DISNEY'S VERSION OF PINOCCHIO published by Grosset & Dunlap and measures 7" x 9". The book contains full color illustrations and is copyright 1939 Walt Disney Enterprises.
Item B: PINOCCHIO CARDBOARD FIGURE, probably used as a wall decoration has no identification markings but stands 10" tall. Circa 1940.

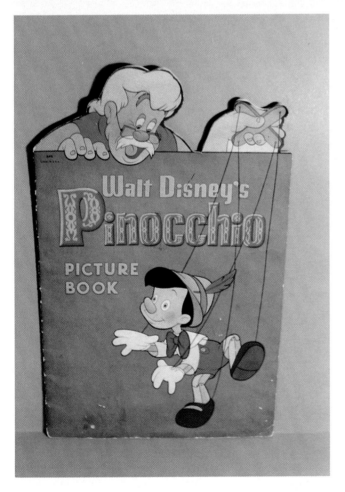

PLATE 474
WALT DISNEY'S PINOCCHIO PICTURE BOOK is a beautiful die-cut picture book containing all full-color illustrations of the various characters from the movie version of Pinocchio. It measures 9½" x 15" and was published by Whitman, copyright 1939 by Walt Disney Productions.

PLATE 475
PINOCCHIO BISQUE FIGURE, made in Japan and circa 1939, stands 4½" tall and has excellent paint detail, including rosey cheeks. This figure can be found by collectors today in several different sizes. This is one of the larger Pinocchio bisques. See *Character Toys* (Plate 277 for three other known sizes.)

PLATE 476
PINOCCHIO EXPRESS WOODEN PULL TOY
measures approximately 12″ x 10″ and features
the action of Pinocchio riding on a unicycle and
pedaling with his legs as it is pulled along. On
the sides of this very colorful toy are pictures
of Gepetto, Jiminy Cricket, Figaro the Cat and
other characters from the movie. This is a very
hard-to-find version compared to other Pinocchio wooden pull toys. Construction is
lithographed paper labels glued to wood.

PLATE 477
Item A: JIMINY CRICKET WOOD COMPOSI-
TION FIGURE manufactured by the Multi-
Products Company of Chicago and copyright
Walt Disney Productions. He stands 5″ tall.
Item B: JIMINY CRICKET COMPOSITION
BANK manufactured by the Crown Toy and
Novelty Company and marked "Walt Disney
Prod." on back. 6″ tall.

PLATE 478
PINOCCHIO MOVIE THEATRE LOBBY
CARD promoting the 1945 re-release of the
Walt Disney film. This very attractive card
measures 11″ x 14″ and pictures a scene from
the movie, its title logo, and a parade of all the
characters from the movie at the side. It is an
interesting piece of Pinocchio paper
memorabilia.

PLATE 479
Item A: JIMINY CRICKET DOLL from the Disney version of Pinocchio was manufactured by the Knickerbocker Toy Company. This doll has jointed arms and an all-wood composition body. The doll is shown with its original wrist tag.
Item B: ORIGINAL LOBBY CARD MOVIE PICTURE from the Disney film. It measures 11″ x 14″, standard size for these. Date uncertain.

PLATE 480
WALT DISNEY'S PINOCCHIO AND JIMINY CRICKET Better Little Books, copyright 1940 by Walt Disney Productions. This book has a very bright cover and is one of the more difficult Better Little Books to find.

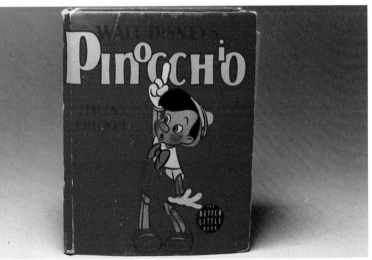

PLATE 481
Item A: FIGARO THE CAT GLAZED CERAMIC FIGURE, circa 1940 and manufactured by Gepetto Pottery. He stands 4″ tall.
Item B: PINOCCHIO AND FIGARO THE CAT GLAZED CERAMIC FIGURE by Gepetto Pottery. On the base of this figure is marked "GEPETTO POTTERY-WALT DISNEY'S PINOCCHIO" circa 1940. This fine ceramic figure stands 4½″ tall.

PLATE 482
GIDDY THE CAT WOOD COMPOSITION
CHARACTER manufactured by the Multi-
Products Company of Chicago. He stands 5″ tall
and is marked "GIDDY" on the front and "Walt
Disney Productions" on the back.

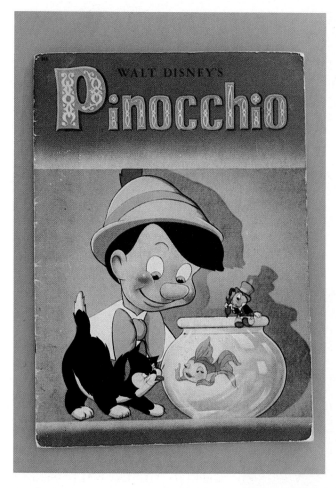

PLATE 483
WALT DISNEY'S PINOCCHIO PICTURE BOOK published by Whitman and copyright 1939-1940 by Walt Disney Prodctions. The extremely colorful book measures 9½″ x 13″ and is filled with full-color
illustrations taken straight from film clips from the show. This is by
far one of the most beautiful of all Pinocchio books.

PLATE 484
PINOCCHIO AND JIMINY CRICKET NURSERY PICTURE manufactured by Lambert Distinctive Pictures and made in the U.S. The picture is in a wooden frame and measures 8½″ x 11″.

PLATE 485
MECHANICAL PINOCCHIO VALENTINE is dated copyright 1939 by W.D.P. and features a very interesting mechanical action. When the heart lever near the back of the carriage is pulled, the figures of Pinocchio and Jiminy Cricket disappear down into the coach.

PLATE 486
GIANT PINOCCHIO DOLL manufactured by the Ideal Toy and Novelty Company. This composition and wood doll measures 20″ tall and has jointed arms, head, and legs. This is the largest of all Pinocchio dolls manufactured by Ideal.

PLATE 487
WOODEN PINOCCHIO DOLL. Although this particular toy is not one of the most attractive designs of Pinocchio, he is still a Disney character collectible. He is of all wood construction and has two blue wooden beads for his arms. The figure stands 5″ tall and is circa 1940. Oddly, this version of the puppet boy has an almost bird-like appearance.

PLATE 488
LARGE STEIFF BAMBI STUFFED DOLL, circa 1940 still has the Steiff button and tag in its ear. The German company manufactured several different styles and sizes of Walt Disney's Bambi character over the years. The doll is all fabric construction and stands 9″ tall.

PLATE 489
BAMBI CHARACTER SHEET MUSIC for the song "Love Is A Song" published by the Broadway Music Company, Inc. of New York. The music measures 9″ x 12″ and is copyright 1942 by Walt Disney Productions.

PLATE 490
BAMBI CHARACTER DOLL manufactured by Steiff of Germany with original button and label in ear and identifying tag on its chest. This version of the Disney deer measures 6″ tall.

PLATE 491
THREE CERAMIC FIGURES FROM WALT DISNEY'S BAMBI manufactured by the American Pottery Company of Los Angeles. All are attractive glazed ceramic.
Item A: BABY THUMPER FIGURE is 3″ tall.
Item B: BROWN THUMPER FIGURE is 4″ tall.
Item C: BABY FLOWER THE SKUNK FIGURE is 3½″ tall.

PLATE 492
BAMBI CHARACTER PITCHER, circa 1940's, was manufactured by the American Pottery Company and it measures 6″ tall. Pictured on the front are Bambi, Thumper, the Owl, and Flower the Skunk. Marked on the bottom is "c. Walt Disney." This is a quality Disney character collectible.

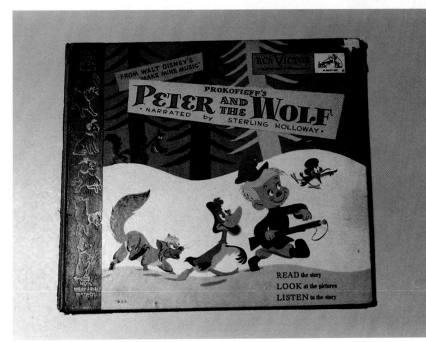

PLATE 493
PETER AND THE WOLF CHILD'S RECORD SET narrated by Disney veteran character voice artist, Sterling Holloway. The 78 r.p.m. record set included a colorful illustrated story book.

PLATE 494
BABY DUMBO GLAZED CERAMIC FIGURE manufactured by the American Pottery Company and circa 1940's stands 5½" tall. He wears a bright yellow baby bonnet on his head and has attractive bright pink ears.

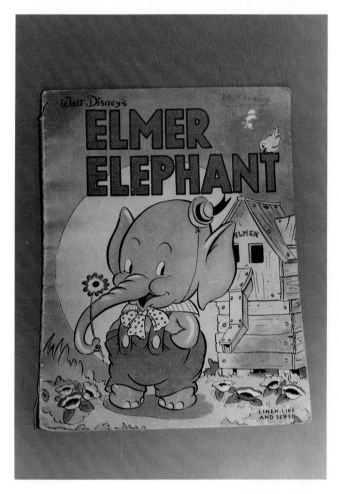

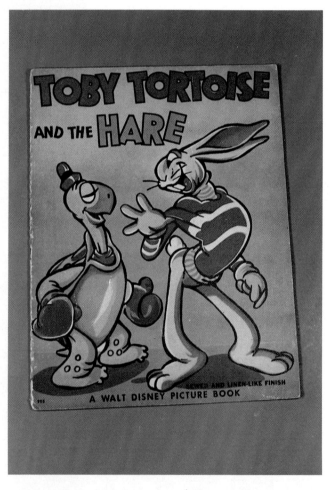

PLATE 495
ELMER THE ELEPHANT LINEN-LIKE BOOK published by Whitman Publishing Company of Racine, Wisconsin. The book measures 9½" x 12" and is copyright 1938 by Walt Disney Enterprises of Hollywood, California. Elmer was one of Disney's mid-1930's characters.

PLATE 496
TOBY TORTOISE AND THE HARE DISNEY CHARACTER LINEN-LIKE BOOK based upon characters featured in the Disney short film "The Tortoise and the Hare." The book is copyright 1938 by Walt Disney Enterprises and measures 9½" x 12¼". It was published as number 928.

PLATE 497
DISNEY CHARACTER CELLULOID PENCIL SHARPENERS circa 1930's and 1940's.
Top row: *Items A,B, and C*: JOE CARIOCA PENCIL SHARPENERS 1¼" long.
Bottom Row:
Item D: DONALD DUCK SHARPENER, 1¼".
Item E: FERDINAND THE BULL SHARPENER, 1".
Item F: PETER FROM PETER AND THE WOLF, 1¼".

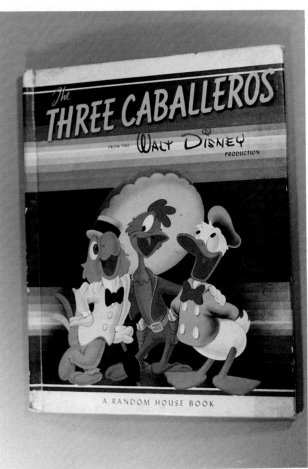

PLATE 498
THE THREE CABALLEROS STORY BOOK by Walt Disney was published by Random House and is copyright 1944 by Walt Disney Productions. This storybook measures 9" x 11" and is illustrated with many full-color pictures.

PLATE 499
JOE CARIOCA CHARACTER GLAZED CERAMIC FIGURE manufactured by the American Pottery Company and circa 1940's. This particular Disney character was featured in the Disney film "The Three Caballeros." The figure stands 6″ tall.

PLATE 500
CINDERELLA JIGSAW PUZZLE manufactured by Jaymar and circa 1950's. The puzzle was cut into extra large pieces so that children could put it together easily. This version pictures Cinderella leaving her slipper behind while the Prince watches her leave.

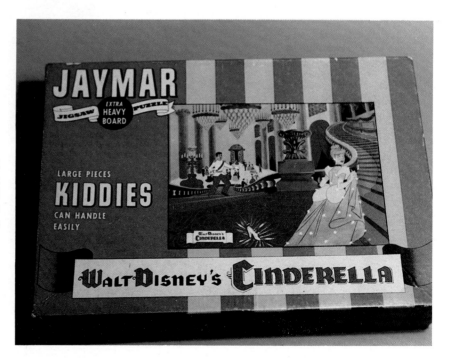

PLATE 501
WALT DISNEY'S CINDERELLA PAINT BOOK published by Whitman Publishing Company of Racine, Wisconsin and copyright 1950 by Walt Disney Productions. The book measures 8½″ x 11″.

PLATE 502
SHEET MUSIC FROM CINDERELLA for the song "Bibbidi-Bobbi-di-Boo" published by the Walt Disney Music Company and copyright 1949. Standard sheet music size.

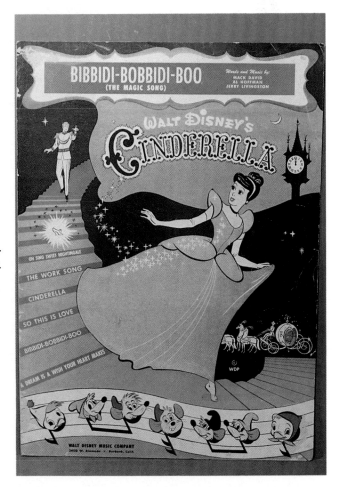

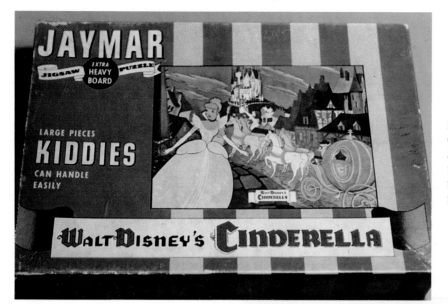

PLATE 503
CINDERELLA PUZZLE manufactured by Jaymar and circa 1950 pictures Cinderella arriving at the ball by pumpkin coach. This set featured extra large pieces so that it could be put together by a child.

PLATE 504
WALT DISNEY'S PETER PAN, A GAME OF ADVENTURE is a 1950's game manufactured by Transogram and copyright Walt Disney Productions.

PLATE 505
WALT DISNEY'S LADY DOLL AND PULL TOY manufactured by the Eldon Company of Los Angeles California. The hard plastic toy measures 10½″ x 10½″ and is based upon the 1954 original Disney film. The string pull for the toy is a small green bone. The toy could be pulled along on the platform as a pull toy or taken off and played with as a doll.

Western Character Collectibles

Whether we live in the North, South, East or West, there is a little bit of cowboy in all of us. Western character collectibles are as singularly American as any category of collecting can be. On television and in the movies, Americans have always loved their cowboys. There's something downright patriotic about a singing cowboy crooning a tune atop his trusty horse as they clippity-clop down a dusty trail. Gene Autry knew that secret and so did Roy Rogers. They are as tried and true as our own best friends, and that is why some collectors just can't let go of them.

Most collectors assume that collecting western character memorabilia is only a man's hobby. This is certainly not the case, for some women today regard Gene and Roy, among others, as being some of the most gallant and masculine of all movie stars who ever were enlarged upon the silver screen.

Western collectors carry their own special passion. Every collecting category has its brazen enthusiasts, but cowboy collectors often manifest the true child at heart. In my travels for this book, I once observed a phenomenon which will always stick out in my mind in regard to this subject. At an impressive antiques-only sale which is held at a fairgrounds just south of Cincinnati, Ohio, my wife and I once witnessed a pleasing sight. The show had just opened and most dealers and collectors

were racing through the seemingly endless rows of outdoor set-ups searching for that special item. Off to the side, away from all the collecting bustle, a car was parked at the edge of the grassy parking lot and its trunk was opened. From the looks of the crowd that had gathered, one would think that the Hope diamond had just been unveiled and offered up for sale. The crowd was so large, I could not see any of the trunk from my vantage point. All of the spectators were intent upon watching this "unofficial" dealer as he rummaged through his trunk. With such a crowd, I assumed the contents had to be good. Upon closer examination, I discovered that the special lure holding the spectators around the trunk like a magnet and away from the huge show that had just opened was something that could only be described as "cowboymania." The man was selling cowboy figures, boxed western playsets and other western toys as fast as he could pull them from his trunk. Whatever had been his form of pre-show publicity, he had certainly drawn a respectable crowd of buyers. The trunk was completely empty in about ten minutes and the buyers moved on to the rest of the show. Cowpokes-at-heart moved away from the trunk with toys in hand and trail-ride smiles on their faces.

Although western character collecting seems a specialty

in itself, there are many collectors who specialize within this field. Some collectors only search for Hopalong Cassidy or Roy Rogers items. Some only collect boxed play sets or toy guns. One collector who was a contributor to this volume took me upstairs into the master bedroom where he had laid out about 100 guns all over the carpet! I was free to pick and choose from all of the great western firearms and it was quite a choice. Guns weren't even this collector's true specialty, but it seems he had just never been able to pass one by.

Most of the western heroes mentioned in this chapter made their claims to fame in the movies. Those good old black and white action films were great enough to make cowboy lovers of us all. And as with any successful influence that Hollywood made upon our lives, slick toy marketing was soon to follow.

Two exceptions to this movie influence upon cowboy collecting were the Lone Ranger and Red Ryder. Both of these characters were subjects of successful strips or fictional book series. Although actors may have portrayed the Lone Ranger over the years, we can clearly remember his sharp cartoon likeness. Likewise, Red Ryder, who first appeared in the comics around 1940, stands out as a strong, masculine cartoon hero. (See Plates 507 and 539 to 541.)

The memorabilia devoted to cowboys seems uniquely all-encompassing. Consider Hopalong Cassidy. His representation in this chapter alone brings forth a television chair, hair tonic, a cookie jar, a wallet, birthday cards and invitations, ice cream cones and milk glasses. Now, guns and hats are obvious, but this list above represents items that we would never normally associate with the life of a cowboy. Nevertheless, such items are out in the collectibles marketplace to be found and enjoyed by collectors.

The superstar of western character marketing had to be Hopalong Cassidy. Although Gene Autry toys runs a close second, Hopalong Cassidy is simply easier to collect because so much merchandise with his likeness painted on or molded into it was produced. Who would think that a western hero's face would belong on a box of ice cream cones? (See Plate 518.) How many of us ever saw a cowboy in the movies eating an ice cream cone? Such unusual tie-ins were all a part of creative merchandising. Good cowboys meant good business and good residuals. America capitalized fully on its cowboys and we never looked better when we did so.

Western character collectors always find Big and Better Little Books to be a solid staple of their collection. The covers of the volumes devoted to western characters were colorful, vivid and packed with action designs. The Red Ryder volumes are undoubtedly the most colorful and graphic on the cover (See Plates 506 and 525). Running a close second to these are the Gene Autry books pictured in Plate 530. Some collectors display their Big Little Books as a background for figures and guns placed in front of them. Other collectors display them on shelves grouped by titles and subjects.

Collectors cannot make their way through this chapter without spending a little time to focus upon the guns. In today's society, there are factions of people who believe that toy guns are the psychological root of all evil in regard to child behavior. Granted with some of the fantasy-world warlords and supercreatures things may have gotten out of hand. But, back to the good old days of the cowboy. What would he have been

without his gun? It was an absolute necessity to keep from being scalped, robbed or bitten by a rattlesnake. A shiny six-gun was a tool of the trade. Besides, when a cowboy shot his gun actually at somebody, the old feller usually just fell off the roof and into the nearest watering trough. Now, how many kids had their behavior altered or lost any sleep over **that**!?

The author's favorite gun in this chapter is the Hopalong Cassidy Gold Plated Cap Pistol shown in Plate 524. Now, this is a gun that could have been worn proudly! No plain old metal barrel like most of the other kids guns had, no sir! This one appears to be solid gold. From the looks of it, it just had to shoot those make-believe bullets a little straighter than all the others. The original box is shown with it and has a nice picture of Hoppy atop his trusty horse, Topper. It's an unusual pose of him because his gun is drawn from its holster.

The matching pair of Hoppy guns pictured in Plate 526 is also a most respectable set. These have "ebony" grips with "ivory" sculptures of Hoppy on each. The Gene Autry guns pictured in Plate 531 are of a similar style, only these have ivory handles. The little Gene Autry pistol pictured in Plate 543 has an attractive red handle. The reason for manufacture of this little gun is odd because we seldom caught a glimpse of Gene using such a little gun. Cowboys used their straight-shootin' six-shooters. We seldom saw them fire a little pistol. The Roy Rogers gun shown as Item C of Plate 545 has an unusually long barrel and this gun feels quite nice in the hand. Finally, the sharp, graphic Zorro gun and rifle set cannot be overlooked. This handsome set was manufactured by Daisy and is pictured in Plate 550. It is one of the most complete western sets that this author has seen. Shown with its original box, the fine set includes a holster, gun and belt along with a matching rifle and two Zorro emblazoned gauntlet cuffs. A child did not have to use much imagination when he wore all of this. He WAS Zorro!

Other western collectibles that warrant a special mention are the Lone Ranger movie viewer pictured in Plate 540 and the Roy Rogers Rodeo play set pictured in Plate 548. The movie viewer has a special appeal because its box is very graphic and it is a neatly self-contained 1940's movie memorabilia set. The Roy Rogers play set by Marx speaks for itself. Although the sturdy box that it is packaged in is not terribly interesting in design (Plate 548), the contents of colorful plastic cowboys, horses, bucking broncos, fencing and corrals, American flag, trees, cacti, steers, jeep and detachable saddles all make up a very play-oriented set. Although the picture in Plate 549 only shows a part of the set, it gives collectors a clear idea of the fun content of each of these. While I was setting up for the photograph for this set, it was hard to refrain from playing with them just a little while we posed the picture. Such play sets are not as old as many of the other western character collectibles, nor are they terribly ingenious in their design. But they are certainly fun to play with, even today.

The toys of the western heroes that America has respected and loved remain today as a part of their western legacy. Their story will be permanently preserved in our folklore and their joy will be continually remembered through their toys. Western character collectibles are uniquely American and whether we collect them or not, their history touches us all.

PLATE 506
RED RYDER BETTER LITTLE BOOKS with beautiful color covers . . .circa 1940.
Item A: RED RYDER WAR ON THE RANGE.
Item B: RED RYDER AND THE SECRET CANYON.
Item C: RED RYDER AND CIRCUS LUCK.

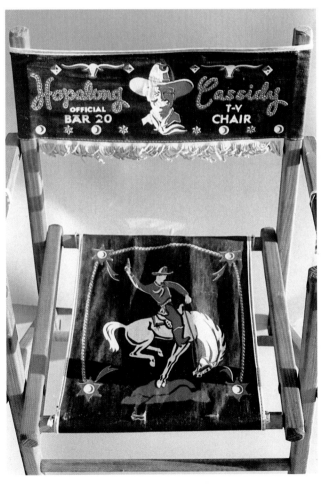

PLATE 507
RED RYDER PLAYMATES CHILDREN'S GLOVES AND MITTENS ADVERTISING POSTER featuring a beautiful black/red/and white picture of Red Ryder with the title logo. This large poster is copyright 1949 by Stephen Slesinger Inc.

PLATE 508
HOPALONG CASSIDY OFFICIAL BAR 20 T-V CHAIR is a cute child's wooden folding lawn chair which could be used as an indoor T-V chair. Decorated with fringe, Hoppy design and a canvas-like seat and back.

PLATE 509
HOPALONG CASSIDY LEATHER WALLET
with painted-on trim and stitching is marked
"Hoppy" in the lower right hand corner.

PLATE 510
HOPALONG CASSIDY COOKIE JAR BARREL. This beautiful
western character item features a colorful decal of Hoppy and Topper on the front of the glazed surface. The piece measures 11″ tall
and has the design of Hoppy's saddle for the lid handle.

PLATE 511
HOPALONG CASSIDY HAIR TRAINER BOTTLE picturing Hoppy
on the front label. The label is copyright 1950 by William Boyd and
was made by Rubicon Preparations Company of New York. 5¼″ tall
4 oz. bottle.

PLATE 512
Item A. TIME MAGAZINE November 27, 1950 issue picturing Hopalong Cassidy on the cover. It is Vol. LVI, No. 22 which originally sold for 20 cents.
Item B: QUICK MAGAZINE picturing Hoppy on the cover is the May 1, 1950 issue which originally sold for 10 cents. Magazines with western heroes on the cover make excellent backgrounds for toy displays.

PLATE 513
Item A: HOPALONG CASSIDY BIRTHDAY CARD for a six-year-old picturing a color drawing of Hoppy and two children on the front. The card is 6″ tall.
Item B: HOPALONG CASSIDY BIRTHDAY PARTY INVITATION manufactured by Buzza Cardozo of Hollywood, California. The invitation is 4″ tall and is circa 1950.

PLATE 514
Item A: "HOPALONG CASSIDY MUSICAL ROUNDUP" collection of sheet music tunes.
Item B: "HOPALONG CASSIDY SONG FOLIO WITH WORDS AND MUSIC" was published by Consolidated Music Publishers and is copyrighted by Paramount Music Corporation of New York.

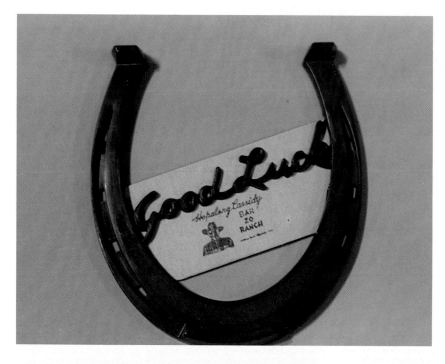

PLATE 515
HOPALONG CASSIDY GOOD LUCK HORSESHOE measures 4″ across and is marked "copyright 1950 by William Boyd". The horseshoe is made of plastic.

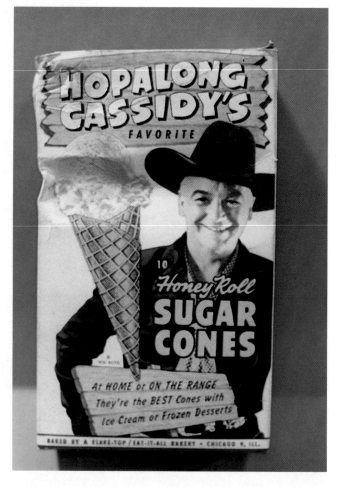

PLATE 516
HOPALONG CASSIDY AND LUCKY AT COPPER GULCH TELEVISION BOOK featured a magic moving picture screen that gave pictures the illusion of "moving" when the wheel on the cover was turned.

PLATE 517
HOPALONG CASSIDY'S FAVORITE HONEY ROLL SUGAR CONES BOX, manufactured by Eat-It-All Bakery of Chicago, Illinois. This 7″ tall box pictures a fine likeness of Hoppy on the front and bears the "c. Wm Boyd" marking.

PLATE 518
HOPALONG CASSIDY GAME manufactured by the Milton Bradley Company of Springfield, Massachusetts features a very colorful game box picturing Hoppy on Topper. The game is marked "copyright 1950 by William Boyd".

PLATE 519
Item A: HOPALONG CASSIDY CHARACTER MILK GLASS, approximately 6″ tall with Hoppy and his horse pictured on front.
Item B: HOPALONG CASSIDY CHARACTER GLASS, approximately 5″ tall with Hoppy's signature and picture on the front.

PLATE 520
HOPALONG CASSIDY TELEVISION PUZZLES manufactured by the Milton Bradley Company of Springfield, Massachusetts. The box that this set of four puzzles came in was designed to depict a television set with Hoppy on the picture tube. The puzzles are copyright 1950 and they measure 12″ square.

PLATE 521
CISCO KID BREAD LABELS promoting Tip Top Bread. Each of the labels measures 3″ across and pictures the Cisco Kid in various movie scenes. Each states at the bottom that Tip Top Bread is "Cisco Kid's Choice."

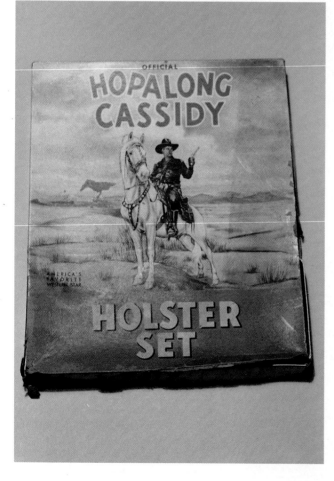

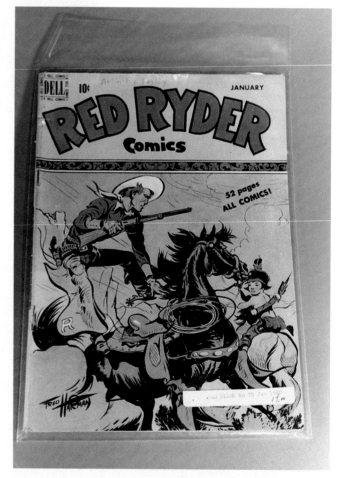

PLATE 522
HOPALONG CASSIDY OFFICIAL HOLSTER SET "America's Favorite Western Star" picturing Hoppy with his gun drawn in a western pose and sitting proudly atop his horse. Price in guide is for box only.

PLATE 523
RED RYDER COMIC published in January of 1950 is issue number 78 and sold for 10 cents. It was published by Dell Publishing Company.

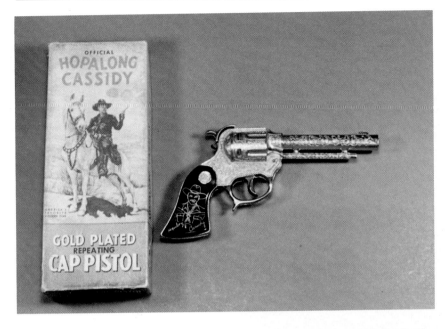

PLATE 524
HOPALONG CASSIDY GOLD PLATED
REPEATING CAP PISTOL manufactured by
the All Metal Products Company of Wyandotte,
Michigan. This most attractive gun has a
beautiful gold-like finish and fine black handles
with the outline of Hoppy on both sides. Shown
here with its original box.

PLATE 525
RED RYDER CHARACTER BETTER LITTLE
BOOKS:
*Item A: RED RYDER THE FIGHTING
WESTERNER*
*Item B: RED RYDER AND LITTLE BEAVER
ON HOOFS OF THUNDER* book by Fred
Harman.
*Item C: RED RYDER AND THE SQUAW-
TOOTH RUSTLERS.*

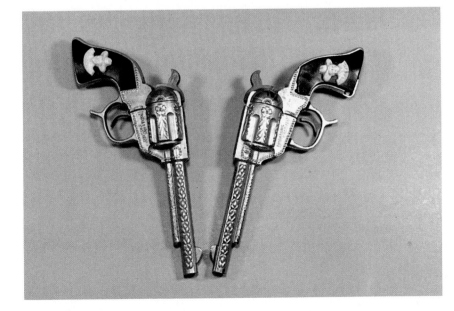

PLATE 526
PAIR OF HOPALONG CASSIDY GUNS, each
9″ long, with Hopalong Cassidy's name molded onto the body of the gun and his picture in
white plastic applied to the handle. What a
proud set!

PLATE 527
WESTERN HERO BIG AND BETTER
LITTLE BOOKS . .
*Item A: TIM McCOY IN THE
WESTERNER* featuring movie photos
inside, Big Little Books. Circa 1930.
*Item B: GUN JUSTICE FEATURING
KEN MAYNARD* copyright 1934 Big
Little Books.
*Item C: TIM McCOY AND THE SAN-
DY GULCH STAMPEDE* copyright
1939, Better Little Books.

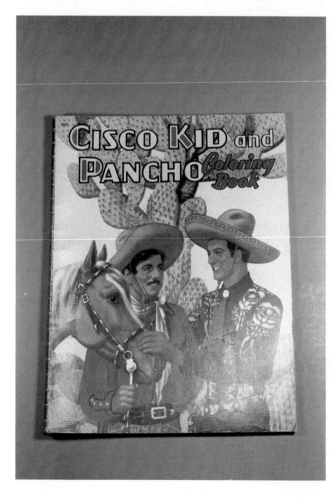

PLATE 528
CISKO KID AND PANCHO COLORING BOOK, oversize with large
pages, published by the Saalfield Publishing Company of Akron, Ohio.

PLATE 529
THE LONE RANGER CHALK STATUE, probably given as a carnival prize stands an impressive 16″ tall and is painted with bright
colors.

PLATE 530
GENE AUTRY BETTER LITTLE BOOKS
(clockwise from top left)
Item A: GENE AUTRY AND THE MYSTERY OF PAINT ROCK CANYON Better Little Books, c. 1947.
Item B: GENE AUTRY AND THE RAIDERS OF THE RANGE Better Little Books, c. 1946.
Item C: GENE AUTRY AND THE RED BANDIT'S GHOST Better Little Books, c. 1949.
Item D: GENE AUTRY AND THE LAND GRAB MYSTERY Better Little Books, c. 1948.

PLATE 531
Item A: GENE AUTRY CHARACTER WESTERN TOY GUNS with his name on the body and the double horseshoe symbol on the handles. These handsome guns measure 9″ long.
Item B: GENE AUTRY PICTURE ARCADE CARD.

PLATE 532
Item A: GENE AUTRY AND THE THIEF RIVER OUTLAWS copyright 1944 by Whitman Publishing and measuring 6″ x 8″ with colorful dust jacket.
Item B: GENE AUTRY 78 R.P.M. RECORD SET featuring 4 records recorded by the singing cowboy on the Okeh Records Label by CBS.

PLATE 533
Item A: TOM MIX AND TONY PINBACK BUTTON, 2″ across.
Item B: BUTTERMILK (Dale Evans' horse) TIN PIECE, 2½″ tall.
Item C: TOM MIX PLAY WATCH, 2″ across with picture of Tom in the center of the face.

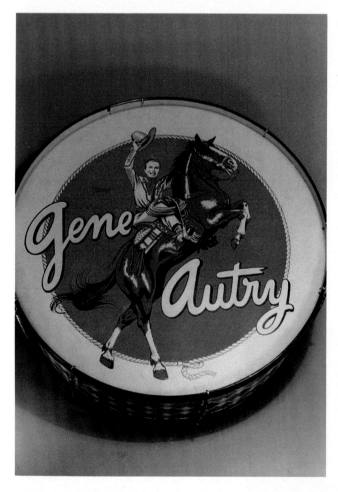

PLATE 534
GENE AUTRY WESTERN CHARACTER BASS DRUM from a trap set, approximately 24″ across with a fine pose of Gene and horse on the drum head. Price in guide is for complete drum and trap set.

PLATE 535
GENE AUTRY COMIC published by Dell Publishing is standard comic book size. This 1950's issue sold originally for 10 cents.

PLATE 536
THE LONE RANGER BIG AND BETTER LIT-
TLE BOOKS . . .
*Item A: THE LONE RANGER AND THE RED
RENEGADES* Better Little Books, copyright
1939.
*Item B: THE LONE RANGER AND THE
SILVER BULLETS* Better Little Books,
copyright 1946.
*Item C: THE LONE RANGER AND HIS
HORSE SILVER* Big Little Books, copyright
1939.

PLATE 537
WESTERN CHARACTER BIG AND BETTER
LITTLE BOOKS . . .
*Item A: THE LONE RANGER FOLLOWS
THROUGH* Better Little Books, c. 1941.
*Item B: GENE AUTRY IN PUBLIC COWBOY
NUMBER 1* a Big Little Book, c. 1938 by Whit-
man Pub. Co.
Item C: GENE AUTRY LAW OF THE RANGE
Better Little Book published in 1939 picturing
the singing cowboy on the cover with his guitar.

PLATE 538
Item A: "GOODBYE LITTLE DARLIN' GOOD-
BYE" SHEET MUSIC by Johnny Marvin and
Gene Autry and published by T.B. Harms Com-
pany of New York.
Item B: "I'M GETTING A MOON'S EYE VIEW
OF THE WORLD" SHEET MUSIC picturing
a very young Gene Autry, published by Calumet
Music Company.

PLATE 539
Item A: THE LONE RANGER AND THE TEXAS RENEGADES HARD-COVER BOOK published by Grosset and Dunlap, 1938 and copyright by The Lone Ranger Inc. The book measures 7″ x 10″.
Item B: THE LONE RANGER PAINT BOOK published by the Whitman Publishing Company and copyright 1941 by The Lone Ranger, Inc. This book measures 8½″ x 11″.

PLATE 540
THE LONE RANGER RIDES AGAIN MOVIE SET manufactured by Acme Plastics and copyright 1940 by The Lone Ranger, Inc. The colorful box measures 9½″ x 8″ and shows the Lone Ranger riding Silver. The set included a plastic movie viewer and several sets of still movie strips that could be viewed, each showing different scenes.

PLATE 541
THE LONE RANGER GAME HI-YO-O-O-O-O SILVER! manufactured by the Parker Brothers Company of Salem, Massachusetts and marked "copyright 1938 by the Lone Ranger Inc."

PLATE 542
THE LONE RANGER CHALK STATUE showing the Lone Ranger on Silver is one of the more unusual western character chalk pieces. It is 12″ tall.

PLATE 543
Item A: GENE AUTRY CHARACTER FILM distributed by Carmel Hollywood Films is 8mm and packaged in an attractive 3″ square box. *Item B:* GENE AUTRY PISTOL with red grips measures 6½″ long and has Gene Autry's signature on the frame.

PLATE 544
ROY ROGERS CHARACTER BETTER LIT-
TLE BOOKS . . .
*Item A: ROY ROGERS AND THE MYSTERY
OF THE HOWLING MESA* Better Little Books,
c. 1948.
*Item B: ROY ROGERS AND THE MYSTERY
OF THE LAZY M* Better Little Books, c. 1949.
*Item C: ROY ROGERS AND THE DEADLY
TREASURE* Better Little Books, c. 1947.

PLATE 545
Item A: (top) ROY ROGERS GUN measuring
9″ long with RR markings.
Item B: ROY ROGERS GUN AND HOLSTER,
small size, 5″ gun manufactured by Wyandotte
Toys.
Item C: ROY ROGERS GUN, 9″ long with nar-
row barrel.
Item D: ROY ROGERS ARCADE PICTURE
CARD (facial view)
Item E: ROY ROGERS ARCADE PICTURE
CARD (Roy on Trigger)

PLATE 546
BETTER LITTLE BOOKS OF WESTERN
CHARACTERS (tall format)
Item A: ROY ROGERS RANGE DETECTIVE
Better Little Books c. 1950.
*Item B: ROY ROGERS AND THE SNOW-
BOUND OUTLAWS* Better Little Books, c.
1949.
*Item C: GENE AUTRY AND THE BANDITS
OF SILVER TIP* Better Little Books, c. 1949.
*Item D: GENE AUTRY AND THE RANGE
WAR* copyright 1950 and published by Better
Little Books.

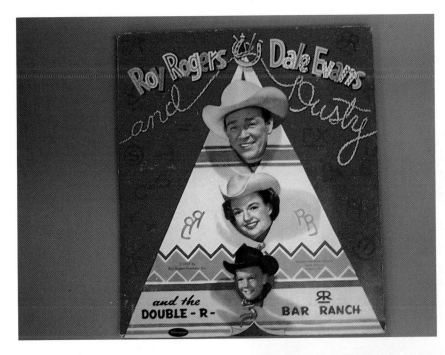

PLATE 547
ROY ROGERS, DUSTY, AND DALE EVANS PAPER DOLL BOOK featuring a colorful cover was published by Whitman and is circa 1950.

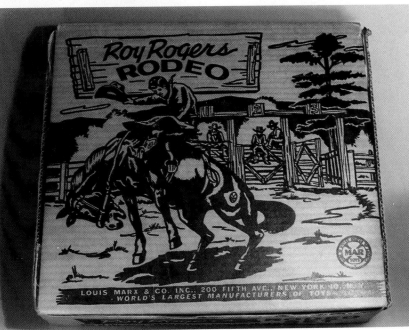

PLATE 548
ROY ROGERS RODEO CARDBOARD CARRYING BOX for the large Roy Rogers set manufactured by the Louis Marx Co. of New York.

PLATE 549
ROY ROGERS RODEO PLASTIC WESTERN CHARACTER SET contained in box shown in Plate 548. The set included corral fencing horses of all types, a jeep, several cacti, cowboys, Roy, an American flag and flagpole, western trees, saddles and halters, steers, and miscellaneous other western accessories. These Marx sets were built to last for long hours of play.

PLATE 550
ZORRO CHARACTER RIFLE, GUN, AND HOLSTER SET was manufactured by the Daisy Manufacturing Company of Plymouth, Michigan and billed as the "OFFICIAL SHOOTING OUTFIT". The set was also copyright by Walt Disney Productions. Included in the set was the "harmless" rifle, a black belt, and two gauntlet cuffs. A fantastic set!

PLATE 551
ORIGINAL BOX for the Zorro Official Shooting Outfit pictured in Plate 550.

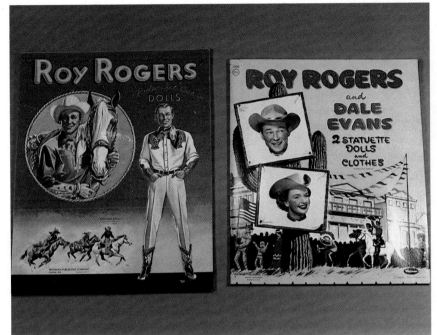

PLATE 552
ROY ROGERS PAPER DOLL SETS
Item A: (left)*ROY ROGERS RODEO CUT-OUTS* published by Whitman and copyright 1948 by the Rohr Company.
Item B: (right) *ROY ROGERS AND DALE EVANS 2 STATUETTE DOLLS AND CLOTHES* is copyright 1956 by Frontiers, Inc. and also published by Whitman Publishing.

PLATE 553
ROY ROGERS RODEO PLATE manufactured by Rodeo (by Universal) and also marked "Union made U.S.A." Ths glazed ceramic plate is very thick and rugged, probably designed for many years of child use. It measures 6¼″ in diameter.

PLATE 554
Item A: ROY ROGERS AND DALE EVANS THERMOS JUG with
lithographed picture of Roy and Trigger (yellow sky version.)
Item B: ROY ROGERS AND DALE EVANS THERMOS JUG with blue
sky in the background.

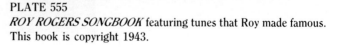

PLATE 555
ROY ROGERS SONGBOOK featuring tunes that Roy made famous.
This book is copyright 1943.

Kewpie Collectibles

Kewpies. Nearly everybody has some idea of what that term applies to, but many of the notions are wrong. Some might think that they are any representations of the little fellow who stings us all with his love-poisoned arrows around Valentine's Day. Wrong. Those are Cupids. Still others subscribe to the misconception that the "Kewpie doll" is a generic term. In the late 1940's and the early 1950's, the term began to apply to any type of carnival junk that was given away at fairs and amusement parks which even closely resembled a doll. This author has heard misinformed dealers and collectors call chalk statues, plaster figures and even plastic swinging toys on sticks given away as carnival prizes "Kewpie dolls." How wrong they are! The carnival merchandise given away over the years no more closely resembles a true "Kewpie" than a finger painting does a Rembrant! There is simply no comparison.

A certain friendship and mutual respect seems to bind together today's Kewpie character collectors. They all seem to have much in common. Today's specialist in the Kewpie collecting field has a tremendous respect for and devotion to the artistry of Rose O'Neill combined with what can best be described as a "passion" for collecting anything associated with her designs. To be a Kewpie collector seems to go far beyond the simple gathering of elfin-like creatures upon a shelf. The devoted Kewpie collector often knows the life of O'Neill backwards and forwards and nearly all of them can chronologically date a Kewpie collectible upon sight, even if it has no markings.

Rose O'Neill is seldom regarded simply as the cartoonist who created the comic strip series "Kewpie Korner" which first appeared around 1917. That series lasted only several years and it alone was certainly not enough to give her the timeless artistic status which her work enjoys today. What, then, made O'Neill so special if it was not her cartooning ability?

To begin, Rose was never really a cartoonist. Some artists are satisfied simply with that title. Rose O'Neill was not. She was an illustrator and one of the very finest in her day. Her character-inspired collectibles are sought by today's collectors who hope to piece together representations of every aspect and genre of O'Neill's art. That is no easy task because Rose was gifted in nearly all of the visual fine arts. Kewpie collectors seek examples of her earliest work just after the turn of the century (the first Kewpies appeared in magazines about

1909) and they follow her artistic career through Scootles, a later human child character who interacted with the Kewpies. Finally, they even seek examples of O'Neill's last creation, Ho-Ho, a little happy Buddha who appeared about 1940.

Rose O'Neill is today revered by her Kewpie collectors as much as Walt Disney is by Disneyana enthusiasts, but there the similarity between the two ends. It is doubtful that Walt Disney ever admitted to being the greatest artist in his own studio at any given time. He was a creator and a motivator, so he surrounded himself with very talented artists who could carry out his concepts and ideas. In contrast, Rose O'Neill remained the sole artist of her characters throughout her lifetime. Tremendous success, fame and fortune never removed her from her art. In fact, success seemed to compel her to create more and do more. She is an example of all we believe about the starving artist set in complete reverse. The more she achieved, the more she knew she must continue to achieve. What intrinsic control Walt Disney may have lost over the manifestation of his ideas when he set his drawing pad and pencils aside for loftier pursuits, Rose O'Neill never relinquished. She remained the creator and true alter-ego of her Kewpies until the day she died.

Because of this close relationship of the artist to her characters, Kewpie collectors have a kind of ongoing romance with Rose O'Neill. They tend to talk about her more than they do themselves and Rose seems to be as important to them as the toys they are collecting.

As was mentioned earlier in the introduction to this volume, Kewpie collectors gather each spring in Branson, Missouri, for the annual "Kewpiesta." This event is more like a family reunion than it is a collector's convention and collectors talk about Rose, meet fellow enthusiasts, show their own collections in contests, buy, sell, trade and in general, learn.

General collectors of toys and character merchandise may not have an understanding of the scope of Rose O'Neill's talents. Aside from the fact that she was renowned in her own day as a gifted illustrator, Rose was also a talented sculptor. In one of the best biographies ever written upon the subject of Rose O'Neill by Rowena Godding Ruggles, *The One Rose*, the author presents a photograph of Rose working upon the very first statue of her Scootles character. It is an impressive sight that one so talented as an illustrator could likewise be as gifted in the art of sculpting.

In addition to her gifts in the fine arts, Rose also qualifies as poet and writer. The little poems which introduced her characters and gave them their literary essence were written by Rose. This writing ability only helped to heighten the popularity of her illustrations as they appeared in magazines and papers.

The most extensive selection of Rose O'Neill's Kewpie character collectibles can be divided into two areas: bisque figures and china pieces. Kewpie bisque figures sometimes seem to be an endless parade of Rose's artistry. Advanced and seasoned collectors of Kewpie memorabilia agree that all Kewpie bisques were not "created equal." The German bisque pieces manufactured prior to World War I are far superior to those that were made in Japan.

The German bisque figures have excellent paint detailing on them and their design, poses and overall quality is superior to their Japanese counterparts. Although most Kewpie bisque figures are marked with either paper labels or stickers or stamped into the mold, it is not difficult to identify German bisque pieces. Check out the details on the face. German bisque Kewpie figures usually have a certain brightness about them in their expression which is achieved through excellent brush detail, especially around the eyes and mouth. There are seldom any paint imperfections to be found on the German figures.

Kewpie bisque items range from the very simple to the most ornate. The most common bisque figures are generally those found with "straight" poses, that is, the Kewpie is not engaged in any unique action. (Note the hugging Kewpies picture in Plate 556.) When a Kewpie bisque design is worked into something practical like a bud vase or toothpick holder, the rarity of the item increases and so does its price (and value). Figurines generally do not command the same high prices from collectors that vases, card holders, and such items as toothpick holders do.

Notice the guitar-playing Kewpie pictured in Plate 558. The design itself is stunning on its own, but the subtle pastel finish makes it an exquisite Kewpie collectible of lasting value. The beautiful pair of bud vases pictured in Plates 587 and 588 are probably the rarest of all Kewpie items pictured in this chapter. Identical in height and a matched set, this Kewpie Farmer and Kewpie Soldier are a handsome and captivating pair.

From bisque figures, we move to fine china. Rose O'Neill's Kewpies never looked better graphically than they do on a piece of Royal Rudolstadt Prussian china. Usually these pieces are done with attractive pastel backgrounds and bright, graphic and playful Kewpies and Kewpie scenes decorating them. The china set featuring Chief Wag and other Kewpies decorating the daisy and pink china pastel background is shown in Plate 562. Other fine examples of beautiful Kewpie character china pieces are shown in Plates 566, 586, 589, 601 and 607. The variety found in these examples proves that there are many pieces of individually different sets which can be collected today. Most would have a rare beauty even without characters on them and the addition of O'Neill's Kewpies makes them all the more fantastic.

Jasperware is not in the same family as china, but is certainly just as desired among Kewpie collectors, if not more so. Jasperware Kewpie designs usually present a deeply colored ceramic surface decorated with Kewpie motifs and flowers. Examples of fine Kewpie Jasperware can be seen in Plates 583 through 585 and in Plate 609. Jasperware examples are usually quite rare and they command high prices in today's collectibles market. Their beauty seems almost classical with the mythological-looking Kewpie figures, ornate flowers and scroll-like handles applied to each piece. Jasperware examples shown in this book are either blue or green.

Of course, no discussion of Kewpies could be complete without taking a look at the dolls. After all, it is the misnomer of the "Kewpie doll" that began our discussion. It is only fitting that we should take a closer look at what the real Kewpie dolls were like. First, Kewpie dolls generally are manufactured in one of two materials: wood composition or bisque. Wood composition Kewpie dolls are pictured in Plates 557, 559, 563,

572 and 573. Composition dolls worthy of special attention are the large 9″ bride and groom set with crepe paper original clothes in Plate 559, the bright 11″ Kewpie in Plate 563 with the red heart label, and the saucy little Kewpie lady in Plate 573 with the stunning clothes.

Bisque Kewpie dolls are shown in Plates 565, 600, 606 and 608. The doll in Plate 608 is particularly interesting because she has painted-on shoes. Most Kewpie bisque figures do not.

A third, less expansive family of Kewpie dolls exists and those are the ones made out of celluloid. Celluloid is a man-made brittle plastic-like substance which cracked easily and was popular for toy production during the 1920's through the 1940's. It was a cheap, easy to mold, lightweight material, but it certainly was not durable and it just did not last. Collectors today are lucky to find dolls in good condition made of this substance. Celluloid Kewpie dolls are pictured in Plates 564 and 580, with unauthorized or knock-off celluloid dolls pictured in Plates 571, 574, 577, 578 and 591. The giant 23″ celluloid Kewpie doll pictured in Plate 564 is one of the largest versions to ever be found.

From dolls we move to an area that is more unique. Rose O'Neill's characters made great subjects for use in advertising and they never looked better than when they appeared on tin lithographed ice cream trays. A fine collection of these is displayed in Plates 592 through 594, and in Plates 596 and 597 and in Plate 599. All of these feature Kewpie characters as a part of their design, and the coloring on many of them is superb. This is not an area of Kewpie collecting to enter into if you're a novice or on a tight budget. Kewpie trays can often command soaring prices in the marketplace. They are great display items with beautiful designs and graphics, so some serious collectors consider them objects of art. These have been known to sell for "fine art" prices.

There are some Kewpie collectibles of wonderful quality that have not been mentioned in this text but are pictured in the photography of this chapter. The author wishes to let the reader "discover" these on his or her own.

For every Kewpie collectible, there is a collector whose destiny it is to seek it out, find it and then cherish it. With her impish smile and her "Kewpish" heart, Rose O'Neill would enjoy watching today's collectors make over her characters in such a big way. She would be flattered that her characters remain popular among some even four decades after her death.

A critical time is approaching for Rose O'Neill's legacy and memory to be preserved. Some of her collectors today are first-generation fans who actually remember her works in magazine, book and newspaper print. A second generation of collectors has taken over who does not remember the artist as a part of their own lifetime, but who regards her past art as significant and who likewise seeks to preserve it. It is the passing and preserving of her memory to today's current generation of young people that must take place in order to insure Rose a spot among the great American illustrators of all time. Her name does not appear in the history books and no one has written a song about her to air on "MTV." How then will her legacy be passed on?

The same way it all started. Somewhere, in the great fantasyland that is "Kewpieville," the next generation will surely introduce itself to Scootles, Kewpie Doodle Dog and all of the Kewpies as it rediscovers the simple and beautiful magic that Rose created. It all starts with acquiring that first Kewpie doll or bisque figure and then the O'Neill magic and passion is rekindled once again.

Yes, Rose's legacy will surely be preserved. There are still enough undiscovered Kewpie treasures out there to "hook" yet another generation of Rose O'Neill fans. May the supply never dwindle!

PLATE 556
EMBRACING KEWPIES BISQUE FIGURE presents the Rose O'Neill characters in a cute pose. This particular figure (all one piece) is approximately 3½" tall.

PLATE 557
KEWPIE TALCUM POWDER CONTAINER DOLL still sports its original red heart label, with a paper label on its back marked "Rose O'Neill, c. 1913". Also, this 6½" figure has a paper label on its feet which indicated it was manufactured by "La Compagnie Vendome, Paris and New York."

PLATE 558
"KEWPIE SERENADE" BUD VASE is an exquisite example of bisque artistry with its adorable guitar-playing figure and the beautiful pastel colors decorating the rest of the vase.

PLATE 559
KEWPIE BRIDE AND GROOM made of wood composition are very rare lovers, indeed! They are most unique because of their original crepe paper clothes and the perfect condition of the often cracked composition. The figures are a large 9″ tall and are circa 1912 to 1913. They both wear clothes made entirely of crepe paper!

PLATE 560
KEWPIE HANDKERCHIEF BOX AND HANKIE. The beautiful, full color handkerchief box features a bright lid design and the hankie inside is just as special. The box originally would have held a set of hankies, not just the single one shown. The box is marked "copyright 1910, 1911, 1912 Crowell Publishing Company, 1913 Frederick A Stokes Company, and 1914 Rose O'Neill." Box measures 6¼″ square. It originally held three hankies.

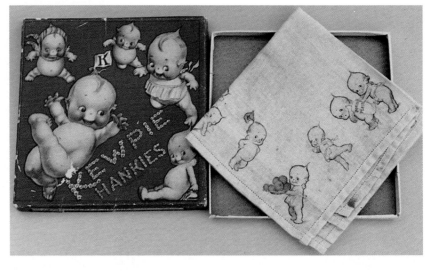

PLATE 561
Item A: SCOOTLES METAL FIGURE is 6½″ tall and is manufactured in pot metal. This particular piece has a bronze-like finish with little green metal flakes incorporated into the surface. He is marked "Scootles" and "c. Rose O'Neill" on the bottom of his feet.
Item B: SCOOTLES TIN PAIL features bright lithograph scene of Scootles and several different Kewpies building sand castles on the beach. This 3″ tall pail bears the design marking "KEWPIE BEACH" and is also marked and signed "c. 1937 by Rose O'Neill."

PLATE 562
GERMAN TEA SET FEATURING THE KEWPIES . . .This beautiful tea set is of the highest quality and is one that could have been proudly used upon the finest of tables! The pieces are marked "c. Rose O'Neill Wilson" and "Kewpie/Germany" with the pieces measuring 5″ for the teapot, 5″ in diameter for the plates and 3″ high for the sugar bowl. It is very unusual to find such a complete set of pieces. (Note-only a part of the complete set is shown. The collector actually owns all four-piece place settings!

PLATE 563
Item A: COMPOSITION KEWPIE DOLL with jointed arms stands 11″ tall and has the official Kewpie heart-shaped label on its chest. *Item B: JELL-O AND THE KEWPIES* BOOK, 6″ tall and copyright 1915.

PLATE 564
CELLULOID KEWPIE DOLL with jointed arms measures a full 2 feet tall. It's the largest known version to have been produced in this material. What a giant!

PLATE 565
KEWPIE DOLL dressed and shown with original box. This pretty little Kewpie is 7" tall and is shown with her original box which measures 8½" x 4½". She is shown dressed in her original flower-printed dress with a lace and satin trim along with her lace and satin trimmed bonnet. These are the little girls that Kewpie collector's dreams are made of!

PLATE 566
Item A: KEWPIE FABRIC DOLL manufactured by Richard G. Krueger, Inc. and marked "c. Rose O'Neill."
Item B: KEWPIE SUGAR BOWL marked "ROYAL RUDOLSTADT c. R.O. Wilson/Kewpie/Germany". The bowl is 3¼" in diameter.

PLATE 567
CHALK SAILOR KEWPIE DOLL designed in the style of Rose O'Neill's Kewpie characters stands 14" tall and is posed with a salute. Although this character is in sailor garb and does not have wings, he was certainly inspired by Rose O'Neill's characters.

PLATE 568
Item A: GERMAN BISQUE KEWPIE PLACE
CARD HOLDER measures a petite 2″ tall and
has a Kewpie holding a flower.
Item B: BISQUE KEWPIE CHARACTER
TOOTHPICK HOLDER is also 2″ tall and
features a mandolin-playing Kewpie leaning next
to a pretty basket. This piece is dated 1915 and
marked "c. O'Neill."

PLATE 569
THE KEWPIE KUTOUTS BOOK by Rose O'Neill. Marked inside
is "Verse and pictures by Rose O'Neill" and copyright 1912, 1913
by the Frederick A. Stokes Company of New York. This book
measures 7½″ x 11″.

PLATE 570
HO-HO CHARACTER CHALK PIECE by Rose O'Neill was made
in limited quantities and planned for commercial distribution in
the U.S. in the early 1940's. He was the last creation of Rose O'Neill
and is circa 1940. The figure measures 5½″ tall.

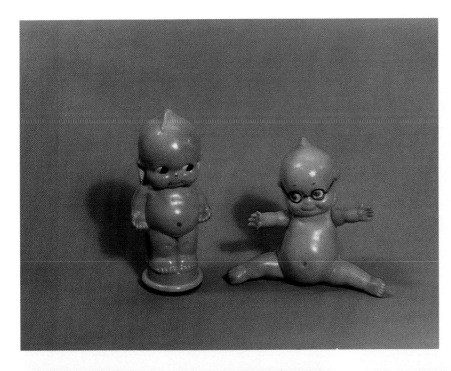

PLATE 571
Item A: CELLULOID PENCIL SHARPENER bears no Kewpie markings as it is probably a knock-off Kewpie imitation. The celluloid figure has a small removable metal pencil sharpener built into its base. The figure is 3″ tall.
Item B: CELLULOID KEWPIE FIGURE with jointed arms is also an unmarked knock-off Japanese Kewpie item. Oddly, this little imitation Kewpie fellow wears a pair of glasses, something rarely seen on actual Kewpie dolls. The doll measures 2½″ tall.

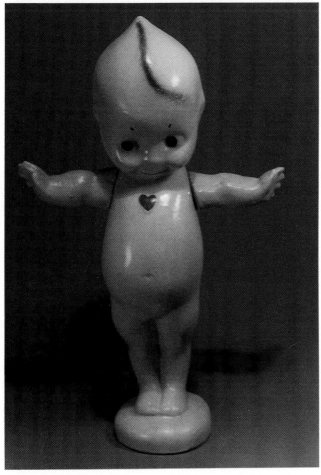

PLATE 572
COMPOSITION KEWPIE DOLL FIGURE with mint condition paint and red heart on its chest has jointed arms and stands approximately 12″ tall. Often such examples are found with very cracked finishes.

PLATE 573
LARGE KEWPIE DOLL dressed in what appears to be her original bathing clothes! This beautiful little gal is all composition with a circular base.

PLATE 574
KEWPIE CHARACTER CELLULOID DOLL FIGURE with movable arms stands approximately 3″ tall and is probably a Japanese piece. She has painted-on features and wears a 1920's version red bathing cap. The doll bears no visible identification markings.

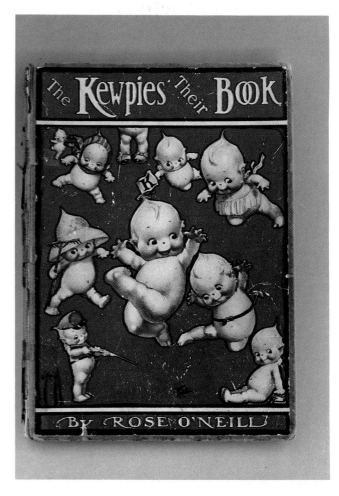

PLATE 575
KEWPIE DOLL BOX measures 8½″ x 4½″ and features a color-lithographed label glued onto a pulp-type box. The box is marked "c. 1913 by Rose O'Neill" and it also contains several lines of Kewpie verse.

PLATE 576
KEWPIE BOOK is actually titled *THE KEWPIES THEIR BOOK* and is copyrighted 1913 by the Crowell Publishing Company. Publisher inside is listed as Frederick A. Stokes Company, and it is dated 1913. The book measures 8″ x 11″ and contains 80 pages of black, white and red pictures.

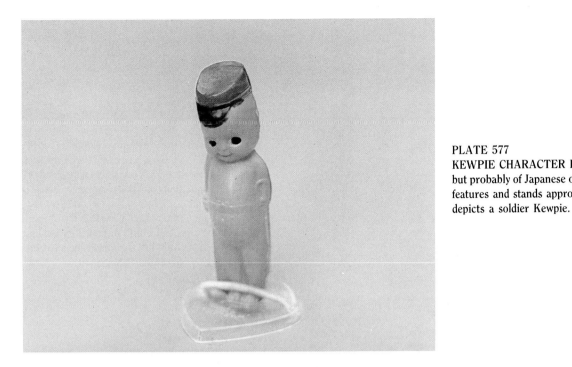

PLATE 577
KEWPIE CHARACTER FIGURE, unmarked, but probably of Japanese origin has painted-on features and stands approximately 3″ tall. He depicts a soldier Kewpie.

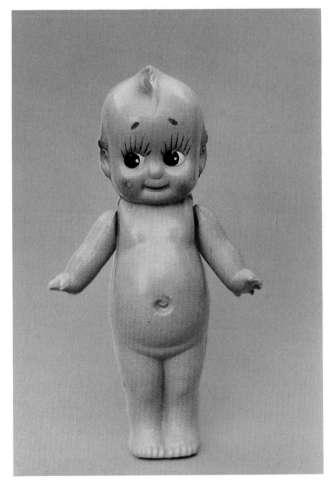

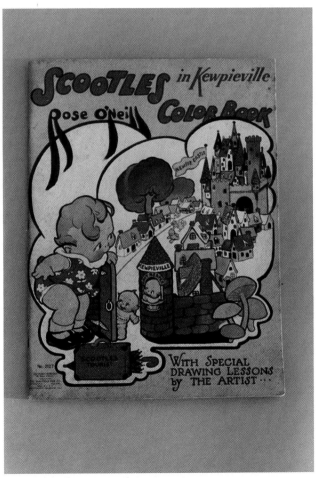

PLATE 578
CELLULOID JOINTED-ARM KEWPIE is marked as made in Occupied Japan. This bright piece measures 7″ tall.

PLATE 579
SCOOTLES IN KEWPIEVILLE COLOR BOOK by Rose O'Neill is circa 1920 and features a fantastic color cover! This, in the author's opinion, is one of the most beautiful books pictured in this volume. The book contains full-color illustrations that are as beautiful as those on the cover.

PLATE 580
Item A: CELLULOID KEWPIE DOLL with jointed arms bears a red-heart label on its chest that reads "KEWPIE Reg. U.S. PAT. OFF. SAXONY." and has a design label on the back with the date 1913. This larger figure stands 4″ tall. Condition of labels on such dolls is important.
Item B: CELLULOID KEWPIE DOLL with jointed arms and a red heart label on its chest that reads "KEWPIE Germany" and a label on its back which reads "Kewpie, 1913." 3″ tall.

PLATE 581
Item A: KEWPIE CHARACTER VALENTINE GREETING CARD is signed O'Neill on lower left-hand corner of the heart. It measures 4″ x 5″ and features beautiful Kewpie art work.
Item B: KEWPIE CHARACTER VALENTINE GREETING CARD, also signed O'Neill shows a tumbling Kewpie and measures 4″ x 5″. Illustrations of both cards are of extremely high quality.

PLATE 582
KEWPIE CHARACTER GLASS CANDY CONTAINER is a highly collectible piece because of its rarity among candy containers and its general appeal to Kewpie enthusiasts. It stands 3″ tall and is circa 1920. On the bottom is marked "Geo. Borgfeltdt & Co., Kewpies Reg. U.S. Pat." A rare piece when found in any condition, this one is unusual because it still has about 90% original paint.

PLATE 583
JASPERWARE KEWPIE CLOCK, styled in a dome shape design is made in Germany with this particular design having a German mechanism, also. Some of these had American mechanisms in them. It is marked on the reverse "Rose O'Neill Kewpie, Germany copyrighted" and is an extremely desirable Kewpie collectible.

PLATE 584
Item A: COVERED JASPERWARE KEWPIE SUGAR BOWL (left) is 3½" tall and marked "Rose O'Neill, Kewpie, Germany." Three seated Kewpies are pictured on front.
Item B: KEWPIE JASPERWARE CREAMER is 2¾" tall and matches the sugar bowl. The front is decorated with Kewpies, flowers and butterflies. The creamer has similar markings to the sugar bowl.

PLATE 585
JASPERWARE KEWPIE PITCHER is blue with white Kewpie figures pictured on the front. One Kewpie is Chief Wag, one is a cook, and two are regular Kewpies. The piece is marked, "ROSE O'NEILL/KEWPIE/GERMANY/ Copyrighted." The piece is 4½" tall and is a fine example of the beauty of German Jasperware design.

PLATE 586
KEWPIE CREAM PITCHER measures 4½″ tall and is marked on the base "copyrighted Rose O'Neill Wilson/KEWPIE/GERMANY" and also bears the stamp of Prussia-Royal Rudolstadt china. This beautiful pitcher dates from 1918 to 1920.

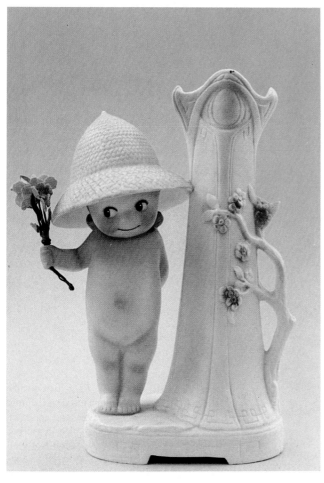

PLATE 587
BISQUE KEWPIE FARMER BUD VASE. This 6½″ tall vase is painted in beautiful soft pastels and the quality is superb. The little Farmer Kewpie holds a tiny flower arrangement. Circa date is 1913.

PLATE 588
BISQUE SOLDIER KEWPIE is of German manufacture, and is circa 1913. This pristine example is marked "Germany" and stands 6½″ tall. Bud vases are popular among collectors because they add an unusual variety to figurine collections.

PLATE 589
KEWPIE CHINA PLATE is 5½″ in diameter and is marked "c. Rose O'Neill Wilson, Kewpie; Germany" and it pictures Carpenter Kewpie and Chief Wag at play. The china itself features a bright daisy pattern with a pastel mauve background.

PLATE 590
KEWPIE "TRAVELLER" BISQUE FIGURE complete with umbrella and suitcase. This figure stands 4″ tall and is a perfect example of the quality detail and design of many of the Kewpie products manufactured in Rose O'Neill's day. Marked "O'Neill 4859" and circa 1912 to 1913.

PLATE 591
MINIATURE CELLULOID KNOCK-OFF KEWPIE PIECES. These small celluloid pieces are unmarked but were obviously intended to be patterned after O'Neill's characters. All have circular cardboard bases and jointed arms held on by elastic. Probably of Japanese origin, they range in size from approximately 2½″ to 4″.

PLATE 592
KEWPIE ICE CREAM TRAY advertising
"Langenfeld's Ice Cream, Made In Watertown."
A Kewpie golfer takes a break for some ice
cream as two other Kewpies frolic on a large
platter of Neopolitan ice cream in the
background. This tray measures 13¼" square.

PLATE 593
Item A: KEWPIE PURITY ICE CREAM TRAY.
It is signed "O'Neill" and measures 13" x 10¼".
An unusual example of a cute Kewpie.
Item B: KEWPIE TRAY advertising "Standard
Ice Cream" with the slogan "Goodness, How
you'll like it!" Four Kewpies are pictured as they
frolic on a large strawberry. Manufactured by
Parker-Brawner Company and circa 1920. The
tray measures 13¼" x 13¼".

PLATE 594
KEWPIE ICE CREAM TRAY advertising
"Mowry's Golden Glow Ice Cream." The two
Kewpies pictured on this tray are "Careful of
His Voice" and "Always Wears His Overshoes."
The tray measures 13½" square and is
copyright Rose O'Neill with a circa date of the
mid 1920's. Both Kewpies are pictured as
dreaming of sundaes that are floating inside of
bubbles. The tray was manufactured by Parker-
Brawner Company of Washington D.C.

PLATE 595
KEWPIE DIVIDED CHILD'S PLATE features the Kewpie, "Careful of His Complexion" working in the garden. Marked as "ROMA, Italian porcelain, it measures 7½″ in diameter. Exact date uncertain, but probably circa 1920. The other Kewpies pictured on the plate are "Chief Wag" and two playing leap-frog.

PLATE 596
KEWPIES TIN LITHOGRAPHED TRAY shows 12 Kewpies picking blackberries. Signed "O'Neill," this tray was manufactured by the H. D. Beach Company of Ohio. Marked "c. R.O.W." and circa 1924. This same company is the one which produced many of the famous Coca-Cola trays. 13″ x 10½″.

PLATE 597
KEWPIES TIN LITHOGRAPHED TRAY shows 11 Kewpies making lemonade and is the perfect companion to the one shown at left. Markings are identical to those of the tray at left. Lithography on both of these trays is vivid and beautiful.

PLATE 598
Item A: KEWPIE CHARACTER PLANTER, manufactured in glazed ceramic is unmarked and a common Kewpie item. These were manufactured in several colors, but the most common designs are the pink or blue versions.
Item B: KEWPIE FLOWER SIFTER stands 3½″ tall. The piece is not decorated with Kewpie characters, but it does have "KEWPIE" marked on the front.

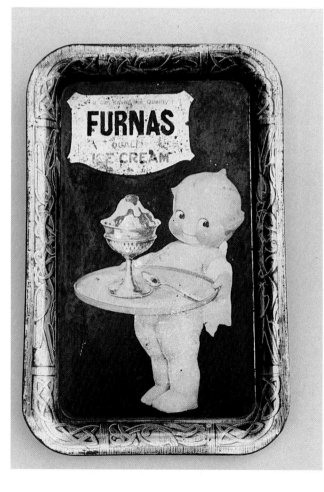

PLATE 599
KEWPIE-STYLE FURNAS ICE CREAM TRAY shows an upright Kewpie holding a strawberry sundae. This tray measures 17½″ x 11½″ and is one of the more common Kewpie tray designs. There are no markings.

PLATE 600
KEWPIE BRIDE AND GROOM SET is marked "Germany, O'Neill" on each piece. The bridal gown of the bride is netting in style of "Chantilly lace" while the groom has on a tuxedo made of crepe paper. 5″ and 4½″ tall, circa 1913. A romantic pair!

PLATE 601
KEWPIE GERMAN TEA SET
Item A: KEWPIE CHARACTER CREAMER, measures 2¾″ from base to top and pictures Kewpies at play on the sides.
Item B: KEWPIE TEAPOT with Careful-of-His-Voice and Always-Wears-His-Overshoes on the front. Two other Kewpies are pictured on the reverse. 5½″ tall and copyrighted "Rose O'Neill Wilson."
Item C: KEWPIE CHARACTER SUGAR BOWL (with lid replacement) made in Germany and 3¼″ tall. Kewpies are pictured around the sides.

PLATE 602
SOAP KEWPIE in original box measures 4½″ tall and the box declares that "Soap Kewpie dear to play with me, it's fun to take a bath you see". The box is marked "copyright R.O. Wilson", and is "warrented Best Pure Baby Soap." An attractive, rare Kewpie collectible because of the expendable nature of character soaps.

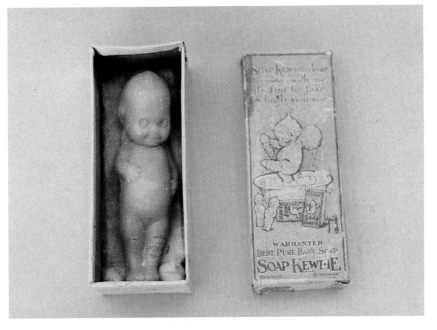

PLATE 603
KEWPIE CAMERA bears the popular name of Kewpie only, with no character decorations. These cameras were distributed widely by the Sears Roebuck Company and came in four different sizes. Box is marked as "Truphoto Daylight Loading Kewpie Kamera". This camera was manufactured by Conley.

PLATE 604
KEWPIE ALPHABET BOWL manufactured by
the D.E. McNichol Company of East Liverpool,
Ohio. This fine and rare piece features a 4″
figure of Chief Wag in the center and alphabet
letters printed around the rim. The bowl is circa 1920 as this company manufactured until the
mid-1920's. The piece measures 7½″ across. It
is a most desirable Kewpie item because of its
design and rarity.

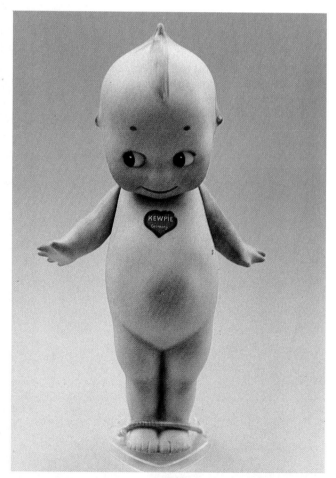

PLATE 605
Item A: KEWPIE AD CARD for royal society, this cute Kewpie
features a flocked red Christmas cap and is dated "Copyrighted 1913"
by Rose O'Neill.
Item B: KEWPIE LETTER OPENER with a 2½″ Kewpie on top is
marked on reverse "Kewpie Pewter".

PLATE 606
LARGE BISQUE KEWPIE doll is 6″ tall and still wears the bright
red original heart label which reads "KEWPIE Germany". The arms
are jointed bisque and the standard paint finish on the bisque is
beautiful.

Item A: KEWPIE CHARACTER CHINA BOWL, marked ROYAL RUDOLSTADT-PRUSSIA and circa 1913 or later. Two Kewpies are shown on inside bottom of bowl and four Kewpies frolic around inside rim. It measures 6¼" in diameter and features splendid colors and a soft glaze.
Item B: KEWPIE BOWL showing Chief Wag talking to three little Kewpies sitting on a log. This bowl also measures 6¼" in diameter and it is marked "c. Rose O'Neill Wilson, Kewpie, Germany".

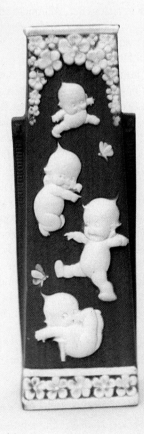

PLATE 608
SMALL GERMAN BISQUE KEWPIE has jointed arms and measures approximately 4" tall. Most Kewpie collectors agree that German bisque Kewpie figures are among the best quality of all collectibles in their field.

PLATE 609
JASPERWARE KEWPIE BUD VASE is green with four light pink Kewpies (one carpenter Kewpie and thee regular) shown on the front. This beautiful piece is marked "Rose O'Neill/Kewpie/Germany". Jasperware among Kewpie collectors is a "specialty within a specialty" area.

The Collector's Resource Guide

This chapter is written for the frustrated collector who has gone too long between shows and flea markets and who believes that there may be no relief in sight. First of all, there is comforting advice from those with experience. Patience will win out. When the slow show seasons of fall and winter have waned away, there will be many bright days for tramping the pavement and bargaining for those special toys. The intention of this chapter is to add to the character toy collector's knowledge and resourcefulness, opening up several options other than simply attending antique and toy shows.

I am certain that each of the methods and activities mentioned here will precipitate sizable agreement from some collectors and disagreement from others. What works for one person may not work for another. However, these are resourceful techniques that are presented here and many of them have worked quite well for other serious collectors.

To begin, we should discuss the "All-American attic myth." We have all heard it . . . it's the toy collector's version of the big fish story. Anyone who has ever collected toys at one time or another has caught himself at times staring blankly upward towards the attic of an old house in the neighborhood and wondering just what might still be left up there. Sure, there are plenty of stories to support the myth that there are still literally thousands of pristine, untouched Victorian and pre-war attics remaining which have escaped fire, salvage, new families and spring cleaning for the past 60 to 100 years. Rest assured, they are a real rarity. Consider that each time a house is sold, the chances of someone completely removing all items from the attic storage are very high. Add to this point the fact that Americans change houses today almost as quickly as they trade cars. Even if Americans only sold their homes once every twenty years (and realtors will agree that is a ridiculously conservative estimate) the attics filled with the toys we are looking for will have had a strong chance of being completely cleaned out at least three to five times. Somewhere along the line, there's a good chance all the good stuff, including old toys, has been removed.

But, there are enough true attic stories around to keep us hunting. I know of a collector in Kentucky who found several rare and beautiful items of Disneyana and a collection of Big Little Books that had survived virtually untouched for 50 years in the attic of a wealthy family. One of the items he found was a rare Steiff 1930's Mickey Mouse riding a go-cart. (This toy was pictured in Volume I). I also know of a local dealer who discovered a wonderfully preserved 1930's Disney ad calendar sealed up between the walls of a garage that was being demolished. Still another non-collector was having foam insulation blown into her attic and had to admit that she had never taken a peek up there. As she took a first and last look at her attic after six inches of foam had been blown in, she noticed a furry arm sticking up out of the insulation material.

She decided to rescue this "drowning" fellow and the resulting find was a large, hump-backed, circa 1900, fully-jointed teddy bear. When she learned of his fine value, he was immediately sent on a journey eastward to New York. This non-collector today still admits "Who know's what's up there under the rest of all that insulation?" Such interesting stories are adequate fuel for the imagination of the adventurous, so the search goes on.

I have heard of collectors who stuff mailboxes with business cards and leaflets in the neighborhoods that they consider to be prime toy territory. Don't use the mailbox! Postal authorities frown upon unauthorized use of their property and it's probably very illegal. If a collector is the adventurous sort and he suspects that an old house might be filled with old toys in the attic, he owes himself a try. If the lure of the "All-American attic myth" is just too strong, then he should go ahead. No reason to be shy. He should walk right up to the old door, ring the bell and proceed with an explanation about his curiosity and purpose. If he gets the door immediately slammed in his face (as is likely to happen in some cases) assume that the people weren't the sort to hang on to old toys anyway. If the resident should happen to actually listen to the brave collector, then he's gained an audience that just might result in the promise of old toys.

Another method for sparking the collector's urge to buy toys from private individuals is the classified ads placed in the local newspaper. A want ad might read as follows:

"Wanted. Any old toys.

Highest prices paid!

Call me at 000-0000."

If a collector places an ad such as this, he has made a serious error. The words "old toys" mean to many people simply "used toys" and as we all know, they are not the same thing. Advertising nebulously for "old toys" means the collector will get calls for anything Junior got last Christmas that he is tired of playing with. If a collector does choose to place an ad in a local paper, he should be honest, direct and mention specifics. A good ad might read!

"Wanted. Dick Tracy and Flash Gordon

Toys from the 1930's and the 1940's.

Will pay good prices! Call me at

000-0000."

In talking with dealers and collectors who use this approach, they agree that it's best not to advertise such phrases as "highest prices paid." In a way, the advertiser is being dishonest from the start since no one actually knows what the highest prices ever really are. The collector should simply state honestly that he will pay a reasonable amount of good money, his hard-earned cash.

Advertising collectors should not expect the phone to start ringing off the wall immediately. A single run of the ad will not do the trick. The ad needs to run over a long period so the idea sinks in, perferably a month or so. Also, collectors should not expect a flood of replies. In moderate-sized cities where mainly one newspaper prevails, advertisers are lucky if they get one or two solid replies per week that the ad runs. This may sound like the proverbial hunt for the needle in the haystack, but if the collector is patient, one fantastic lead may result in the purchase of a rare toy that was well worth the wait!

Another method of acquiring toys is by mail auction. This is a concept that has been increasing in popularity over the past decade, especially in the east. Several current nostalgia auction companies cater to mail-bid buyers and toy collectors. These companies normally put out quarterly auction catalogues with descriptive information and photographs of all items up for bid. They normally charge bidders as subscribers to their catalogue mailing list in order to offset production costs of the illustrated catalogues. The addresses of several of these auction houses are listed in the back of this book.

Most mail auctions require that bidders either mail in a bid sheet or phone on the last day of the auction to place a bid. Generally, the quality of items offered in these is excellent and the selection of rare items is often very impressive. Prices for toys range from modest to expensive depending upon the condition, rarity and appeal that the item has toward very advanced collectors.

Bidders should be forewarned that these companies serve a national pool of collectors linked up by phone on one evening and the bidding can get quite fervid. When the bidding gets tough, a collector may have to part with a significant amount of cash to acquire that special toy. There are seldom any "sleepers" (low-bid items going far below actual value) but the quality of the toys is usually exceptional and the prices reflect the old phrase "You get what you pay for."

Yet another way of procuring toys is by mail order. This process requires a certain measure of caution because ordering toys by mail can often put the collector in a very blind, vulnerable position. Reputable mail order antique toy dealers should always list their phone numbers so that additional information can be given to collectors desiring it. Some dealers may even furnish photographs of items in their stock, although this is an exception and certainly not the rule. The most important thing about mail order when viewed from the collector's standpoint is that return and refund privileges MUST be guaranteed by the dealer. If a dealer will not give such assurances to the prospective buyer, then he may have something to hide.

Mail order toy buying may be a good alternative for aggressive, resourceful collectors or those who live in remote, rural areas. All collectors should understand that buying antique toys by mail is often fun and satisfying (as close as we adults will ever get to sending in our box-tops and waiting for the postman again) but it does carry with it some risk.

Many dealers and collectors who contributed to this book both buy and sell toys by mail. All of these individuals encourage mail inquiries. When sending want lists or descriptions of items for sale, they ask that collectors please include a self-addressed, stamped envelope. Toy dealers have livings to earn, too, and excessive postage can often be extra overhead expense.

The list at the end of this chapter is by no means all-inclusive. There are many fine and reputable mail order antique toy dealers across the country who are not listed here. Those with the very best selections usually advertise heavily in two major toy publications, *Antique Toy World* and *Collector's Showcase*. Their names also often appear in regional and national general-line antique trade papers and tabloids.

As an additional service to collectors, I've included a list of "rainy day" activities for the toy lover in all of us. Some of these may appear obvious, but I'm always amazed at collectors who tell me that they've never tried some of these things that I mention. Being an educator by profession, I decided that some readers might enjoy my list of "rainy day activities for the toy collector."

Suggested Activities

1. Visit or write local antique dealers in your area and personally let them know what your specialty is.
2. Visit your local library and consult the back copies of *The Reader's Guide to Periodical Literature*. Look for magazine articles of your favorite characters or ones dealing with your specialty. Take notes and make copies. These make excellent supplements to your library on toy collectibles.
3. Start a written inventory of your character toy collection. You may have been putting it off forever, but a rainy day is the best time to start!
4. Contact your insurance agent and check on the coverage that your homeowner's policy provides for your collectibles. Most basic policies have provisions that severely limit the amount of coverage to only the new replacement value of an equivalent item. Simply put, if your valuable, favorite Buck Rogers gun is stolen or burns up, most policies will only buy you a **new toy gun** (not a collectible replacement). What a horror that is! Considering the fact that many private collections represent a value surpassing that of the family car, checking on insurance would be a wise, smart move. Most companies offer the option of riders to cover valuables such as collectibles.
5. Call your family members, both distant and close, and mention to them exactly what you're collecting these days. You never know what Uncle George might find when he next cleans out the garage.
6. While you're visiting the library, scan all the auction listings for rural and out-of-town newspapers that you never read at home. You never know . . .
7. Read. Read. And then read some more. You can never be too knowledgeable in your area of collecting. Remember, knowledge can often turn into dollars when it saves you from paying too much for a toy or when it tips you off that a certain item is a tremendous bargain. Toy collectors need to be educated and there aren't many colleges around that offer degrees in collecting.
8. Take a rainy day for maintenance of your collection. Play with your wind-up toys; they need the exercise. Wax old lithographed tin toys and buff them to a good shine, but be careful not to scar or dull the finish. Always work with a test spot on an unseen portion of the toy first. Take

time to wrap or frame old paper collectibles. Air and moisture are bitter enemies of pulp-type paper books, so collectors should take care to preserve them.

9. Write a classified ad for your local paper explaining that you are a collector and tell what you're looking for. Listing your phone number is much better than listing your address - for obvious reasons.

10. Photograph your collection. If time and money does not permit a piece by piece photo inventory, then at least photograph each wall of your collection. A photograph is an accurate, instant inventory of your collection.

11. Research your own collection of toys. I know of a serious collector who has an old library card catalogue packed with literally thousands of cards detailing information about his collection. He also has filed and inventoried each item in his collection with a decimal system number. Each toy has a tiny tag on it with the identifying number and he has immediate access to all the information he has ever gathered on any toy. His system is by far the most sophisticated, useful and advanced form of independent research that I have ever seen. All of us could use such a system of organization and resourcefulness.

12. Design a toy collector business card for yourself. Cards are a definite, tangible reminder to the strangers that you meet as to exactly who you are and what you are looking for. Unless you have a post office box or want to hand out your personal address to the world, it is best to include only your phone number on these. Design a picture or logo which is "catchy" and will represent your interests to all those future contacts that you will meet. Business cards are a useful tool for the resourceful toy collector.

13. Take a day to "dream." Write down a concise, specific "want list" which describes all of the toys that you are currently looking for and list generally the broad price range that you are willing to pay. Make lots of copies and ship them out to toy and antique dealers who advertise and cater to mail order. You may be pleasantly surprised at the response.

14. Take the time to subscribe to all those toy collecting periodicals and papers that you've been putting off. Magazines and newspapers may not be as much fun to purchase as old toys, but in the long run the information you gain and retain will make you a much better, more informed collector.

15. Try rearranging your collection in some new way. Use this as an excuse to get in there and play with your toys. Some collectors feel afraid to touch their old toys, but look at it this way . . . when you're gone from this world, somebody else will have to deal with your collection. You might as well enjoy what you have while you have it. Be creative; work toys in and around with the furniture scheme. Don't clutter, but display. Remember, effective lighting can do a lot for a collection.

As was mentioned, none of these suggestions are brand new or earth shattering. However, they do offer the resourceful collector several interesting options as to how to improve both the quality of a personal collection and the collector's own ability to acquire additional toys by creative and interesting ways.

Finally, as the collector continues to expand his knowledge by reading periodicals more and visiting the public library frequently as a research base, he should not overlook the prospects of the weekly local farm and estate auctions taking place nearby. Getting to know local auctioneers well and letting them know that you are a serious collector may be the best bit of public relations that a toy lover will ever do. Respected and recognized collectors often get "tips" from auctioneers who know first-hand that an unsusual toy is going up for sale. Getting advance notice of when these toys will be selling certainly never hurts.

Also, collectors should not forget to scan local and regional publications for toys at auction coming up for sale soon. I once knew a collector who spotted an ad in a regional antique paper which mentioned that a "Mickey Mouse piano" was going to be auctioned that upcoming weekend in an estate sale. The collector decided that it was probably a common toy from the 1950's or 1960's, but he phoned a good collecting friend to tip him off that such a toy was going up for sale Saturday. Since this particular collector was a doubter, he turned all initiative over to his friend. Subsequently, the collector's friend phoned that auctioneer and found out that the toy was the very rare and desirable mint-in-the box Mickey and Minnie Mouse piano from the 1930's (pictured on this book's cover and in plate 199.) The friend left a bid of $150 on the toy and assumed that the piano would sell for an astounding price.

Auction day came with snowy weather. The crowd in attendance was small. The collector's friend won the piano with his bid of $150 and immediately made arrangements to pick it up the next day. The piano is worth four to six times what he paid for it and the collecting friend was grateful to the fellow collector who tipped him off. I learned a personal lesson from this story for, you see, I was that doubting collector who didn't follow through but passed the opportunity along. It pays to check out all leads. We never know when we'll encounter that once-in-a-lifetime find.

Use the information in this resource guide to help expand your collecting methods and your collection. Even the well-seasoned, advanced collector can use a new angle now and then.

Price Guide Introduction

The price guide for *Character Toys and Collectibles, Second Series* is presently in the same format as the one for the first volume. Readers must realize that although price guides appear to be highly objective because of their numerical focus, they are acually quite subjective in nature and obviously represent some educated estimating. The finest of all price guides can only be at best an accurate representation of estimates in today's quickly changing toy marketplace.

Contrary to what some readers of price guides often believe, such books are not written to help the author and his associates acquire toys cheaply by setting low prices. Nor are they written to make fortunes for the contributors by setting extremely unrealistic high values for toys that will be sold in the future. These are both myths that have no place in this book.

This guide is simply intended to let collectors, both novice and advanced, know generally what all of the toys pictured in this book are worth in today's toy marketplace. It is not intended to actually set prices for dealers or collectors. Most of us know from experience that the actual selling price of a toy depends on many things. For the collector's general consideration, here are several factors that I think go into establishing the selling price of a toy:

1. Condition of the toy.
2. Seller's disposition at time of sale. Is he in a good mood or a bad mood? Has it been a good or bad day for him?
3. Buyer's disposition at time of sale. What is his mood like? Is he kind and congenial or a real rat? This makes a difference.
4. Seller's current stock. How many of these toys does the dealer have in stock? If he has only one and thinks it's rare, that's one thing. If he has a dozen more just like it under the table, that's another.
5. Seller's attachment to the toy. Does he really want to part with it?
6. Seller's knowledge of current toy values.
7. Buyer's knowledge of current toy values.
8. Seller's experience in toys. Is he a general-line antiques dealer or one who specializes in only antique toys?
9. Perceived rarity of toy by both parties.
10. Regional fluctuations in the toy market. What is "Big" in one area may not be somewhere else.

These ten factors all go into establishing the actual selling price of any given toy on any day. Any one of these factors can alter the price drastically, so the collector should be aware of them and realize that this price guide can only be just that - a guide. The price estimates printed here are sound ones, but they are just estimates. Obviously, they are, in part subjective and open to debate and scrutiny.

Pricing has been arrived at through samplings of similar toys selling at shows and in auctions. Actual prices that collectors paid to acquire such toys has been taken into account in some instances, but they have not been the sole standard. The author's own knowledge of today's current toy market was the bottom line on all pricing, so as that plaque that reportedly sat upon Harry Truman's desk read, "THE BUCK STOPS HERE."

Collector's should use this guide as a basis for forming their own pricing opinions. If collectors choose to quote this book's prices as a base for bargaining with dealers, that's fine. But they should then be prepared for the dealer to offer his own price references. No two books are alike and no two price guides are identical. Whether authors choose to admit it or not, price guides are subjective and usually based upon some form of estimating. Collectors should realize that they are using "educated estimates" here and their purpose is to be used as a tool to lead buyers and sellers through the maze of bargains and busts that are available today in the toy collecting marketplace.

The same working definition for FINE and MINT CONDITION TOYS as appeared in Volume I will be used again in this volume.

FINE CONDITION - the toy contains all parts; it was once played with or used, but the nature of the wear is very slight and does not distract from the toy's display potential. The toy must be reasonably clean and in working order. Most old toys are found in this condition, because they were once used.

MINT CONDITION - the toy is clean, bright and contains its original shine or luster. It may or may not have ever been used, but regardless of whether it was played with or not, it shows no signs of wear - AT ALL! It is complete and among many collectors, mint condition also applies to mint-in-box (M.I.B.) condition, meaning that the toy is still within its original packaging. It is a real rarity to find toys in true mint condition.

Photograph	Item	Fine Condition Value	Mint Condition Value
PLATE 1	Brownies Bowling Set	$ 100.00	$ 210.00
PLATE 2	Brownie Wood Puzzle	65.00	145.00
PLATE 3-A	*The Brownies At Home* Book	45.00	75.00
PLATE 3-B	*Another Brownie* Book	40.00	70.00
PLATE 4	Brownie Wooden Band Figures	95.00	200.00
PLATE 5	Eastman Brownie Camera	65.00	125.00
PLATE 6	Brownie Plate	45.00	100.00
PLATE 7	Buster Brown Cast-Iron Toy	375.00	700.00
PLATE 8-A	Yellow Kid Sheet Music	35.00	60.00
PLATE 8-B	Buster Brown Dictionary	18.00	40.00
PLATE 9	Buster Brown Valentine	15.00	30.00
PLATE 10	Foxy Grandpa Book	40.00	70.00
PLATE 11-A	Foxy Grandpa Doll	110.00	300.00
PLATE 11-B	Foxy Grandma Doll	110.00	300.00
PLATE 12	Toonerville Trolley Candy Container	75.00	150.00
PLATE 13	Happy Hooligan Planter	55.00	85.00
PLATE 14-A	Happy Hooligan Pencil Holder	65.00	135.00
PLATE 14-B	Kayo Wooden Figure	25.00	45.00
PLATE 15	Foxy Grandpa Figure	60.00	120.00
PLATE 16	Katzenjammer Kids Cast-Iron Pull Toy	750.00	1,300.00
PLATE 17	Katzenjammer Kids Hockey Game	30.00	50.00
PLATE 18	Katzenjammer Kids Puzzle Set	55.00	110.00
PLATE 19	Spark Plug Toy	350.00	725.00
PLATE 20	*All The Funny Folks* Book	45.00	85.00

Photograph	Item	Fine Condition Value	Mint Condition Value
PLATE 21	Barney Google Book	$ 35.00	$ 75.00
PLATE 22	Andy Gump Arcade Car	500.00	900.00
PLATE 23	Gumps Ginger Ale Bottle	35.00	75.00
PLATE 24	Mutt Gasoline Card	35.00	70.00
PLATE 25	*Bringing Up Father* Book	65.00	135.00
PLATE 26	Jiggs Chalk Figure	50.00	85.00
PLATE 27	Bringing Up Father Music	20.00	45.00
PLATE 28	Maggie & Jiggs Wind-Up	625.00	1,100.00
PLATE 29	Maggie & Jiggs Salt & Pepper Figures	60.00	125.00
PLATE 30-A	Jiggs Doll	150.00	320.00
PLATE 30-B	Maggie Doll	150.00	320.00
PLATE 31-A	Ching Chow Figure	45.00	90.00
PLATE 31-B	Lord Plush Bottom Figure	45.00	90.00
PLATE 31-C	Mr. Bailey Figure	45.00	90.00
PLATE 32-A	*Tillie the Toiler* Book	25.00	75.00
PLATE 32-B	*Mutt and Jeff* Book	45.00	85.00
PLATE 33-A	Andy Gump Nodder	50.00	95.00
PLATE 33-B	Rachel Nodder	50.00	90.00
PLATE 33-C	Chester Gump Nodder	50.00	90.00
PLATE 34-A	Felix The Cat Figure	35.00	75.00
PLATE 34-B	Micky Wood Toy	50.00	85.00
PLATE 35-A	Felix Sheet Music	15.00	40.00
PLATE 35-B	Felix Jointed Chad Valley	80.00	175.00
PLATE 36-A	Felix Chad Valley Doll	75.00	135.00
PLATE 36-B	2" Felix Celluloid	25.00	65.00

Photograph	Item	Fine Condition Value	Mint Condition Value	Photograph	Item	Fine Condition Value	Mint Condition Value
PLATE 37-A	Maggie and Jiggs Valentine	$ 15.00	$ 25.00	PLATE 88-A	L'il Abner/Daisy Mae Bookends	$ 40.00	$ 70.00
PLATE 37-B	Felix Valentine	10.00	20.00	PLATE 88-B	L'il Abner Can Bank	15.00	35.00
PLATE 38	Felix Jointed-Arm Chalk	50.00	105.00	PLATE 89	Shmoos Salt & Pepper Figures	35.00	55.00
PLATE 39	Felix Tin Wind-Up	300.00	600.00	PLATE 90	L'il Abner Packaged Puzzles	35.00	65.00
PLATE 40	Felix Three Piece Place Setting	65.00	125.00	PLATE 91	Nancy and Sluggo Game	25.00	45.00
PLATE 41	Felix The Cat Game	12.00	20.00	PLATE 92-A	Annie Christmas Card	8.00	15.00
PLATE 42-A	*Bringing Up Father* - Softcover	45.00	75.00	PLATE 92-B	Dick Tracy Christmas Card	8.00	15.00
PLATE 42-B	*Bringing Up Father* - 3rd Series	45.00	75.00	PLATE 92-C	Gasoline Alley Card	8.00	15.00
PLATE 43-A	Happyfats Tea Service	75.00	120.00	PLATE 93-A	Nancy and Sluggo Card	8.00	15.00
PLATE 43-B	Happyfats Boy Bisque Doll	60.00	95.00	PLATE 93-B	Comic Hero Card	8.00	15.00
PLATE 43-C	Happyfats Girl Bisque Doll	60.00	95.00	PLATE 93-C	The Gumps Christmas Card	8.00	15.00
PLATE 44-A	Happyfats Girl Bisque	35.00	60.00	PLATE 94-A	Sandy Bisque Figure	45.00	75.00
PLATE 44-B	Happyfats Boy Bisque	35.00	60.00	PLATE 94-B	Orphan Annie Nodder	60.00	110.00
PLATE 45	Reg'lar Fellers Pencil Box	15.00	28.00	PLATE 94-C	Daddy Warbucks Nodder	60.00	90.00
PLATE 46	Scrappy Christmas Lights	65.00	110.00	PLATE 94-D	Annie Miniature Figure	25.00	45.00
PLATE 47	Scrappy Christmas Lights	65.00	110.00	PLATE 94-E	Sandy Miniature Figure	20.00	40.00
PLATE 48-A	Scrappy Bank	20.00	40.00	PLATE 94-F	Orphan Annie Bisque Figure	30.00	50.00
PLATE 48-B	Scrappy Bank	20.00	40.00	PLATE 94-G	Sandy Bisque Figure	25.00	45.00
PLATE 49	Uncle Wiggily Tin Car	1,400.00	2,200.00	PLATE 95	Orphan Annie Sheet Music	20.00	65.00
PLATE 50-A	Uncle Wiggily Book	12.00	25.00	PLATE 96	Little Orphan Annie Paint Box	65.00	100.00
PLATE 50-B	Uncle Wiggily Book	12.00	25.00	PLATE 97	Orphan Annie Pull Toy	50.00	75.00
PLATE 51	Uncle Wiggily Crazy Car	250.00	500.00	PLATE 98	Oilcloth Orphan Annie Doll	75.00	140.00
PLATE 52	Peter Rabbit Lionel Handcar	325.00	600.00	PLATE 99-A	Oilcloth Sandy Doll	60.00	85.00
PLATE 53	Flip The Frog Coloring Book	60.00	100.00	PLATE 99-B	Orphan Annie Oilcloth Doll	85.00	120.00
PLATE 54	Uncle Wiggily Storybook	20.00	35.00	PLATE 100	Orphan Annie Coloring Book	20.00	45.00
PLATE 55	Gasoline Alley Game	35.00	65.00	PLATE 101	Orphan Annie Wood Composition Doll	165.00	350.00
PLATE 56-A	Moon Mullins Figure	18.00	40.00	PLATE 102	Annie and Sandy Wall Pocket	75.00	120.00
PLATE 56-B	Uncle Wiggily Figure	18.00	40.00	PLATE 103	The Pop-Up Orphan Annie Book	85.00	200.00
PLATE 57	Snuffy Smith Shakers	20.00	45.00	PLATE 104	Pop-Up Orphan Annie Book	85.00	200.00
PLATE 58	Betty Boop String Holder	65.00	135.00	PLATE 105-A	Orphan Annie Watch	150.00	250.00
PLATE 59	Bimbo Boxed Figures	120.00	200.00	PLATE 105-B	Orphan Annie Rummy Cards	50.00	75.00
PLATE 60	Betty Boop Candy Box	50.00	85.00	PLATE 106-A	Orphan Annie Yellow Pull Toy	60.00	85.00
PLATE 61-A	Betty Boop Bridge Cards	15.00	30.00	PLATE 106-B	Orphan Annie White Pull Toy	60.00	85.00
PLATE 61-B	Bimbo Flip Cards	10.00	20.00	PLATE 107	Orphan Annie Tea Set	85.00	150.00
PLATE 62	Betty Boop Wall Pocket	65.00	110.00	PLATE 108	Orphan Annie Big Little Books (price each)	20.00	40.00
PLATE 63	Betty Boop Celluloid Wind-up	200.00	600.00	PLATE 109	Orphan Annie Table Cloth	80.00	120.00
PLATE 64	Moon Mullins & Kayo Soap	75.00	120.00	PLATE 110	Orphan Annie Knitting Set	70.00	120.00
PLATE 65-A	Bimbo Figure	15.00	40.00	PLATE 111	Orphan Annie Knitting Set	70.00	120.00
PLATE 65-B	Koko The Clown Figure	20.00	45.00	PLATE 112	Orphan Annie China Tea Set	175.00	350.00
PLATE 65-C	Betty Boop Figure	20.00	45.00	PLATE 113-A	Orphan Annie Doll	50.00	100.00
PLATE 66-A	Bimbo Japanese Figure	20.00	40.00	PLATE 113-B	Sandy Tin Toy	100.00	165.00
PLATE 66-B	Betty Boop Bisque Figure	25.00	40.00	PLATE 114	Orphan Annie Crayon Set	50.00	90.00
PLATE 66-C	Bimbo Bisque Figure	20.00	40.00	PLATE 115	Little Orphan Embroidery Set	85.00	150.00
PLATE 67	Buttercup Composition Figure	100.00	175.00	PLATE 116-A	Orphan Annie Knitting Outfit	65.00	100.00
PLATE 68	Jeff Chalk Figure	30.00	55.00	PLATE 116-B	Little Orphan Annie Moccasins	35.00	60.00
PLATE 69	Betty Boop Carnival Figure	35.00	60.00	PLATE 117	Little Orphan Annie Hankie Holder	65.00	110.00
PLATE 70	Buttercup & Spare Ribs Tin Wind-Up Toy	850.00	1,400.00	PLATE 118-A	Orphan Annie Crayon Book	25.00	50.00
PLATE 71	Henry Celluloid Wind-up	250.00	600.00	PLATE 118-B	Orphan Annie Coloring Book	25.00	65.00
PLATE 72	Henry and the Swan Wind-up	300.00	750.00	PLATE 119-A	Annie Bead Game Toy	35.00	65.00
PLATE 73-A	Henry Paint Book	15.00	35.00	PLATE 119-B	Annie Embroidery Spool	15.00	25.00
PLATE 73-B	Henry Wonder Book	5.00	15.00	PLATE 119-C	Orphan Annie Dime Register Bank	80.00	125.00
PLATE 74	Henry Doll	20.00	65.00	PLATE 119-D	Little Orphan Annie Napkin Ring	45.00	65.00
PLATE 75	Denny Dimwit Figure	35.00	70.00	PLATE 120-A	Orphan Annie "Big Big Book"	45.00	75.00
PLATE 76-A	Favorite Funnies Puzzle	10.00	25.00	PLATE 120-B	The Great Big Orphan Annie Book	45.00	65.00
PLATE 76-B	Funnies Jigsaw Puzzle	10.00	20.00	PLATE 121	Little Orphan Annie Crayons Set	35.00	65.00
PLATE 77	Movie Komics Viewer	55.00	80.00	PLATE 122-A	Orphan Annie Jacks Set	30.00	55.00
PLATE 78	Little Lulu Book	10.00	22.00	PLATE 122-B	Orphan Annie Wall Pocket	90.00	125.00
PLATE 79	Joe Palooka Boxing Gloves	45.00	90.00	PLATE 123-A	Wooden Sandy, 3½"	40.00	70.00
PLATE 80	Humphrey Doll	85.00	115.00	PLATE 123-B	Wooden Annie Figure	65.00	95.00
PLATE 81	Joe Palooka Bicycle Pump	25.00	45.00	PLATE 123-C	Sandy Wooden Doll, 4"	50.00	75.00
PLATE 82	Blondie's Jalopy	675.00	1,400.00	PLATE 124	Orphan Annie Boxed Figures	125.00	275.00
PLATE 83	Blondie Stroller	65.00	90.00	PLATE 125	Celluloid Orphan Annie Doll	175.00	300.00
PLATE 84-A	Uncle Walt Doll	65.00	95.00	PLATE 126	Little Orphan Annie Bubble Set	65.00	125.00
PLATE 84-B	Skeezix Oilcloth Doll	50.00	85.00	PLATE 127-A	Junior Commandos Coloring Book	25.00	55.00
PLATE 84-C	Camel Doll	35.00	65.00	PLATE 127-B	Orphan Annie Paint & Crayon Book	35.00	60.00
PLATE 84-D	Pal Doll	35.00	65.00				
PLATE 85-A	L'il Abner Book	15.00	35.00				
PLATE 85-B	Joe Palooka Book	15.00	35.00				
PLATE 86-A	Pappy Yokum Doll	45.00	85.00				
PLATE 86-B	Mammy Yokum Doll	45.00	85.00				
PLATE 87	L'il Abner Coloring Book	15.00	35.00				

Photograph	Item	Fine Condition Value	Mint Condition Value
PLATE 128	Little Orphan Annie Hardcover		
	Books/Cupples and Leon (ea.)	$ 25.00	$ 55.00
PLATE 129	Orphan Annie Travel Game	45.00	80.00
PLATE 130	Orphan Annie Stove	45.00	90.00
PLATE 131	Little Orphan Annie		
	Little Library	65.00	100.00
PLATE 132	Skippy Sheet Music	15.00	35.00
PLATE 133	Mortimer Snerd Crazy Car	250.00	550.00
PLATE 134	Charlie McCarthy Doll	95.00	225.00
PLATE 135	Charlie McCarthy Doll	110.00	240.00
PLATE 136-A	*Charlie McCarthy Meets*		
	Snow White Book	25.00	45.00
PLATE 136-B	Time Magazine with		
	Charlie McCarthy	10.00	20.00
PLATE 137	Charlie McCarthy Lobby Card	15.00	35.00
PLATE 138	Charlie McCarthy Puzzles	25.00	45.00
PLATE 139-A	Charlie McCarthy		
	Game of Topper	35.00	65.00
PLATE 139-B	Charlie McCarthy Glass	10.00	35.00
PLATE 140-A	McCarthy Talking Card	25.00	40.00
PLATE 140-B	McCarthy Talking Card	25.00	40.00
PLATE 140-C	McCarthy Talking Card	25.00	40.00
PLATE 141-A	Charlie McCarthy Play Money	12.00	25.00
PLATE 141-B	Mortimer Snerd Teeth	10.00	25.00
PLATE 141-C	Charlie McCarthy Valentine	15.00	25.00
PLATE 142-A	A Day With Charlie (book)	20.00	45.00
PLATE 142-B	Charlie McCarthy Comic	12.00	22.00
PLATE 143-A	Charlie McCarthy Scrapbook	25.00	45.00
PLATE 143-B	Charlie McCarthy Poster	35.00	65.00
PLATE 144-A	Literary Digest, 1938	10.00	20.00
PLATE 144-B	Movie Life Magazine	10.00	22.00
PLATE 144-C	Joke Book with Charlie	10.00	20.00
PLATE 145-A	Charlie McCarthy Fan Card	30.00	55.00
PLATE 145-B	Charlie Punch-Out Premium	35.00	55.00
PLATE 146-A	Charlie McCarthy Book	25.00	45.00
PLATE 146-B	Charlie McCarthy Stencil	20.00	35.00
PLATE 147	Charlie McCarthy Dancer	70.00	125.00
PLATE 148-A	Flying Hats Game	20.00	35.00
PLATE 148-B	Mortimer Snerd Puppet	20.00	40.00
PLATE 149-A	Arcade Postcard	5.00	15.00
PLATE 149-B	Charlie McCarthy Birthday Card	10.00	20.00
PLATE 149-C	Arcade Card	5.00	15.00
PLATE 149-D	Charlie McCarthy Matches Set	15.00	30.00
PLATE 150-A	Charlie McCarthy		
	Pencil Sharpener	20.00	45.00
PLATE 150-B	Charlie Pin-Back Button	15.00	35.00
PLATE 150-C	Color Movie Slide	35.00	75.00
PLATE 150-D	Charlie McCarthy Pin -		
	Back Figure	15.00	30.00
PLATE 150-E	Charlie McCarthy Ring	15.00	35.00
PLATE 150-F	Charlie McCarthy		
	Pencil Sharpener	15.00	30.00
PLATE 151	McCarthy Question &		
	Answer Game	20.00	45.00
PLATE 152	Put and Take Bingo Game	25.00	45.00
PLATE 153	Chase and Sandborn Ad	20.00	35.00
PLATE 154	Original Boxes for Howdy Doody		
	Character Marionettes (each)	25.00	60.00
PLATE 155-A	Mr. Bluster Marionette	50.00	90.00
PLATE 155-B	Howdy Doody Marionette	50.00	90.00
PLATE 156-A	Princess Summer-Fall-Winter-		
	Spring Marionette	50.00	90.00
PLATE 156-B	Clarabell Marionette	50.00	90.00
PLATE 157-A	Flub-A-Dub Figure	15.00	30.00
PLATE 157-B	Howdy Doody Magic Puzzle Ball	15.00	30.00
PLATE 157-C	Howdy Doody Ball	10.00	20.00
PLATE 158-A	Howdy Doody Mitten Kit	10.00	25.00
PLATE 158-B	Howdy Doody Bee-Nee Kit	15.00	30.00
PLATE 158-C	Howdy Doody Slipper Kit	10.00	25.00
PLATE 159-A	Howdy Doody Jello Boxes	5.00	12.00
PLATE 159-B	Palmolive Howdy Doody		
	Premium	15.00	25.00

Photograph	Item	Fine Condition Value	Mint Condition Value
PLATE 159-C	Howdy Doody Bandages	$ 10.00	$ 20.00
PLATE 159-D	Howdy Doody Frosty Spray	5.00	8.00
PLATE 160-A	Flub-A-Dub Hand Puppet	10.00	25.00
PLATE 160-B	Flub-A-Dub Marionette	75.00	150.00
PLATE 161	Howdy Doody Carnival Game	20.00	45.00
PLATE 162	Howdy Doody Swim Ring	20.00	35.00
PLATE 163	Howdy Doody Game	30.00	60.00
PLATE 164	Howdy Doody Glass Lamp Shade	50.00	75.00
PLATE 165-A	Howdy Doody Cup	8.00	15.00
PLATE 165-B	Howdy Doody Bowl	10.00	20.00
PLATE 165-C	Howdy Doody Plate	10.00	25.00
PLATE 166	Howdy Doody Book	5.00	10.00
PLATE 167	Howdy Doody Umbrella	25.00	45.00
PLATE 168	Howdy Doody Ceramic Bank	15.00	25.00
PLATE 169	Howdy Doody Picture Set	45.00	70.00
PLATE 170-A	Howdy Doody Coloring Book	12.00	22.00
PLATE 170-B	Howdy Doody Follow-The-Dots	10.00	20.00
PLATE 170-C	Howdy Doody Coloring Book	10.00	20.00
PLATE 171-A	Howdy Doody Picture	4.00	10.00
PLATE 171-B	TV Guide - Howdy Doody	5.00	12.00
PLATE 171-C	Howdy Doody Picture	4.00	10.00
PLATE 172	Howdy Doody Sand Set	20.00	35.00
PLATE 173	Howdy Doody Bubble Pipes	15.00	25.00
PLATE 174	Howdy Doody Ukelele	20.00	45.00
PLATE 175-A	Howdy Doody Coloring Book	10.00	20.00
PLATE 175-B	Howdy Doody Coloring Book	12.00	22.00
PLATE 176	Howdy Doody On Trapeze	70.00	135.00
PLATE 177	Trapeze Toy (box only)	30.00	50.00
PLATE 178-A	Clarabell Push Puppet	15.00	35.00
PLATE 178-B	Howdy Doody Push Puppet	15.00	35.00
PLATE 179-A	Howdy Doody Bubble Bath	12.00	23.00
PLATE 179-B	Howdy Doody Nite Light	15.00	25.00
PLATE 180	Howdy Doody Wrist Watch	75.00	150.00
PLATE 181	Charlie McCarthy Knock-Off		
	Salt & Pepper Set	15.00	30.00
PLATE 182	Joe Penner's Duck Goo-Goo	45.00	70.00
PLATE 183	Amos 'N Andy Ash Tray	60.00	95.00
PLATE 184	Phil Silvers Game	20.00	40.00
PLATE 185	J. Fred Muggs Toy	40.00	75.00
PLATE 186	Groucho Marx Goggles	15.00	30.00
PLATE 187-A	Elmer Fudd Planter	30.00	60.00
PLATE 187-B	Porky Pig Planter	30.00	60.00
PLATE 188	Bugs Bunny Alarm Clock	70.00	150.00
PLATE 189	Porky Pig Wrist Watch	110.00	200.00
PLATE 190-A	Leave It To Beaver Slate	12.00	22.00
PLATE 190-B	Leave It To Beaver Book	4.00	8.00
PLATE 190-C	Leave It To Beaver		
	Coloring Book	12.00	22.00
PLATE 191	Jackie Gleason Bus Driver's		
	Outfit	50.00	85.00
PLATE 192	Leave It To Beaver Game	10.00	20.00
PLATE 193-A	Paul Winchell Record	10.00	20.00
PLATE 193-B	Jerry Mahoney Keychain	5.00	10.00
PLATE 193-C	TV Digest with Jerry Mahoney	8.00	15.00
PLATE 194-A	Farfel Cup	8.00	15.00
PLATE 194-B	Shari Lewis Magic Slate	8.00	18.00
PLATE 194-C	Lambchop Doll	8.00	23.00
PLATE 195	I Dream of Jeannie Doll	60.00	100.00
PLATE 196	Fred & Dino Battery Operated		
	Toy	85.00	175.00
PLATE 197-A	Fred Flintstone Squeak Toy	10.00	18.00
PLATE 197-B	Dinosaur Squeak Toy	8.00	15.00
PLATE 197-C	Barney Rubble Squeak Toy	10.00	18.00
PLATE 198-A	Herman Munster Puppet	8.00	20.00
PLATE 198-B	Munsters Paper Dolls	7.00	15.00
PLATE 198-C	Munsters Gum Box	12.00	22.00
PLATE 199	Mickey Mouse Piano	750.00	1,800.00
PLATE 200	Disney Lead Figures (each)	12.00	25.00
PLATE 201	Santa Claus Hand Car	650.00	1,400.00
PLATE 202	Mickey Mouse Scatter Ball	80.00	150.00
PLATE 203	Mickey Mouse Scatter Ball	80.00	150.00
PLATE 204	Mickey Celluloid Wind-Up	800.00	1,500.00

Photograph	Item	Fine Condition Value	Mint Condition Value
PLATE 205	Mickey Mouse Watering Can	$ 75.00	$ 135.00
PLATE 206	Mickey Mouse Lusterware Tea Set	85.00	160.00
PLATE 207	Mickey Mouse Sweeper	65.00	135.00
PLATE 208	Mickey Mouse Pencil Case	35.00	75.00
PLATE 209	Mickey Mouse Waste Basket	90.00	150.00
PLATE 210-A	Mickey Mouse Movie Jecktor	80.00	140.00
PLATE 210-B	Mickey Mouse Sand Sifter	70.00	165.00
PLATE 211	Mickey Mouse Blocks	65.00	125.00
PLATE 212	Mickey Mouse Lead Figure	250.00	600.00
PLATE 213-A	Mickey Mouse Big Little Book	15.00	35.00
PLATE 213-B	Mickey Mouse Better Little Book	10.00	25.00
PLATE 214-A	Mickey Mouse Roll-A-Toy	75.00	150.00
PLATE 214-B	Goofy Bisque Figure	35.00	60.00
PLATE 215	Mickey Mouse Saxophone	90.00	150.00
PLATE 216	Mickey Alphabet Book	50.00	85.00
PLATE 217	Mickey & Minnie Bisque Pair	125.00	200.00
PLATE 218	Mickey Toothbrush Holder	125.00	350.00
PLATE 219	Minnie Toothbrush Holder	125.00	350.00
PLATE 220-A	Minnie Toothbrush Holder	135.00	300.00
PLATE 220-B	Mickey Toothbrush Holder	135.00	300.00
PLATE 221	Mickey & Minnie Figures (pair)	70.00	120.00
PLATE 222	Mickey Ash Tray	70.00	135.00
PLATE 223	Mickey Mouse Print Shop	40.00	75.00
PLATE 224	Mickey Coming Home Game (complete)	85.00	150.00
PLATE 225	Mickey Game Board Only	40.00	85.00
PLATE 226	Mickey Pencil Case and Ruler	45.00	80.00
PLATE 227	Mickey Die-Cut Coloring Book	65.00	95.00
PLATE 228	Mickey Mouse Stories	50.00	85.00
PLATE 229-A	Patriot China Plate	40.00	75.00
PLATE 229-B	Patriot China Cup	25.00	55.00
PLATE 230	Mickey and Donald Book	70.00	110.00
PLATE 231	1st Donald Book ever published	100.00	200.00
PLATE 232-A	Donald Duck Pail	40.00	85.00
PLATE 232-B	Donald Duck Pail	35.00	70.00
PLATE 233	Mickey Mouse Pail	60.00	100.00
PLATE 234	Mickey Mouse Band Drum	75.00	130.00
PLATE 235	Mickey Mouse Old Maid Cards	30.00	65.00
PLATE 236	Mickey and Gang Puzzle	35.00	70.00
PLATE 237	Mickey and Minnie (pair)	20.00	45.00
PLATE 238-A	Mickey Drummer Figure	30.00	65.00
PLATE 238-B	Mickey Mouse Brush	35.00	60.00
PLATE 238-C	Mickey Cardboard Soldier	15.00	30.00
PLATE 239	Mickey Pail and Shovel	50.00	85.00
PLATE 240	Mickey Celluloid Wind-up	400.00	700.00
PLATE 241-A	Lusterware Cream Pitcher	25.00	40.00
PLATE 241-B	Beetleware Mickey Cup	15.00	25.00
PLATE 242-A	Mickey Mouse Postcard	15.00	30.00
PLATE 242-B	Mickey Mouse Birthday Card	15.00	30.00
PLATE 243	Mickey Ash Tray	50.00	80.00
PLATE 244	Mickey & Pluto Ash Tray	75.00	140.00
PLATE 245-A	Mickey Mouse Cup	25.00	40.00
PLATE 245-B	Pluto Cream Pitcher	25.00	35.00
PLATE 245-C	Minnie Mouse Cup	25.00	40.00
PLATE 246-A	Mickey Mouse Film	15.00	25.00
PLATE 246-B	Mickey Mouse Film	15.00	30.00
PLATE 246-C	Mickey Mouse Watch	300.00	550.00
PLATE 246-D	Mickey Mouse Club Tag	15.00	30.00
PLATE 247	Mickey Pop-Up Book	125.00	200.00
PLATE 248	Mickey Pop-Up Book	125.00	200.00
PLATE 249	Wooden Minnie Doorstop	45.00	75.00
PLATE 250	Mickey Race Car	125.00	275.00
PLATE 251	Mickey Mouse Watering Can	65.00	120.00
PLATE 252	Mickey Soap Set	70.00	135.00
PLATE 253-A	Mickey Dime Bank	45.00	90.00
PLATE 253-B	Mickey Book Bank	45.00	70.00
PLATE 254	Mickey Alarm Clock	325.00	500.00
PLATE 255	Mickey Talkie Jecktor	135.00	220.00
PLATE 256-A	Minnie Valentine	15.00	25.00
PLATE 256-B	Mickey Party Horn	35.00	65.00

Photograph	Item	Fine Condition Value	Mint Condition Value
PLATE 257	Mickey & Donald Tea Set	$ 65.00	$ 110.00
PLATE 258-A	Mickey Mouse Handkerchief	20.00	40.00
PLATE 258-B	Mickey Mouse Slide Set	20.00	35.00
PLATE 258-C	Mickey Mouse Lantern Slide Set	20.00	35.00
PLATE 259	Post Toasties with Mickey	60.00	125.00
PLATE 260	Mickey on Modern Mechanix	10.00	20.00
PLATE 261-A	Mickey Ice Cream Figures	65.00	110.00
PLATE 261 B	Dental Appointment Card	20.00	35.00
PLATE 261-C	Mickey Mouse Bread Card	12.00	25.00
PLATE 262	Mickey Mouse Candle Holders	60.00	100.00
PLATE 263	Mickey Mouse Cut-Outs Set	50.00	100.00
PLATE 264-A	Donald Paint Box	15.00	30.00
PLATE 264-B	Mickey Bread Label/Card	12.00	25.00
PLATE 264-C	Mickey Mouse Letterhead	15.00	25.00
PLATE 265	Mickey Mouse Trivet	60.00	135.00
PLATE 266	Mickey Mouse Bow & Arrow Set	80.00	150.00
PLATE 267	Mickey Mouse Tin Pail	75.00	135.00
PLATE 268-A	Mickey Mouse Magic Slate	25.00	40.00
PLATE 268-B	Mickey Mouse Movie Jecktor Rolls	15.00	25.00
PLATE 268-C	Donald Duck Pencil Sharpener	20.00	40.00
PLATE 269	Mickey Celluloid Figure	200.00	450.00
PLATE 270	Donald & Mickey Drum	70.00	125.00
PLATE 271	Mickey Mouse Ski Jump	80.00	120.00
PLATE 272	Mickey Mouse Wall Pocket	85.00	135.00
PLATE 273	Mickey Mouse Post Toasties Ad Poster	120.00	200.00
PLATE 274	Mickey Mouse Library of Games	35.00	70.00
PLATE 275	Mickey Mouse Small Sand Pail	35.00	65.00
PLATE 276	Mickey Mouse Black Board	70.00	125.00
PLATE 277	Mickey Mouse Pull Toy	35.00	70.00
PLATE 278	Mickey Mouse Tool Chest	40.00	95.00
PLATE 279	Mickey Mouse Tool Box	65.00	120.00
PLATE 280	Mickey Mouse Character Lights	45.00	80.00
PLATE 281	Victory March Book	25.00	60.00
PLATE 282	Mickey & Minnie Large Tin Sand Pail	55.00	90.00
PLATE 283	Donald Duck Lionel Hand Car	650.00	1,250.00
PLATE 284-A	Donald Duck Rubber Figure	70.00	120.00
PLATE 284-B	Donald Duck & Shovel	65.00	90.00
PLATE 285	Donald Watering Can	45.00	80.00
PLATE 286	Donald Duck Bread Wrapper	15.00	35.00
PLATE 287	Donald Duck Pull Toy	125.00	250.00
PLATE 288	Celluloid Donald Wind-Up Nodder	150.00	375.00
PLATE 289-A	Donald with Umbrella Wind-Up	125.00	200.00
PLATE 289-B	Donald Duck Drummer	225.00	400.00
PLATE 290	Donald Duck on Rocking Chair	300.00	600.00
PLATE 291	Donald Duck Nite Lite	60.00	120.00
PLATE 292	Donald Duck Ceramic Planter	150.00	300.00
PLATE 293-A	Donald Duck Napkin Ring	25.00	35.00
PLATE 293-B	Donald Duck Pencil Sharpener	20.00	35.00
PLATE 294	Donald Duck Tea Tray	15.00	30.00
PLATE 295	Donald Duck Paint Box	10.00	25.00
PLATE 296	Donald Duck Lamp	125.00	220.00
PLATE 297	Donald Duck Cloth Doll	75.00	150.00
PLATE 298	Donald Duck Pull Toy	40.00	85.00
PLATE 299	Donald Duck Camera	25.00	65.00
PLATE 300	Donald Duck Wind-Up Car	65.00	125.00
PLATE 301-A	Donald Duck Wind-Up Figure	30.00	50.00
PLATE 301-B	Goofy Wind-up Figure	30.00	50.00
PLATE 302	Donald Duck Sand Shovel	85.00	150.00
PLATE 303	Donald Duck Lars Doll	300.00	650.00
PLATE 304	Donald Duck Party Game	40.00	70.00
PLATE 305	Donald Duck Party Game	40.00	70.00
PLATE 306	Donald Duck Plush Doll	200.00	400.00
PLATE 307	Disneyland Melody Player	75.00	125.00
PLATE 308	Donald Duck Figure	15.00	25.00
PLATE 309	Donald Duck Pillow Case	65.00	95.00
PLATE 310	Donald Nephews Wind-Up	50.00	70.00
PLATE 311	Donald Hot Water Bottle	25.00	55.00
PLATE 312	Donald Duck Sand Pail	70.00	120.00

Photograph	Item	Fine Condition Value	Mint Condition Value
PLATE 313	Donald The Skier	$ 100.00	$ 175.00
PLATE 314-A	Donald on Motorcycle	40.00	80.00
PLATE 314-B	Goofy Line Mar Wind-Up	75.00	150.00
PLATE 315-A	Donald Duck Juice Can	10.00	25.00
PLATE 315-B	Donald Duck Rubber Ball	20.00	35.00
PLATE 315-C	Donald Duck Register Bank	35.00	75.00
PLATE 315-D	Donald Duck Pop Corn	5.00	20.00
PLATE 316-A	Pluto Bisque Figure	30.00	50.00
PLATE 316-B	Pluto Mechanical Valentine	15.00	30.00
PLATE 317-A	Schuco Donald Wind-Up (1960's)	95.00	150.00
PLATE 317-B	Pluto Line Mar Lantern	60.00	100.00
PLATE 318	Pluto Plush Doll	125.00	225.00
PLATE 319	Pluto Friction Toy	25.00	60.00
PLATE 320	Pluto Action Toy	110.00	140.00
PLATE 321	Pluto Magic Slate	15.00	25.00
PLATE 322	Disneyland Express	100.00	150.00
PLATE 323	Mickey Mouse Meteor Train	200.00	300.00
PLATE 324	Mousketeer Television	65.00	120.00
PLATE 325-A	Ludwig Von Drake Go-Cart	40.00	75.00
PLATE 325-B	Professor Ludwig Von Drake Wind-Up	50.00	95.00
PLATE 326	Ludwig Von Drake Chalkboard	20.00	40.00
PLATE 327	Uncle Scrooge Bank	12.00	20.00
PLATE 328-A	Harold Lloyd Doll	75.00	110.00
PLATE 328-B	Jackie Coogan Figure	65.00	95.00
PLATE 329-A	Movie Camera	25.00	50.00
PLATE 329-B	Harold Lloyd Wind-Up	200.00	400.00
PLATE 329-C	Ed Wynn Firechief Figure	50.00	85.00
PLATE 330	Harold Lloyd Sparkler	95.00	145.00
PLATE 331	Movie-Land Keeno	35.00	75.00
PLATE 332	Deanna Durbin Doll	225.00	400.00
PLATE 333	Sonja Henie Doll	200.00	425.00
PLATE 334	Charlie Chaplin Game	45.00	95.00
PLATE 335-A	Charlie Chaplin Glove Box	35.00	60.00
PLATE 335-B	Charlie Chaplin Candy Container	85.00	145.00
PLATE 336	Charlie Chaplin Coloring Book	25.00	45.00
PLATE 337	Charlie Chaplin Wind-Up	600.00	1,000.00
PLATE 338	W.C. Fields Doll	250.00	500.00
PLATE 339	Jackie Cooper Doll	160.00	280.00
PLATE 340-A	Rudy Valee Valentine	10.00	20.00
PLATE 340-B	Ed Wynn Fire Chief Siren	30.00	65.00
PLATE 341	Our Gang Storybook	35.00	55.00
PLATE 342	Movieland Cut-Ups	55.00	90.00
PLATE 343	Milton Berle Funny Car	100.00	250.00
PLATE 344	Fanny Brice Premium	65.00	95.00
PLATE 345	Fanny Brice Baby Snooks Doll	150.00	325.00
PLATE 346-A	Shirley Temple Book	20.00	45.00
PLATE 346-B	Shirley Temple Book	25.00	45.00
PLATE 347	Shirley Temple Doll	375.00	600.00
PLATE 348	Shirley Temple Christmas Book	25.00	45.00
PLATE 349	Judy Garland Doll	225.00	400.00
PLATE 350	Jane Withers Doll	175.00	325.00
PLATE 351	Shirley Temple Book	25.00	45.00
PLATE 352-A	Dr. DeFoe Doll	150.00	250.00
PLATE 352-B	Nurse Doll	130.00	200.00
PLATE 353	Margaret O'Brien Doll	150.00	280.00
PLATE 354	Shirley Temple Paper Dolls	35.00	65.00
PLATE 355	Shirley Temple Books (set)	75.00	110.00
PLATE 356	Shirley Temple Scrap Book	35.00	60.00
PLATE 357-A	Rhonda Fleming Paper Dolls	15.00	30.00
PLATE 357-B	Betty Grable Paper Dolls	15.00	30.00
PLATE 358-A	Gloria Jean Paper Dolls	15.00	30.00
PLATE 358-B	Claudette Colbert Paper Dolls	15.00	25.00
PLATE 359-A	Rock Hudson Paper Dolls	15.00	25.00
PLATE 359-B	Jane Powell Cut-Out Dolls	15.00	25.00
PLATE 360-A	Dionne Quint Doll, Yvonne	150.00	225.00
PLATE 360-B	Dionne Quint Doll, Cecile	150.00	225.00
PLATE 360-C	Dionne Quint Doll, Annette	150.00	225.00
PLATE 360-D	Dionne Quint Doll, Emilie	150.00	225.00
PLATE 360-E	Dionne Quint Doll, Marie	150.00	225.00
PLATE 361-A	Dionne Quint Picture Album	20.00	35.00
PLATE 361-B	Dionne Quint Book	15.00	27.00
PLATE 362	Dionne Quint Doll Set	$ 600.00	$1,000.00
PLATE 363	Popeye Dippy Dumper	350.00	675.00
PLATE 364	Bluto Dippy Dumper	350.00	675.00
PLATE 365	Popeye & Bluto Wind-Up	125.00	250.00
PLATE 366	Popeye Pop-Up Book	120.00	175.00
PLATE 367	Popeye Pop-Up Book	120.00	175.00
PLATE 368	Popeye Pop-Up Book	120.00	175.00
PLATE 369	Popeye Hat	35.00	65.00
PLATE 370	Popeye Celluloid Doll	70.00	150.00
PLATE 371	Popeye Wood Composition Doll	250.00	550.00
PLATE 372	Popeye Modeling Clay	20.00	40.00
PLATE 373	Popeye Party Game	20.00	45.00
PLATE 374	Dick Tracy Pistol	55.00	80.00
PLATE 375	Dick Tracy Riot Car	65.00	95.00
PLATE 376	Dick Tracy Card Game	20.00	45.00
PLATE 377	Sparkle Plenty Christmas Lights	65.00	120.00
PLATE 378	Popeye Chalk	25.00	38.00
PLATE 379	Dick Tracy Coloring Book	15.00	25.00
PLATE 380	Popeye Crayon Set	20.00	30.00
PLATE 381	Popeye Tank Wind-Up	140.00	250.00
PLATE 382	Dick Tracy Police Station	150.00	265.00
PLATE 383	Popeye Celluloid Napkin Ring	20.00	35.00
PLATE 384	Popeye Telescope	65.00	110.00
PLATE 385	Popeye Picture Book	45.00	70.00
PLATE 386	Popeye Pencil Sharpeners (each)	20.00	35.00
PLATE 387	Terry & The Pirates Coloring Book	15.00	25.00
PLATE 388	Terry & The Pirates Big Book	25.00	40.00
PLATE 389	Batman Belt	15.00	30.00
PLATE 390	Batman & Robin Bookends	35.00	75.00
PLATE 391	Superman Tank Wind-Up	150.00	250.00
PLATE 392-A	Dick Tracy Book	12.00	25.00
PLATE 392-B	Dick Tracy Book	12.00	25.00
PLATE 392-C	Dick Tracy Book	12.00	35.00
PLATE 392-D	Dick Tracy Book	12.00	35.00
PLATE 393-A	Tarzan Book	15.00	30.00
PLATE 393-B	Tarzan Book	15.00	30.00
PLATE 393-C	Tarzan Book	15.00	30.00
PLATE 394-A	Tarzan Book	20.00	35.00
PLATE 394-B	Tarzan Book	20.00	35.00
PLATE 394-C	Tarzan Book	20.00	35.00
PLATE 395	Flash Gordon Pencil Box	20.00	35.00
PLATE 396	Mary Marvel Toss Bag	10.00	20.00
PLATE 397	Terry & The Pirates Book	20.00	40.00
PLATE 398-A	Flash Gordon Book	15.00	28.00
PLATE 398-B	Flash Gordon Book	15.00	28.00
PLATE 398-C	Flash Gordon Book	15.00	28.00
PLATE 399	Atomic Disintegrator Gun	40.00	85.00
PLATE 400-A	Terry and The Pirates Book	10.00	25.00
PLATE 400-B	The Shadow Book	12.00	25.00
PLATE 400-C	Terry and The Pirates Book	12.00	27.00
PLATE 400-D	Terry and The Pirates Book	10.00	25.00
PLATE 401	Jack Armstrong Propeller Gun	65.00	100.00
PLATE 402-A	Jack Armstrong Book	10.00	25.00
PLATE 402-B	Jack Armstrong Atomic Bomb Sight	25.00	40.00
PLATE 402-C	Jack Armstrong Book	12.00	25.00
PLATE 403	Superman Costume	15.00	45.00
PLATE 404	Buck Rogers Battle Cruiser	65.00	115.00
PLATE 405-A	Buck Rogers Big Little Book	12.00	27.00
PLATE 405-B	Buck Rogers Big Little Book	12.00	27.00
PLATE 406	Buck Rogers Destroyer	65.00	115.00
PLATE 407	Captain Marvel Booklets	60.00	120.00
PLATE 408	Captain Marvel Tie Clip	18.00	35.00
PLATE 409	Captain Video Game	20.00	45.00
PLATE 410	Buck Rogers Pop-Up Book	75.00	175.00
PLATE 411	Buck Rogers Pop-Up Book	75.00	175.00
PLATE 412	Captain Marvel Ski Jump	15.00	35.00
PLATE 413	Three Little Pigs Tea Set	75.00	140.00
PLATE 414	Three Little Pigs Toothbrush Holder	50.00	95.00
PLATE 415	Three Little Pigs Pail	35.00	65.00

Photograph	Item	Fine Condition Value	Mint Condition Value
PLATE 416-A	Big Bad Wolf Game Board	$ 25.00	$ 50.00
PLATE 416-B	Three Little Pigs Pail	45.00	75.00
PLATE 417	Three Little Pigs Figure Set	45.00	80.00
PLATE 418	Three Little Pigs Cut-Outs	15.00	30.00
PLATE 419	Three Little Pigs Ash Tray	55.00	90.00
PLATE 420	Three Little Pigs Sand Pail	45.00	75.00
PLATE 421	Ferdinand The Bull Chalk Figure	20.00	30.00
PLATE 422	Ferdinand The Bull Lobby Card	50.00	70.00
PLATE 423	Ferdinand The Bull Figure	20.00	30.00
PLATE 424	Wise Little Hen Book	35.00	50.00
PLATE 425	Snow White Target Game	75.00	125.00
PLATE 426	Snow White Target Game	75.00	125.00
PLATE 427	Snow White Cut-Outs	20.00	35.00
PLATE 428-A	Grumpy Bisque Figure	30.00	50.00
PLATE 428-B	Bashful Bisque Figure	30.00	50.00
PLATE 429	Snow White Writing Tablet	25.00	45.00
PLATE 430	Dopey Composition Doll	150.00	220.00
PLATE 431-A	Doc Toothpick Holder	65.00	150.00
PLATE 431-B	Snow White Toothpick Holder	75.00	150.00
PLATE 431-C	Dopey Toothpick Holder	65.00	150.00
PLATE 432	Snow White Lobby Card	35.00	65.00
PLATE 433	Snow White Lobby Card	35.00	65.00
PLATE 434	Snow White & Dwarfs (small partial set)	55.00	100.00
PLATE 435	Happy Marionette	100.00	250.00
PLATE 436-A	Snow White Marionette	125.00	275.00
PLATE 436-B	Dopey Marionette	100.00	250.00
PLATE 437	Grumpy Bookends	125.00	200.00
PLATE 438	Dopey Doll	85.00	135.00
PLATE 439	Snow White Lamp (with shade)	70.00	150.00
PLATE 440	Snow White Game	55.00	75.00
PLATE 441	Snow White & Doc Plate	25.00	50.00
PLATE 442	Snow White School Bag	15.00	45.00
PLATE 443-A	Snow White Book	25.00	45.00
PLATE 443-B	Bashful Book	25.00	45.00
PLATE 444-A	Sneezy Book	25.00	45.00
PLATE 444-B	Dopey Book	25.00	45.00
PLATE 445	Snow White Lantern Slides	85.00	125.00
PLATE 446	Snow White & The Seven Dwarfs Book	25.00	50.00
PLATE 447	Dopey American Pottery Figure	70.00	150.00
PLATE 448-A	Snow White Postcard	15.00	30.00
PLATE 448-B	Snow White Postcard	15.00	30.00
PLATE 448-C	Ferdinand Postcard	15.00	30.00
PLATE 449	Snow White Valentine	15.00	25.00
PLATE 450	Dopey Knickerbocker Doll	75.00	135.00
PLATE 451	Snow White Aluminum Kitchen Ware	70.00	135.00
PLATE 452	Snow White Pull Toy	90.00	165.00
PLATE 453	Grumpy Knickerbocker Doll	75.00	135.00
PLATE 454	Grumpy Figure (clay)	35.00	75.00
PLATE 455	Doc Hanky	10.00	20.00
PLATE 456-A	Snow White Pencil Sharpener	15.00	30.00
PLATE 456-B	Snow White Napkin Ring	20.00	45.00
PLATE 456-C	Snow White Napkin Ring	20.00	45.00
PLATE 456-D	Dopey Pencil Sharpener	15.00	35.00
PLATE 457	Snow White Dwarfs Plate	35.00	65.00
PLATE 458	Snow White Tapestry Rug	95.00	165.00
PLATE 459	Musical Dwarfs & Snow White Set	175.00	350.00
PLATE 460-A	Dopey Plate	15.00	30.00
PLATE 460-B	Dopey Lincoln Log Figure	20.00	45.00
PLATE 460-C	Dopey Plate	10.00	15.00
PLATE 461	English Snow White Cards	45.00	75.00
PLATE 462-A	Snow White Figure & Candy	85.00	135.00
PLATE 462-B	Grumpy Figure & Candy	75.00	125.00
PLATE 463-A	Snow White Pail	40.00	75.00
PLATE 463-B	Dopey Ceramic Egg Cup	20.00	35.00
PLATE 464	Original Grumpy Cel	750.00	1,800.00
PLATE 465-A	Bashful Glass	8.00	15.00
PLATE 465-B	Happy Glass	8.00	15.00

Photograph	Item	Fine Condition Value	Mint Condition Value
PLATE 466	Pepsodent's Moving Picture Machine	$ 65.00	$ 125.00
PLATE 467	Bashful 3-Piece Ceramic China Set	40.00	75.00
PLATE 468	Snow White Book	20.00	45.00
PLATE 469	Snow White Movie Poster	35.00	75.00
PLATE 470	3 Dwarfs Picture Set	45.00	75.00
PLATE 471	Doc Cloth Mask	30.00	65.00
PLATE 472-A	Pinocchio Chalk Figure	15.00	25.00
PLATE 472-B	Dopey Chalk Figure	15.00	25.00
PLATE 473-A	Pinocchio Book	20.00	45.00
PLATE 473-B	Pinocchio Cardboard Figure	15.00	30.00
PLATE 474	Pinocchio Die-Cut Book	25.00	60.00
PLATE 475	Pinocchio Figure, 4½"	30.00	65.00
PLATE 476	Pinocchio Express Pull Toy	200.00	300.00
PLATE 477-A	Jiminy Cricket Figure	45.00	80.00
PLATE 477-B	Jiminy Cricket Bank	75.00	125.00
PLATE 478	Pinocchio Movie Theatre Lobby Card	25.00	60.00
PLATE 479-A	Jiminy Cricket Coll	125.00	300.00
PLATE 479-B	Pinocchio Lobby Card	25.00	60.00
PLATE 480	Pinocchio Book	15.00	30.00
PLATE 481-A	Figaro The Cat Figure	35.00	70.00
PLATE 481-B	Pinocchio & Figaro Figure	75.00	150.00
PLATE 482	Giddy The Cat Figure	30.00	50.00
PLATE 483	Pinocchio Book	25.00	50.00
PLATE 484	Pinocchio Picture	10.00	20.00
PLATE 485	Pinocchio Valentine	15.00	25.00
PLATE 486	Pinocchio Ideal Doll, 20"	500.00	900.00
PLATE 487	Pinocchio Wooden Figure	20.00	45.00
PLATE 488	Steiff Bambi (large)	50.00	90.00
PLATE 489	Bambi Sheet Music	10.00	20.00
PLATE 490	Bambi Doll, Steiff	30.00	60.00
PLATE 491-A	Baby Thumper Figure	50.00	85.00
PLATE 491-B	Brown Thumper Figure	55.00	90.00
PLATE 491-C	Baby Flower the Skunk	30.00	85.00
PLATE 492	Ceramic Bambi Pitcher	60.00	120.00
PLATE 493	Peter and The Wolf Album	15.00	30.00
PLATE 494	Baby Dumbo Ceramic Figure	75.00	150.00
PLATE 495	Elmer Elephant Book	20.00	55.00
PLATE 496	Toby Tortoise Book	20.00	35.00
PLATE 497-A	Joe Carioca Pencil Sharpener	15.00	30.00
PLATE 497-B	Joe Carioca Pencil Sharpener	15.00	30.00
PLATE 497-C	Joe Carioca Pencil Sharpener	15.00	30.00
PLATE 497-D	Donald Duck Pencil Sharpener	15.00	30.00
PLATE 497-E	Ferdinand the Bull Pencil Sharpener	25.00	45.00
PLATE 497-F	Peter & The Wolf Pencil Sharpener	12.00	20.00
PLATE 498	Three Caballeros Book	35.00	65.00
PLATE 499	Joe Carioca American Pottery Figure	85.00	150.00
PLATE 500	Cinderella Puzzle	5.00	15.00
PLATE 501	Cinderella Book	10.00	20.00
PLATE 502	Cinderella Sheet Music	5.00	10.00
PLATE 503	Cinderella Puzzle	5.00	15.00
PLATE 504	Peter Pan Game	15.00	25.00
PLATE 505	Lady Doll and Pull Toy	30.00	60.00
PLATE 506-A	Red Ryder Better Little Book	10.00	20.00
PLATE 506-B	Red Ryder Better Little Book	10.00	20.00
PLATE 506-C	Red Ryder Better Little Book	10.00	20.00
PLATE 507	Red Ryder Ad Poster	30.00	65.00
PLATE 508	Hopalong Cassidy TV Chair	65.00	110.00
PLATE 509	Hopalong Cassidy Wallet	10.00	20.00
PLATE 510	Hopalong Cassidy Cookie Barrel	85.00	175.00
PLATE 511	Hopalong Cassidy Hair Trainer	10.00	25.00
PLATE 512-A	Hoppy On Time Magazine	10.00	20.00
PLATE 512-B	Hoppy On Quick Magazine	5.00	15.00
PLATE 513-A	Hopalong Cassidy Birthday Card	10.00	20.00
PLATE 513-B	Hopalong Cassidy Party Invitation	5.00	15.00
PLATE 514-A	Hopalong Cassidy Musical Roundup	12.00	25.00

Photograph	Item	Fine Condition Value	Mint Condition Value
PLATE 514-B	Hopalong Cassidy Song Folio	$ 12.00	$ 25.00
PLATE 515	Hopalong Cassidy Good Luck Horseshoe	12.00	20.00
PLATE 516	Hopalong Cassidy Television Book	25.00	50.00
PLATE 517	Hopalong Cassidy Sugar Cones	20.00	45.00
PLATE 518	Hopalong Cassidy Game	35.00	70.00
PLATE 519-A	Hopalong Cassidy Tall Milk Glass	15.00	30.00
PLATE 519-B	Hopalong Cassidy Milk Glass	10.00	25.00
PLATE 520	Hopalong Cassidy Television Puzzles	40.00	75.00
PLATE 521	Cisco Kid Bread Labels (each)	5.00	12.00
PLATE 522	Hopalong Cassidy Holster (box only)	12.00	28.00
PLATE 523	Red Ryder Comic	10.00	20.00
PLATE 524	Hopalong Cassidy Gold Pistol	45.00	65.00
PLATE 525-A	Red Ryder Better Little Book	10.00	25.00
PLATE 525-B	Red Ryder Better Little Book	10.00	25.00
PLATE 525-C	Red Ryder Better Little Book	10.00	25.00
PLATE 526	Hopalong Cassidy Pistols	50.00	95.00
PLATE 527-A	Tim McCoy Book	10.00	25.00
PLATE 527-B	Ken Maynard Book	10.00	25.00
PLATE 527-C	Tim McCoy Book	10.00	25.00
PLATE 528	Cisco Kid Book	10.00	18.00
PLATE 529	Lone Ranger Statue	20.00	40.00
PLATE 530-A	Gene Autry Better Little Book	15.00	25.00
PLATE 530-B	Gene Autry Better Little Book	15.00	25.00
PLATE 530-C	Gene Autry Better Little Book	15.00	25.00
PLATE 530-D	Gene Autry Better Little Book	15.00	25.00
PLATE 531-A	Gene Autry Guns	50.00	80.00
PLATE 531-B	Gene Autry Arcade Card	5.00	15.00
PLATE 532-A	Gene Autry Book	12.00	25.00
PLATE 532-B	Gene Autry Records	15.00	30.00
PLATE 533-A	Tom Mix Button	15.00	30.00
PLATE 533-B	Buttermilk Tin Piece	5.00	15.00
PLATE 533-C	Tom Mix Play Watch	10.00	25.00
PLATE 534	Gene Autry Drum Trap Set	40.00	70.00
PLATE 535	Gene Autry Comic Book	6.00	18.00
PLATE 536-A	Lone Ranger Book	10.00	25.00
PLATE 536-B	Lone Ranger Book	10.00	25.00
PLATE 536-C	Lone Ranger Book	10.00	25.00
PLATE 537-A	Lone Ranger Book	14.00	30.00
PLATE 537-B	Gene Autry Book	12.00	25.00
PLATE 537-C	Gene Autry Book	12.00	25.00
PLATE 538-A	Gene Autry Sheet Music	10.00	25.00
PLATE 538-B	Gene Autry Sheet Music	10.00	25.00
PLATE 539-A	Lone Ranger Book	25.00	50.00
PLATE 539-B	Lone Ranger Paint Book	20.00	40.00
PLATE 540	Lone Ranger Movie Set	50.00	75.00
PLATE 541	Lone Ranger Game	35.00	75.00
PLATE 542	Lone Ranger Chalk Statue	25.00	40.00
PLATE 543-A	Gene Autry Film	5.00	15.00
PLATE 543-B	Gene Autry Pistol	25.00	40.00
PLATE 544-A	Roy Rogers Better Little Book	12.00	25.00
PLATE 544-B	Roy Rogers Better Little Book	12.00	25.00
PLATE 544-C	Roy Rogers Better Little Book	12.00	25.00
PLATE 545-A	Roy Rogers Pistol	25.00	40.00
PLATE 545-B	Roy Rogers Gun and Holster	20.00	40.00
PLATE 545-C	Roy Rogers Gun	30.00	60.00
PLATE 545-D	Roy Rogers Arcade Card	5.00	15.00
PLATE 545-E	Roy Rogers Arcade Card	5.00	15.00
PLATE 546-A	Roy Rogers Book	10.00	22.00
PLATE 546-B	Roy Rogers Book	10.00	22.00
PLATE 546-C	Gene Autry Book	10.00	22.00
PLATE 546-D	Gene Autry Book	10.00	22.00
PLATE 547	Roy Rogers & Dale Evans Book	12.00	22.00
PLATE 548	Roy Rogers Rodeo Set	75.00	130.00
PLATE 549	Roy Rogers Rodeo Set	75.00	130.00
PLATE 550	Zorro Gun Set	70.00	125.00
PLATE 551	Zorro Gun Set	70.00	125.00
PLATE 552-A	Roy Rogers Paper Doll Set	15.00	30.00

Photograph	Item	Fine Condition Value	Mint Condition Value
PLATE 552-B	Roy Rogers Paper Doll Set	$ 15.00	$ 30.00
PLATE 553	Roy Rogers Rodeo Plate	15.00	30.00
PLATE 554-A	Roy Rogers Yellow Thermos	10.00	15.00
PLATE 554-B	Roy Rogers Blue Thermos	10.00	15.00
PLATE 555	Roy Rogers Song Book	20.00	30.00
PLATE 556	Embracing Kewpies Figure	120.00	250.00
PLATE 557	Kewpie Talcum Powder	135.00	250.00
PLATE 558	Kewpie Serenade Bud Vase	300.00	500.00
PLATE 559	Kewpie Bride and Groom Set	400.00	800.00
PLATE 560	Kewpie Hankie in Box	135.00	200.00
PLATE 561-A	Scootles Statue	150.00	300.00
PLATE 561-B	Scootles Tin Pail	125.00	300.00
PLATE 562	Kewpie Tea Set	200.00	500.00
PLATE 563-A	Composition Kewpie Doll	150.00	300.00
PLATE 563-B	Jello Kewpie Book	30.00	65.00
PLATE 564	Giant Celluloid Kewpie Doll	200.00	450.00
PLATE 565	Kewpie Doll & Original Box	225.00	450.00
PLATE 566-A	Kewpie Fabric Doll	80.00	165.00
PLATE 566-B	Kewpie Sugar Bowl	70.00	130.00
PLATE 567	Chalk Sailor Kewpie	65.00	120.00
PLATE 568-A	Kewpie Place Card Holder	125.00	175.00
PLATE 568-B	Kewpie Toothpick Holder	140.00	210.00
PLATE 569	Kewpie Kutouts Book	100.00	200.00
PLATE 570	Ho-Ho Chalk Figure	40.00	80.00
PLATE 571-A	Celluloid Pencil Sharpener	35.00	65.00
PLATE 571-B	Jointed Celluloid Figure	30.00	60.00
PLATE 572	Kewpie Doll Figure	65.00	110.00
PLATE 573	Dressed Kewpie Doll	150.00	300.00
PLATE 574	Celluloid Doll	35.00	65.00
PLATE 575	Kewpie Doll Box	40.00	75.00
PLATE 576	*The Kewpies Their Book*	110.00	250.00
PLATE 577	Kewpie Celluloid Soldier	30.00	75.00
PLATE 578	Jointed Celluloid Doll	35.00	65.00
PLATE 579	*Scootles In Kewpieville* Book	85.00	175.00
PLATE 580-A	Kewpie Figure, Celluloid 4"	60.00	100.00
PLATE 580-B	Kewpie Figure, Celluloid 3"	40.00	75.00
PLATE 581-A	Kewpie Valentine Card	25.00	50.00
PLATE 581-B	Kewpie Valentine Card	25.00	50.00
PLATE 582	Kewpie Candy Container	90.00	150.00
PLATE 583	Jasperware Kewpie Clock	350.00	550.00
PLATE 584-A	Jasperware Sugar Bowl	200.00	400.00
PLATE 584-B	Jasperware Creamer	200.00	400.00
PLATE 585	Jasperware Kewpie Pitcher	250.00	450.00
PLATE 586	Kewpie Cream Pitcher	85.00	150.00
PLATE 587	Kewpie Farmer Bud Vase	600.00	1,000.00
PLATE 588	Bisque Soldier Kewpie Vase	600.00	1,000.00
PLATE 589	Kewpie China Plate	75.00	125.00
PLATE 590	Kewpie Traveler Bisque	90.00	150.00
PLATE 591	Celluloid Figures (each)	20.00	40.00
PLATE 592	Kewpie Ice Cream Tray	200.00	320.00
PLATE 593-A	Kewpie Purity Ice Cream Tray	250.00	450.00
PLATE 593-B	Standard Ice Cream	275.00	500.00
PLATE 594	Kewpie Ice Cream Tray	200.00	520.00
PLATE 595	Kewpie Divided Dish	80.00	140.00
PLATE 596	Kewpie Blackberry Tray	350.00	650.00
PLATE 597	Kewpie Lemonade Tray	350.00	650.00
PLATE 598-A	Kewpie Planter	25.00	45.00
PLATE 598-B	Kewpie Flower Sifter	50.00	110.00
PLATE 599	Furnas Ice Cream Tray	200.00	350.00
PLATE 600	Kewpie Bride and Groom	200.00	400.00
PLATE 601-A	Kewpie Creamer	75.00	125.00
PLATE 601-B	Kewpie Teapot	85.00	150.00
PLATE 601-C	Kewpie Sugar Bowl	75.00	125.00
PLATE 602	Soap Kewpie in Box	75.00	135.00
PLATE 603	Kewpie Camera	60.00	125.00
PLATE 604	Kewpie Alphabet Bowl	100.00	175.00
PLATE 605-A	Kewpie Ad Card	35.00	65.00
PLATE 605-B	Kewpie Letter Opener	25.00	75.00
PLATE 606	Large Bisque Kewpie Doll	150.00	350.00
PLATE 607-A	Kewpie Bowl	65.00	135.00
PLATE 607-B	Kewpie Bowl	65.00	135.00
PLATE 608	Bisque Kewpie w/painted shoes	200.00	375.00
PLATE 609	Jasperware Bud Vase	250.00	450.00

Price Guide - First Edition

Photograph	Item	Fine Condition Value	Mint Condition Value
PLATE 1	Buster Brown Tea Set	$ 85.00	$ 125.00
PLATE 2	Buster Brown Game	110.00	165.00
PLATE 3	Buster Brown Bank	77.00	130.00
PLATE 4	Foxy Grandpa Card	35.00	50.00
PLATE 5	Foxy Grandpa Game	100.00	150.00
PLATE 6	Foxy Grandpa Bank	82.00	135.00
PLATE 7	Barney Google Wind-Up	800.00	1,400.00
PLATE 8	Spark Plug Wood Toy	150.00	225.00
PLATE 9-A	Spark Plug Doll	275.00	450.00
PLATE 9-B	Barney Google Doll	275.00	450.00
PLATE 10	Barney Google Game	55.00	90.00
PLATE 11-A	Barney Google Music	10.00	25.00
PLATE 11-B	Spark Plug Rubber Toy	20.00	45.00
PLATE 12	Spark Plug Wood Toy	75.00	150.00
PLATE 13	Toonerville Trolley Toy	750.00	900.00
PLATE 14	Powerful Katrinka Wind-Up	750.00	1,000.00
PLATE 15-A	Tiny Toonerville Trolley	200.00	450.00
PLATE 15-B	Cast Metal Toonerville Trolley	125.00	225.00
PLATE 16	Toonerville Trolley Game	65.00	110.00
PLATE 17	Toonerville Game Board Only	25.00	50.00
PLATE 18	Metal Toonerville Trolley	125.00	200.00
PLATE 19	Moon Mullins & Kayo Wind-Up	400.00	600.00
PLATE 20	Andy Gump Arcade Car	800.00	1,100.00
PLATE 21	Andy Gump Mirror Brush	35.00	65.00
PLATE 22	Bringing Up Father Bisques	150.00	300.00
PLATE 23	Uncle Walt & Skeezix Bisques	150.00	300.00
PLATE 24	Moon Mullins Bisque Set	150.00	300.00
PLATE 25	Mutt & Jeff Doll Pair	400.00	600.00
PLATE 26	Mutt & Jeff Iron Bank	75.00	125.00
PLATE 27	Mutt & Jeff Figures (Pair)	75.00	125.00
PLATE 28-A	Felix 4" Jointed Wood Doll	75.00	140.00
PLATE 28-B	Felix Wood Figure	35.00	60.00
PLATE 29	Spark Plug Candy Cont.	80.00	125.00
PLATE 30-A	Happy Hooligan Toy Figures	35.00	50.00
PLATE 30-B	Barney Google & Spark Plug	75.00	175.00
PLATE 31	Felix Tin Pull Toy	200.00	450.00
PLATE 32	Felix The Cat 13" Doll	250.00	500.00
PLATE 33	Felix 8" Jointed Wood Doll	100.00	165.00
PLATE 34	Betty Boop & Mickey Mouse Plate	75.00	100.00
PLATE 35	Felix China Tea Set (Two Plates)	35.00	75.00
PLATE 36	Moon Mullins & Kayo Bisque	40.00	80.00
PLATE 37	Henry on Trapeze Wind-Up	300.00	600.00
PLATE 38	Komic Kamera Film Set	65.00	100.00
PLATE 39-A	Felix on Scooter Wind-Up	350.00	550.00
PLATE 39-B	Felix the Cat Pencil Case	25.00	45.00
PLATE 40	Marx Merry Makers Band	425.00	700.00
PLATE 41-A	Charlie Chaplin Pencil Case	25.00	45.00
PLATE 41-B	Charlie Chaplin Plastic Toy	35.00	60.00
PLATE 42	Chaplin Tin & Cast Iron Wind-Up	700.00	1,100.00
PLATE 43-A	Chaplin Lead Figure	25.00	50.00
PLATE 43-B	Chaplin Novelty Toy	30.00	45.00
PLATE 44	Chaplin Wind-Up	300.00	575.00
PLATE 45	Maggie Chalk Statue	35.00	65.00
PLATE 46	Amos 'n Andy Puzzle	25.00	45.00
PLATE 47	Fresh Air Taxi Cab Wind-Up	500.00	750.00
PLATE 48	Amos 'n Andy Card Party Set	25.00	50.00
PLATE 49-A	Dagwood & Kids Figures	45.00	60.00
PLATE 49-B	Blondie Paint Set	7.00	15.00
PLATE 50	Joe Penner Wind-Up	250.00	400.00
PLATE 51-A	Andy Tin Wind-Up Toy	250.00	500.00
PLATE 51-B	Amos Tin Wind-Up Toy	250.00	500.00
PLATE 52	Skeezix Stationery Box	20.00	35.00
PLATE 53	The Gumps Book	30.00	45.00
PLATE 54-A	Skeezix & Walt Book	15.00	25.00
PLATE 54-B	Bringing Up Father Paint Book	20.00	35.00
PLATE 55	Blondie's Peg Set	25.00	40.00
PLATE 56	Dagwood Tin Wind-Up Plane	200.00	375.00
PLATE 57-A	Blondie Paint Book	$ 16.00	$ 23.00
PLATE 57-B	Blondie Paint Book	16.00	23.00
PLATE 58-A	Dagwood Lead Figure	15.00	20.00
PLATE 58-B	Blondie Lead Figure	15.00	20.00
PLATE 58-C	Li'l Abner Lead Figure	15.00	20.00
PLATE 58-D	Orphan Annie Lead Figure	15.00	20.00
PLATE 58-E	Sandy Lead Figure	15.00	20.00
PLATE 59	Bonzo Wind-Up Scooter	250.00	425.00
PLATE 60	Maggie & Jiggs Lead Figures	35.00	50.00
PLATE 61	Li'l Abner Dogpatch Band	375.00	600.00
PLATE 62	Uncle Walt & Skeezix Bisque	40.00	85.00
PLATE 63	Li'l Abner Vending Machine	200.00	350.00
PLATE 64	Joe Palooka Lunch Box	25.00	50.00
PLATE 65-A	Happy Hooligan Wind-Up	250.00	475.00
PLATE 65-B	Porky Pig Wind-Up	85.00	125.00
PLATE 66	Terry & The Pirates Record	18.00	30.00
PLATE 67	Popular Comics Christmas Cards	30.00	65.00
PLATE 68-A	Fred on Dino Tin Wind-Up	75.00	150.00
PLATE 68-B	Barney on Dino Tin Wind-Up	75.00	150.00
PLATE 69	Mister Magoo Car	70.00	110.00
PLATE 70	Mickey Mouse Lionel Handcar	600.00	950.00
PLATE 71	Mickey Mouse Movie Projector	300.00	500.00
PLATE 72	Mickey Mouse Chritmas Lights	125.00	175.00
PLATE 73	Mickey Mouse Emerson Radio	700.00	1,100.00
PLATE 74-A	Donald Duck Boxed Soap	75.00	100.00
PLATE 74-B	Pluto Boxed Soap	75.00	100.00
PLATE 75-A	Pluto Rubber Figure	50.00	90.00
PLATE 75-B	Mickey Mouse Rubber Figure	90.00	175.00
PLATE 76	Mickey Mouse Steiff Pull Toy	800.00	1,800.00
PLATE 77	Mickey Mouse Night Light	85.00	135.00
PLATE 78	Mickey Mouse Dart Target	50.00	90.00
PLATE 79	Mickey & Minnie Tea Set	85.00	140.00
PLATE 80	Mickey Mouse Knickerbocker Doll	150.00	300.00
PLATE 81	Minnie Mouse Knickerbocker Doll	175.00	400.00
PLATE 82	Mickey & Minnie Toothbrush Holder	90.00	140.00
PLATE 83	Donald Duck Toothbrush Holder	100.00	150.00
PLATE 84-A	Minnie Mouse Bisque Figure	35.00	60.00
PLATE 84-B	Donald Duck Bisque Figure	100.00	250.00
PLATE 84-C	Mickey Mouse Bisque Figure	35.00	60.00
PLATE 85	Mickey & Minnie Toothbrush Holder	100.00	150.00
PLATE 86-A	Pluto Fun-E-Flex Figure	50.00	85.00
PLATE 86-B	Pluto Red Rubber Figure	30.00	65.00
PLATE 87-A	Mickey Celluloid Pencil Sharpener	90.00	140.00
PLATE 87-B	Minnie Bisque Pin Cushion	95.00	150.00
PLATE 88	Mickey Mouse Wood Pull Toy	100.00	250.00
PLATE 89-A	Pluto Wooden Toy	75.00	150.00
PLATE 89-B	Mickey Mouse Wooden Toy	75.00	150.00
PLATE 90	Donald Duck Pull Toy	85.00	175.00
PLATE 91-A	Mickey Mouse Composition Bank	75.00	150.00
PLATE 91-B	Donald Duck Composition Bank	85.00	150.00
PLATE 92-A	Donald Duck Bisque Figure	35.00	50.00
PLATE 92-B	Mickey Mouse with Sax Bisque	60.00	90.00
PLATE 92-C	Donald Duck with Horn Bisque	35.00	50.00
PLATE 92-D	Mickey Mouse Bisque Figure	40.00	65.00
PLATE 93-A	Mickey Mouse China Plate	10.00	20.00
PLATE 93-B	Mickey Mouse China Tea Pot	20.00	40.00
PLATE 93-C	Mickey Mouse China Cup	10.00	20.00
PLATE 94-A	Donald, Mickey & Minnie Bisque Toothbrush Holder	95.00	150.00
PLATE 94-B	Donald Duck Toothbush Holder	95.00	150.00

Photograph	Item	Fine Condition Value	Mint Condition Value
PLATE 95-A	Mickey Mouse Tin Sand Pail	$ 75.00	$ 100.00
PLATE 95-B	Mickey Mouse Band Sand Pail	85.00	125.00
PLATE 96	Disney Character Tin Tray	50.00	75.00
PLATE 97-A	Donald Duck Ceramic Figure	90.00	150.00
PLATE 97-B	Pluto Ceramic Figure	90.00	150.00
PLATE 97-C	Mickey Mouse Ceramic Figure	90.00	150.00
PLATE 98-A	Mickey Mouse Drum	75.00	125.00
PLATE 98-B	Mickey Mouse Band Drum	75.00	125.00
PLATE 99-A	Donald Duck Solid Rubber Figure	90.00	130.00
PLATE 99-B	Donald Duck Hollow Rubber Figure	75.00	125.00
PLATE 100-A	Donald Duck Wagon Pull Toy	75.00	125.00
PLATE 100-B	Donald Duck Pull Toy	75.00	125.00
PLATE 101-A	Donald Duck Card Game	25.00	45.00
PLATE 101-B	Donald Duck Celluloid Figure	80.00	120.00
PLATE 102-A	Mickey Mouse Band Top	100.00	175.00
PLATE 102-B	Mickey & 3 Pigs Tin Top	100.00	200.00
PLATE 103	Easter Parade Toy Set	250.00	500.00
PLATE 104	Disney Character Fire Truck	150.00	300.00
PLATE 105	Mickey Mouse Sled	175.00	400.00
PLATE 106	Disney Dipsy Car	125.00	300.00
PLATE 107-A	Disney Television Car	95.00	150.00
PLATE 107-B	Mickey Mouse Wind-Up Car	100.00	175.00
PLATE 108	Donald Duck Celluloid Wind-Up	600.00	1,000.00
PLATE 109-A	Mickey Mouse Rubber Fire Truck	45.00	75.00
PLATE 109-B	Mickey Black Rubber Figure	60.00	95.00
PLATE 109-C	Mickey Mouse Rubber Tractor	45.00	75.00
PLATE 110-A	Donald Duck Trapeze Toy	100.00	175.00
PLATE 110-B	Disney Wind-Up Carousel	300.00	750.00
PLATE 111-A	Donald Duck Cello. Pencil Sharpener	20.00	35.00
PLATE 111-B	Snow White Cello. Pencil Sharpener	20.00	35.00
PLATE 111-C	Mickey Mouse Pencil Sharpener	30.00	60.00
PLATE 111-D	Pinocchio Pencil Sharpener	20.00	35.00
PLATE 112	Minnie Mouse Rocker Wind-Up	250.00	450.00
PLATE 113	Roll Over Pluto Wind-Up	125.00	200.00
PLATE 114	Pluto Acrobat Wind-Up Toy	135.00	200.00
PLATE 115-A	Disneyland Express Wind-Up Train	35.00	60.00
PLATE 115-B	Mickey & Minnie Mouse Washing Machine	100.00	225.00
PLATE 116	Mickey Mouse Lamp	110.00	200.00
PLATE 117	Mickey Mouse Xylophone Player	150.00	300.00
PLATE 118	Mickey & Minnie Valentine	20.00	35.00
PLATE 119-A	Donald Duck Phone Bank	75.00	110.00
PLATE 119-B	Mickey Mouse Phone Bank	75.00	110.00
PLATE 120-A	Mickey Mouse Ingersoll Pocket Watch	350.00	600.00
PLATE 120-B	Mickey Mouse Scissors	50.00	80.00
PLATE 121	Mickey Mouse Band Giant Drum	120.00	200.00
PLATE 122	Radio Magazine, 1938	15.00	25.00
PLATE 123	Large Mickey Mouse Pull Toy	150.00	275.00
PLATE 124-A	Mickey Beetleware Bowl	15.00	22.00
PLATE 124-B	Mickey Mouse Watch & Stand	50.00	85.00
PLATE 125-A	Mickey Wood Trapeze Toy	20.00	45.00
PLATE 125-B	Mickey Mouse Story Book	35.00	50.00
PLATE 125-C	Mickey Mouse Crayons	20.00	35.00
PLATE 126-A	Minnie Mouse Bisque	50.00	75.00
PLATE 126-B	Mickey Mouse Bisque	50.00	75.00
PLATE 127-A	Mickey Mouse Ash Tray	75.00	125.00
PLATE 127-B	Mickey Mouse Candy Wrapper	35.00	70.00
PLATE 128	Mickey Mouse Jigsaw Puzzle	50.00	90.00
PLATE 129-A	Pluto & Cart Friction Toy	70.00	125.00
PLATE 129-B	Small Pluto Friction Toy	40.00	70.00
PLATE 130-A	Minnie Mouse Ceramic Bank	15.00	25.00
PLATE 130-B	Minnie Mouse China Plate	35.00	60.00
PLATE 130-C	Minnie Mouse Plastic Figure	$ 10.00	$ 20.00
PLATE 131-A	Mickey Mouse Sand Pail	40.00	75.00
PLATE 131-B	Mickey Mouse Sand Shovel	30.00	50.00
PLATE 132-A	Mickey China Sugar Bowl	40.00	60.00
PLATE 132-B	Mickey Mouse China Cup	30.00	50.00
PLATE 133-A	Mickey Mouse Bubble Buster	60.00	100.00
PLATE 133-B	Mickey Mouse Stamp Pad	20.00	35.00
PLATE 134	Walt Disney Paint Book	40.00	65.00
PLATE 135	Donald Duck Knickerbocker Doll	275.00	500.00
PLATE 136-A	Mickey Mouse Comp. Figure	125.00	175.00
PLATE 136-B	Small Mickey Mouse Wire Fig.	35.00	70.00
PLATE 137	Donald Duck Snow Shovel	100.00	175.00
PLATE 138	Mickey Mouse Sugar Set	140.00	250.00
PLATE 139	Donald Duck Schuco Wind-Up	650.00	1000.00
PLATE 140	Disneyland Ferris Wheel	150.00	325.00
PLATE 141	Donald Duck Duet Wind-Up	225.00	500.00
PLATE 142	Mickey Mouse Lionel Circus Train	1,000.00	1,800.00
PLATE 143	Donald Duck Jack-In-The-Box	75.00	135.00
PLATE 144	Mickey Mouse Fireman Doll	30.00	50.00
PLATE 145-A	Mickey Mouse Linen-Like Book	60.00	95.00
PLATE 145-B	Mickey Mouse Activity Book	40.00	80.00
PLATE 146-A	Mickey Mouse Picture Book	65.00	100.00
PLATE 146-B	Mickey Mouse Book One	50.00	85.00
PLATE 147-A	Donald Duck Metal Bank	50.00	90.00
PLATE 147-B	Donald Duck Paint Box	12.00	20.00
PLATE 148-A	Mickey Mouse Fun-E-Flex Fig.	60.00	85.00
PLATE 148-B	Mickey & Minnie Mouse Tray	25.00	55.00
PLATE 148-C	Mickey Mouse Giant Bisque	120.00	275.00
PLATE 149-A	Donald Duck Rubber Car	35.00	65.00
PLATE 149-B	Donald Duck Paint Box	8.00	15.00
PLATE 150-A	Donald Duck Watering Can	35.00	60.00
PLATE 150-B	Mickey Mouse Watering Can	50.00	95.00
PLATE 151	Donald Duck Tin Tea Set	40.00	65.00
PLATE 152	Mickey & Minnie Mouse Washtub	35.00	50.00
PLATE 152-B	Mickey & Minnie Mouse Watering Can	38.00	50.00
PLATE 153	Disney Character Globe	25.00	45.00
PLATE 154-A	Mickey Mouse Party Hat	5.00	10.00
PLATE 154-B	Mickey Plastic Figure	6.00	10.00
PLATE 154-C	Mickey Mouse Plastic Bank	15.00	25.00
PLATE 154-D	Mickey Mouse Jigsaw Puzzle	10.00	20.00
PLATE 155-A	Disney Boxed Puppet	15.00	25.00
PLATE 155-B	Disney Merry-Go-Round Lamp	25.00	40.00
PLATE 156-A	Donald Duck Vacuum	50.00	75.00
PLATE 156-B	Donald Duck Sweeper	50.00	75.00
PLATE 157	Orphan Annie Ceramic Mug	20.00	40.00
PLATE 158-A	Little Orphan Annie Wind-Up	275.00	400.00
PLATE 158-B	Sandy Tin Wind-Up	250.00	350.00
PLATE 159	Orphan Annie Stove	40.00	65.00
PLATE 160	Annie & Sandy Bisque Planter	35.00	65.00
PLATE 161	Captain Midnight Plastic Cup	15.00	25.00
PLATE 162	Orphan Annie Toothbrush Holder	45.00	65.00
PLATE 163-A	Orphan Annie Cup	15.00	25.00
PLATE 163-B	Orphan Annie Mug	15.00	25.00
PLATE 164	Orphan Annie Gameboard (only)	20.00	30.00
PLATE 165	Orphan Annie Game (complete)	40.00	75.00
PLATE 166	Orphan Annie Electric Stove	45.00	65.00
PLATE 167	Orphan Annie Rummy Game	35.00	50.00
PLATE 168	Annie & Sandy Bisque Toothbrush Holder	65.00	95.00
PLATE 169	Orphan Annie Treasure Hunt	25.00	40.00
PLATE 170-A	Annie Booklet-1936	45.00	75.00
PLATE 170-B	Annie Booklet-1937	40.00	65.00
PLATE 171	Annie Booklet-1938	45.00	75.00
PLATE 172-A	Annie Decoder-1936	18.00	30.00
PLATE 172-B	Annie Decoder-1937	18.00	30.00
PLATE 172-C	Annie Decoder-1939	18.00	30.00
PLATE 173-A	Captain Midnight Comic Book	9.00	16.00
PLATE 173-B	Captain Midnight Decoder, 1949	15.00	30.00

Photograph	Item	Fine Condition Value	Mint Condition Value
PLATE 174-A	Membership Certificate Only	$ 5.00	$ 10.00
PLATE 174-B	Orphan Annie Membership Pin	8.00	15.00
PLATE 175-A	Orphan Annie Big Little Book	12.00	25.00
PLATE 175-B	Orphan Annie Pocket Game	25.00	55.00
PLATE 176	Orphan Annie Clothespins	40.00	70.00
PLATE 177-A	Orphan Annie Book	30.00	65.00
PLATE 177-B	Orphan Annie Book	35.00	65.00
PLATE 178	Orphan Annie Ash Tray	75.00	125.00
PLATE 179	Orphan Annie Puzzle	20.00	35.00
PLATE 180	Skippy Character Mug	25.00	40.00
PLATE 181-A	Orphan Annie Book	35.00	65.00
PLATE 181-B	Orphan Annie Book	35.00	65.00
PLATE 182	Skippy Jigsaw Puzzles	25.00	45.00
PLATE 183	Skippy Silverware Set	80.00	125.00
PLATE 184-A	Orphan Annie Hardback Book	35.00	65.00
PLATE 184-B	Orphan Annie Better Little Book	12.00	25.00
PLATE 184-C	Orphan Annie Hardback Book	35.00	65.00
PLATE 185	Orphan Annie Paper Costume	20.00	35.00
PLATE 186	Skippy Wood Comp. Doll	85.00	140.00
PLATE 187	Orphan Annie Hingees	10.00	20.00
PLATE 188	Skippy Puzzles (Framed)	8.00	15.00
PLATE 189	Skippy Bisque Figure	40.00	70.00
PLATE 190-A	Popeye Better Little Book	12.00	25.00
PLATE 190-B	Popeye Wood Jointed Doll	68.00	95.00
PLATE 191	Popeye Cameo Doll	35.00	65.00
PLATE 192	Funny Fire Fighters Toy	500.00	850.00
PLATE 193	Popeye Chase Set	65.00	150.00
PLATE 194	Popeye & Punching Bag Toy	225.00	450.00
PLATE 195-A	Barnacle Bill in Barrel	175.00	285.00
PLATE 195-B	Barnacle Bill Wind-Up	150.00	265.00
PLATE 196	Popeye Card Game	25.00	40.00
PLATE 197	Popeye Wood Hammer Game	20.00	40.00
PLATE 198	Popeye Pipe Toss Game	35.00	60.00
PLATE 199-A	Popeye Pocket Game	25.00	55.00
PLATE 199-B	Popeye Dime Bank	35.00	75.00
PLATE 200	Popeye Walking Wind-Up Toy	145.00	250.00
PLATE 201	Popeye Roof Dancers Toy	450.00	800.00
PLATE 202	Popeye Wood Pull Toy	45.00	80.00
PLATE 203	Popeye The Champ Wind-Up	650.00	1,200.00
PLATE 204	Popeye the Pilot Wind-Up	225.00	400.00
PLATE 205	Popeye Boxed Soap Figures	75.00	120.00
PLATE 206	Popeye Boxed Lantern	75.00	100.00
PLATE 207	Popeye Bubble Set	25.00	45.00
PLATE 208-A	Wimpy Lead Figure	12.00	20.00
PLATE 208-B	Olive Oyl Lead Figure	12.00	20.00
PLATE 208-C	Popeye Lead Figure	12.00	20.00
PLATE 209	Popeye Express Wind-Up	175.00	300.00
PLATE 210	Popeye Spinach Can	15.00	30.00
PLATE 211-A	Popeye Paints Set	15.00	25.00
PLATE 211-B	Popeye On Tricycle Wind-Up	125.00	200.00
PLATE 212-A	Popeye Vinyl Figure	30.00	45.00
PLATE 212-B	Wimpy Vinyl Figure	30.00	45.00
PLATE 212-C	Olive Oyl Vinyl Figure	30.00	45.00
PLATE 213-A	Popeye Metal Brush	20.00	35.00
PLATE 213-B	Popeye Kazoo Pipe	15.00	30.00
PLATE 214	Popeye Jaymar Puzzle	20.00	30.00
PLATE 215	Popeye Sponge Rubber Doll	15.00	25.00
PLATE 216	Popeye Large Wooden Doll	90.00	140.00
PLATE 217	Dick Tracy Wrist Radios	20.00	40.00
PLATE 218-A	Popeye Linen-Like Book	35.00	55.00
PLATE 218-B	Popeye Animated Book	45.00	80.00
PLATE 219-A	Dick Tracy Book	15.00	20.00
PLATE 219-B	Green Hornet Book	12.00	18.00
PLATE 219-C	Charlie Chan Book	12.00	18.00
PLATE 220	Dick Tracy Machine Gun	20.00	35.00
PLATE 221	Sparkle Plenty Bank	300.00	600.00
PLATE 222	Dick Tracy Coloring Book	20.00	30.00
PLATE 223	Dick Tracy Pop-Up Book	75.00	120.00
PLATE 224	Dick Tracy Pop-Up Book	75.00	120.00
PLATE 225	Dick Tracy Toys Set	25.00	40.00
PLATE 226	Dick Tracy Squad Car	70.00	100.00
PLATE 227	Dick Tracy Blacklight Kit	$ 30.00	$ 45.00
PLATE 228	B.O. Plenty Wind-Up Toy	125.00	225.00
PLATE 229	Silly Symphony Christmas Lights	90.00	130.00
PLATE 230-A	Peculiar Penguins Book	35.00	60.00
PLATE 230-B	Silly Symphony Book	20.00	35.00
PLATE 230-C	Silly Symphony Fan	45.00	65.00
PLATE 231	Silly Symphony Lights	100.00	135.00
PLATE 232-A	Three Little Pigs Plate	25.00	40.00
PLATE 232-B	Three Little Pigs Toothbrush Holder	60.00	85.00
PLATE 233-A	Fiddler Pig Chalk Figure	20.00	30.00
PLATE 233-B	3 Pigs Tin Plates (price for 3)	18.00	30.00
PLATE 234	Three Pigs & Wolf Bisques	70.00	125.00
PLATE 235	Schuco 3 Pigs Wind-Ups (Set)	500.00	800.00
PLATE 236-A	Three Pigs Tin Pail	25.00	70.00
PLATE 236-B	Drummer Pig Bisque	20.00	45.00
PLATE 237	Ferdinand Stuffed Doll	100.00	140.00
PLATE 238	Ferdinand & Matador Wind-Up	150.00	350.00
PLATE 239	Ferdinand Wood Comp. Doll	75.00	100.00
PLATE 240-A	Ferdinand Rubber Figure	25.00	50.00
PLATE 240-B	Ferdinand Bisque Figure	15.00	30.00
PLATE 240-C	Ferdinand Tin Wind-Up Toy	70.00	125.00
PLATE 241-A	Ferdinand Jointed Doll	75.00	100.00
PLATE 241-B	Ferdinand Picture Book	30.00	45.00
PLATE 242	Large Ferdinand Figure	25.00	35.00
PLATE 243	Ferdinand Wood Comp. Bank	50.00	85.00
PLATE 244	Snow White Radio	650.00	1,100.00
PLATE 245	Seven Dwarfs Set (Rubber)	210.00	300.00
PLATE 246	Snow White & Dwarfs Blocks	50.00	100.00
PLATE 247	Snow White Puzzle	15.00	30.00
PLATE 248	Doc Dwarf Lamp	65.00	110.00
PLATE 249	Snow White Tin Pail	75.00	125.00
PLATE 250	Doc & Dopey Pull Toy	100.00	175.00
PLATE 251-A	Snow White Planter	15.00	30.00
PLATE 251-B	Snow White Ceramic Bank	15.00	25.00
PLATE 252	Snow White & Dwarfs Bisque Set	120.00	200.00
PLATE 253-A	Grumpy Knickerbocker Doll	90.00	140.00
PLATE 253-B	Dopey Knickerbocker Doll	90.00	140.00
PLATE 254-A	Dopey Dwarf Doll	75.00	95.00
PLATE 254-B	Bashful Dwarf Doll	75.00	95.00
PLATE 254-C	Doc Dwarf Doll	75.00	95.00
PLATE 254-D	Doc Dwarf Doll	55.00	75.00
PLATE 255-A	Dopey Plaster Figure	15.00	25.00
PLATE 255-B	Grumpy Plaster Figure	15.00	25.00
PLATE 255-C	Snow White Plaster Figure	20.00	35.00
PLATE 255-D	Doc Plaster Figure	15.00	25.00
PLATE 255-E	Sneezy Plaster Figure	15.00	25.00
PLATE 256	Snow White Boxed Puzzles	35.00	65.00
PLATE 257-A	Dopey Composition Bank	90.00	130.00
PLATE 257-B	Dopey Linen-like Book	35.00	55.00
PLATE 257-C	Dopey Ceramic Lamp	65.00	90.00
PLATE 258	Seven Dwarfs Book	35.00	65.00
PLATE 259	Snow White Tea Set	40.00	75.00
PLATE 260-A	Sleepy 5" Bisque	50.00	80.00
PLATE 260-B	Sneezy 5" Bisque	50.00	80.00
PLATE 260-C	Dopey 5" Bisque	50.00	80.00
PLATE 261	Snow White Calendar Print	70.00	125.00
PLATE 262	Snow White & Dwarfs Prints (price each)	12.00	20.00
PLATE 263-A	Bashful Boxed Soap Figure	40.00	65.00
PLATE 263-B	Snow White Boxed Soap	55.00	80.00
PLATE 263-C	Sneezy Boxed Soap Figure	40.00	65.00
PLATE 264	Snow White & Dwarfs Display	200.00	350.00
PLATE 265	Snow White Tek Premium Game	65.00	100.00
PLATE 266	Snow White China Tea Set	90.00	150.00
PLATE 267-A	Snow White Movie Mirror Mag.	15.00	30.00
PLATE 267-B	Hollywood Mag.-Snow White Cover	15.00	30.00
PLATE 268-A	Snow White Big Little Book	20.00	35.00

Photograph	Item	Fine Condition Value	Mint Condition Value	Photograph	Item	Fine Condition Value	Mint Condition Value
PLATE 268-B	Bashful Toothpick Holder	$ 75.00	$ 150.00	PLATE 308	Pinocchio Game Board Only	$ 20.00	$ 45.00
PLATE 269	Disneykin Dwarfs (each)	7.00	10.00	PLATE 309-A	Pinocchio Story Book	12.00	25.00
PLATE 270-A	Snow White Book	20.00	35.00	PLATE 309-B	Pinocchio Hardbound Book	35.00	65.00
PLATE 270-B	Snow White Mirror	15.00	35.00	PLATE 310-A	Bambi Ceramic Figure	20.00	30.00
PLATE 271-A	Snow White Scrapbook	50.00	90.00	PLATE 310-B	Baby Bambi Ceramic Figure	45.00	70.00
PLATE 271-B	Snow White Ad Flyer	35.00	65.00	PLATE 310-C	Flower the Skunk Planter	25.00	35.00
PLATE 272	Snow White Mech. Valentines			PLATE 310-D	Bambi Picture Book	20.00	30.00
	(each)	12.00	20.00	PLATE 311-A	Thumper's Girlfriend	30.00	65.00
PLATE 273-A	Snow White Hardbound Book	60.00	85.00	PLATE 311-B	Thumper Ceramic Figure	35.00	70.00
PLATE 273-B	Snow White Linen-Like Book	25.00	40.00	PLATE 311-C	Flower Ceramic Figure	35.00	70.00
PLATE 274-A	Dopey Marx Wind-Up	125.00	200.00	PLATE 311-D	Bambi 8" Ceramic Figure	75.00	150.00
PLATE 274-B	Pinocchio Marx Wind-Up	125.00	200.00	PLATE 312-A	Thumper Storybook	20.00	30.00
PLATE 275-A	Snow White Dime Bank	50.00	100.00	PLATE 312-B	Thumper Pull Toy	100.00	175.00
PLATE 275-B	Dopey Dime Bank	45.00	90.00	PLATE 313-A	Alice in Wond. Tea Tray &		
PLATE 276	Snow White Drinking Glasses				Plates	30.00	45.00
	(set)	80.00	125.00	PLATE 313-B	Alice in Wond. Salt, Pepper &		
PLATE 277-A	Pinocchio 4" Bisque	25.00	50.00		Sugar Bowl	60.00	125.00
PLATE 277-B	Pinocchio 5" Bisque	35.00	60.00	PLATE 314	Disneykins (Small) Each Boxed	5.00	12.00
PLATE 277-C	Pinocchio 3" Bisque	20.00	35.00	PLATE 314	Disneykins (Large) Boxed	7.00	15.00
PLATE 278-A	Dopey Doll-Chad Valley	100.00	140.00	PLATE 315-A	Dalmatian Squeeze Toy	8.00	10.00
PLATE 278-B	Snow White Knickerbocker Doll	100.00	150.00	PLATE 315-B	Dalmatian Pups Figurine Set	20.00	45.00
PLATE 279	Pinocchio Knickerbocker Doll	175.00	350.00	PLATE 316-A	Cinderella Planter	20.00	35.00
PLATE 280-A	Fantasia Ceramic Figure	300.00	500.00	PLATE 316-B	Cinderella Figure Ceramic	10.00	20.00
PLATE 280-B	Fantasia Ceramic Unicorn	100.00	200.00	PLATE 316-C	Cinderella Figure-Plastic	5.00	12.00
PLATE 281-A	Happy Dwarf Birthday Card	8.00	15.00	PLATE 316-D	Cinderella Bank	25.00	35.00
PLATE 281-B	Grumpy Dwarf Get-Well Card	8.00	15.00	PLATE 316-E	Cinderella Storybook	7.00	12.00
PLATE 281-C	Snow White Story Book	35.00	70.00	PLATE 316-F	Cinderella Record	3.00	7.00
PLATE 282	Pinocchio The Acrobat	125.00	250.00	PLATE 317-A	Alice Ceramic Figure	10.00	20.00
PLATE 283-A	Three Pigs Sheet Music	12.00	20.00	PLATE 317-B	Alice Plastic Wallet	8.00	12.00
PLATE 283-B	Snow White Sheet Music	10.00	20.00	PLATE 317-C	Alice in Wond. Planter	25.00	40.00
PLATE 283-C	Pinocchio Sheet Music	10.00	20.00	PLATE 317-D	Alice Story Book	7.00	12.00
PLATE 284	Snow White Night Lamp	75.00	125.00	PLATE 318-A	Peter Pan Planter	20.00	35.00
PLATE 285	Boxed Snow White & Dwarfs			PLATE 318-B	Peter Pan Sewing Cards	18.00	30.00
	Bisque Set	150.00	325.00	PLATE 318-C	Captain Hook Figure	12.00	23.00
PLATE 286-A	Pinocchio Wind-Up Toy	125.00	200.00	PLATE 319	Alice Stand-Up Fig. (Set of 15)	38.00	60.00
PLATE 286-B	Pinocchio Lunch Pail	25.00	50.00	PLATE 320	Dumbo Tin Wind-Up Marx	65.00	125.00
PLATE 287	Pinocchio Tin Tea Set	100.00	150.00	PLATE 321-A	Cinderella & Prince Wind-Up	50.00	85.00
PLATE 288	Pinocchio Lunch Box	25.00	50.00	PLATE 321-B	Mary Poppins Wind-Up	35.00	75.00
PLATE 289-A	Pinocchio 10" Wood Doll	125.00	225.00	PLATE 322	Charlie McCarthy Radio	200.00	400.00
PLATE 289-B	Pinocchio 8" Wood Doll	100.00	150.00	PLATE 323	Mortimer Snerd Puppet	35.00	60.00
PLATE 290-A	Figaro Wood Comp. Figure	20.00	35.00	PLATE 324	Charlie McCarthy Puppet	40.00	70.00
PLATE 290-B	Pinocchio Large Comp. Figure	65.00	125.00	PLATE 325	Charlie McCarthy Wind-Up Car	300.00	500.00
PLATE 290-C	Gepetto Wood Comp. Figure	30.00	75.00	PLATE 326-A	Charlie Tin Wind-Up Toy	130.00	200.00
PLATE 291-A	Gepetto Comp. Figure	30.00	50.00	PLATE 326-B	Mortimer Snerd Wind-Up	130.00	190.00
PLATE 291-B	Pinocchio Comp. Figure	25.00	45.00	PLATE 327-A	Charlie McCarthy Soap	45.00	70.00
PLATE 291-C	Lampwick Comp. Figure	25.00	45.00	PLATE 327-B	Charlie McCarthy Soap	45.00	70.00
PLATE 292	Pinocchio Paint Box	20.00	30.00	PLATE 328	Mortimer Snerd Card Puppet	40.00	65.00
PLATE 293	Pinocchio Composition Bank	50.00	125.00	PLATE 329	Charlie McCarthy Card Puppet	45.00	70.00
PLATE 294	Pin the Nose on Pinocchio			PLATE 330	Charlie McCarthy Rummy Game	20.00	35.00
	Game	65.00	120.00	PLATE 331-A	Charlie McCarthy Figure	18.00	25.00
PLATE 295	Pinocchio Story Book Set	140.00	250.00	PLATE 331-B	Charlie McCarthy Bank	85.00	135.00
PLATE 296-A	Pinocchio Story Book	20.00	35.00	PLATE 332	Charlie & Mort. Private Car	400.00	750.00
PLATE 296-B	Pinocchio Wood Comp. Doll	80.00	135.00	PLATE 333-A	Mortimer Decanter	20.00	40.00
PLATE 297	Pinocchio Character Books (ea.)	18.00	35.00	PLATE 333-B	Charlie Mc. Big Little Book	18.00	30.00
PLATE 298-A	Pinocchio Theatre Valentine	12.00	20.00	PLATE 333-C	Charlie Mc. Decanter	20.00	40.00
PLATE 298-B	Cleo Goldfish Valentine	10.00	20.00	PLATE 334	Howdy Doody Puzzle	8.00	12.00
PLATE 298-C	Pinocchio Figure Valentine	10.00	20.00	PLATE 335	Charlie McCarthy Paint Book	20.00	35.00
PLATE 298-D	Gepetto & Figaro Valentine	12.00	20.00	PLATE 336	Howdy Doody Game	30.00	45.00
PLATE 299-A	Pinocchio & Figaro Planter	35.00	60.00	PLATE 337	Howdy Doody Game	30.00	45.00
PLATE 299-B	Pinocchio Thermometer	30.00	60.00	PLATE 338	Howdy Doody Savings Bank	15.00	25.00
PLATE 300	Figaro Wind-Up by Marx	100.00	200.00	PLATE 339	Howdy Doody Jointed Doll	65.00	90.00
PLATE 301	Pinocchio Prints (pair)	75.00	150.00	PLATE 340	Howdy Doody Clock-A-Doodle	325.00	500.00
PLATE 302	Bambi Prints (pair)	40.00	80.00	PLATE 341	Howdy Doody Ear Muffs	15.00	30.00
PLATE 303	Pinocchio Prints (pair)	75.00	150.00	PLATE 342	Howdy Doody Ovaltine Mug	15.00	25.00
PLATE 303				PLATE 343	Howdy Doody Wind-Up Toy	200.00	400.00
& 301	Prints (Complete set of 4)	200.00	400.00	PLATE 344	Howdy Doody Fun Book	20.00	30.00
PLATE 304-A	Pinocchio Paperback Book	25.00	45.00	PLATE 345-A	Charlie McCarthy Book	20.00	38.00
PLATE 304-B	Pinocchio Comp. Head Puppet	35.00	50.00	PLATE 345-B	Charlie McCarthy Big Little		
PLATE 305-A	Pinocchio Picture Book	45.00	65.00		Book	18.00	30.00
PLATE 305-B	Pinocchio Paint Book	30.00	45.00	PLATE 346	Howdy Doody Doll-16"	140.00	250.00
PLATE 306	Pinocchio Bell-Ring Pull Toy	100.00	250.00	PLATE 346-B	Charlie McCarthy Big Little		
PLATE 307	Pinocchio Boxed Game Compl.	40.00	85.00		Book	18.00	30.00

Photograph	Item	Fine Condition Value	Mint Condition Value
PLATE 347	Howdy Doody Night Light	$ 35.00	$ 50.00
PLATE 348	Howdy & Santa Christmas Light	28.00	45.00
PLATE 349	Flash Gordon Rocket Fighter	90.00	185.00
PLATE 350	Flash Gordon Paint Book	35.00	55.00
PLATE 351	Flash Gordon Feature Book	40.00	65.00
PLATE 352-A	Flash Gordon Air Blaster	75.00	125.00
PLATE 352-B	Flash Gordon Space Compass	20.00	40.00
PLATE 353	Flash Gordon Boxed Vest	75.00	125.00
PLATE 354	Flash Gordon Boxed Vest	75.00	125.00
PLATE 355	Flash Gordon Puzzle	12.00	20.00
PLATE 356	Flash Gordon Puzzle	12.00	20.00
PLATE 357	Flash Gordon Puzzle	12.00	20.00
PLATE 358	Buck Rogers Disintegrator	75.00	125.00
PLATE 359	Captain Video Rocket Set	25.00	45.00
PLATE 360	Rex Mars Planet Pistol Patrol	15.00	35.00
PLATE 361-A	Buck Rogers Attack Ship	35.00	75.00
PLATE 361-B	Venus Duo Destroyer	35.00	75.00
PLATE 362	Buck Rogers U-235 Pistol	65.00	120.00
PLATE 363-A	Flash Gordon Big Little Book	18.00	30.00
PLATE 363-B	Buck Rogers Better Little Book	15.00	25.00
PLATE 364	Buck Rogers Space Rangers Kit	85.00	150.00
PLATE 365	Buck Rogers Space Rangers Kit	85.00	150.00
PLATE 366	Buck Rogers Space Rangers Kit	85.00	140.00
PLATE 367	Buck Rogers Rocket Ship	90.00	175.00
PLATE 368-A	Buck Rogers Battle Cruiser	35.00	75.00
PLATE 368-B	Venus Duo-Destroyer	35.00	75.00
PLATE 369	Flash Gordon Picture Record	20.00	30.00
PLATE 370	Superman Record Set	20.00	35.00
PLATE 371	Superman Statue	25.00	50.00
PLATE 372	Superman Krypto Ray Gun	125.00	250.00
PLATE 373-A	Superman Comic 1941	45.00	75.00
PLATE 373-B	Superman Comic 1943	30.00	55.00
PLATE 374 & 375	Superman Game by Transogram	25.00	45.00
PLATE 376	Captain Marvel Cars (each)	50.00	85.00
PLATE 377	Captain Marvel Picture Puzzle	10.00	20.00
PLATE 378-A	Captain Marvel Horn	10.00	20.00
PLATE 378-B	Captain Marvel Club Patch	8.00	15.00
PLATE 379	Red Ryder Gun & Holster Set	45.00	85.00
PLATE 380	Red Ryder Target Game	50.00	80.00
PLATE 381	Red Ryder Target Game	50.00	80.00
PLATE 382-A	Gene Autry Paint Book	20.00	30.00
PLATE 382-B	Gene Autry Coloring Book	15.00	25.00
PLATE 383	Hopalong Cassidy Pistol & Box	40.00	65.00
PLATE 384	Hopalong Picture Gun Theatre	60.00	100.00
PLATE 385	Hopalong Cassidy Radio	125.00	200.00
PLATE 386	Hopalong Merchandise Ad	45.00	65.00
PLATE 387-A	Gene Autry Rubber Boots	20.00	35.00

Photograph	Item	Fine Condition Value	Mint Condition Value
PLATE 387-B	Hopalong Cassidy Ice Cream Container	$ 10.00	$ 20.00
PLATE 388	Hopalong Cassidy Booklet Set	35.00	65.00
PLATE 389	Hopalong Cassidy Wind-Up	75.00	150.00
PLATE 390	Hopalong Cassidy Automatic Wind-Up Television	45.00	90.00
PLATE 391	Roy Rogers Ranch Lantern	45.00	75.00
PLATE 392-A	Red Ryder Better Little Book	15.00	22.00
PLATE 392-B	Red Ryder Book	18.00	25.00
PLATE 392-C	Red Ryder Book	18.00	30.00
PLATE 393	Buck Jones Book	25.00	35.00
PLATE 394-A	Roy Rogers Mug	15.00	22.00
PLATE 394-B	Roy Rogers Camera	20.00	30.00
PLATE 395	Roy Rogers Guitar	30.00	45.00
PLATE 396	Roy Rogers Lamp	75.00	150.00
PLATE 397-A	Roy Rogers Tin Lunch Box	8.00	15.00
PLATE 397-B	Tom Mix Big Little Books	15.00	25.00
PLATE 398	Tonto Composition Doll	250.00	400.00
PLATE 399	Lone Ranger & Silver Wind-Up (Silver Version)	150.00	225.00
PLATE 400-A	Lone Ranger First Aid Kit	30.00	55.00
PLATE 400-B	Lone Ranger Figure	25.00	40.00
PLATE 401	Hopalong Cassidy Picture	35.00	50.00
PLATE 402-A	Tom Mix Picture Puzzles	25.00	40.00
PLATE 402-B	Tom Mix "Big Big" Book	30.00	45.00
PLATE 403	Hopalong Cassidy Plate	25.00	40.00
PLATE 404	Gene Autry Metal Tray	30.00	45.00
PLATE 405	Lone Ranger w/Silver Wind-Up White Horse	100.00	150.00
PLATE 406	Hopalong Cassidy Cup	10.00	20.00
PLATE 407	Hopalong Cassidy Puzzle	14.00	22.00
PLATE 408	Hopalong Cassidy Puzzle	14.00	22.00
PLATE 409	Hopalong Cassidy Puzzle	14.00	22.00
PLATE 410	Gene Autry Song Book	20.00	35.00
PLATE 411	Davy Crocket Lamp	45.00	75.00
PLATE 412	Lone Ranger Printing Set	30.00	50.00
PLATE 413	Roy Rogers Truck	45.00	75.00
PLATE 414-A	Dale Evans Necklace	5.00	10.00
PLATE 414-B	Hopalong Cassidy Button	7.00	12.00
PLATE 414-C	Roy Rogers Post Card	5.00	10.00
PLATE 415	Zorro Pencil Holder	40.00	65.00
PLATE 416	Red Ryder Picture Record	20.00	30.00
PLATE 417-A	Lone Ranger Better Little Book	15.00	22.00
PLATE 417-B	Lone Ranger Better Little Book	15.00	22.00
PLATE 417-C	Tom Mix Better Little Book	15.00	22.00
PLATE 417-D	Red Ryder Better Little Book	15.00	22.00

Most of the character toys pictured in this book were licensed by the toy manufacturer to the original holders of the character copyrights. Every effort has been made to list these copyright holders whenever the information has been marked on the toy or has become known through other sources.

Bibliography

Ayres, William S., *The Main Street Pocket Guide to Toys,* The Main Street Press, Pittstown, New York, 1984.

Blackbeard, Bill and Martin Williams, (Editors) *The Smithsonian Collection of Newspaper Comics,* Smithsonian Institution Press and Harry N. Abrams, Inc. (Washington, D.C. and New York) 1977.

Eyles, Allen, *The Western,* A.S. Barnes & Co. (New York) 1975.

Finch, Christopher, *The Art of Walt Disney,* Abrams (New York) 1975.

Galewitz, Herb and Don Winslow, *Fontaine Fox's Toonerville Trolley,* Weathervane Books by arrangement with Charles Scribner's Sons (New York) 1972.

Grossman, Gary H., *Saturday Morning T.V.,* Dell Publishing Co. (New York) 1981.

Harman, Kenny, *Comic Strip Toys,* Wallace Homestead, Des Moines, Iowa, 1975.

Harmon, Jim and Donald F. Glut, *The Great Movie Serials,* Doubleday and Company (New York) 1972.

Horn, Maurice (Editor), *The World Encyclopedia of Cartoons,* Chelsea House Publishers, New York, 1980.

Kaonis, Donna, "I Yam What I Yam" (Popeye Article), *Collector's Showcase,* Volume I, Number 6, July/August 1982.

Lesser, Robert, *A Celebration of Comic Art and Memorabilia,* Hawthorn Books (New York) 1975.

Maltin, Leonard, *Of Mice and Magic: A History of American Animated Cartoons,* New American Library (New York) 1980.

Maltin, Leonard, *The Disney Films,* Popular Library (New York) 1978.

Munsey, Cecil, *Disneyana: Walt Disney Collectibles,* Hawthorn Books (New York) 1974.

McMahon, Morgan, *A Flick of the Switch, 1930-1950,* Vintage Radio, (Palos Verdes, CA) 1975.

O'Brien, Richard, *Collecting Toys,* 4th Edition, Books Americana, Florence Alabama, 1985.

Robinson, Jerry, *The Comics: An Illustrated History of Comic Strip Art,* G.P. Putnam's Sons (New York) 1974.

Ruggles, Rowena Godding, *The One Rose,* 1st Edition, Albany, Califonia, 1972.

Schickel, Richard, "Bringing Forth the Mouse" article in *American Heritage* Volume XIX, Number 3, American Heritage Publishing Co., 1968.

Schickel, Richard, *The Disney Version,* Simon and Schuster, New York, 1968.

Schorr, Martyn, L. *A Flick of the Switch, 1930-1959,* Vintage Radio, (Palos Verdes, CA) 1975.

Schroeder, Joseph J., Jr., *The Wonderful World of Toys, Games and Dolls,* DBI Books, Northfield, Illinois, 1971.

Thomas, Bob, *Walt Disney: An American Original,* Simon and Schuster, New York, 1976.

Tumbusch, Tom, *Tomart's Illustrated Disneyana Catalogue and Price Guide,* Tomart Publications, Dayton, Ohio, 1985.

Magazines Devoted To Toys Collecting

Antique Toy World
4419 Irving Park
Chicago, IL 60641
Publisher: Dale Kelley. Monthly black, white and color magazine devoted strictly to toys.

Collector's Showcase
P.O. Box 6929
San Diego, CA 92106
Publishers: Donna and Keith Kaonis. Full color magazine with an emphasis on toys, antique advertising and collectibles. Published every two months.

Mail Bid Collectibles Auction Companies

Hake's Americana and Collectibles
P.O. Box 1444
York, PA 17405
Publishes quarterly and semi-monthly auction catalogues. Also features immediate phone-in sales on a less frequent basis. Contact Ted Hake.

Historicana
1632 Robert Road
Lancaster, PA 17601
Publishes about three auction catalogues per year. Contact: Robert Coup or Michael Goyda.

Dealers and Collectors Interested in Selling or Purchasing Toys by Mail

Dennis Hasty
436 Hillside Ave., #11
Lockland, OH 45215
Buying and selling - TV character memorabilia.

Ken Schmitz
2405 West Carrington
Oak Creek, WI 53154
Buying and selling - Space character toys, westerns, comic characters, figures, books, games, etc.

Marc Belich
2014 South 81st St.
West Alice, WI 53219
Buying and selling - Character toys in all forms.

Louise Henderson
Waynesville, OH
Phone: (513) 885-3940
Buying and selling - Character & general line dolls, Madame Alexander dolls.

Joe & Juanita Reese
511 Dair Ave.
Harrison, OH 45030
Buying and selling - Character collectibles, Madame Alexander dolls, western collectibles, pocket knives.

The Hoosier Peddler
Dave Harris
5400 S. Webster St.
Kokomo, IN 46902
Buying and selling - Rare comic character toys & tin wind-ups, antique advertising; Disneyana.

O.E. & Julia Gernand
Rural Route 2
Yorktown, IN 47396
Buying and selling - Character toys & wind-ups, general line antique toys, all comic characters.

Pin-On
Helene & Foster Pollack
120 Bennetts Farm Rd.
Ridgefield, CT 06877
Buying and selling - Comic character toys, pin-back buttons, popular memorabilia.

Donna Walker
1560 N. Sandburg Terrace
Chicago, IL 60610
Buying only - Orphan Annie, related toys & books exclusively.

Doug Moore
57 Hickory Ridge Cr.
Cicero, IN 46034
Buying and selling - Tin wind-ups, Buddy L, character toys, cast iron toys.

Terry and Jeannie Quadnau
434 Hillside Ave., No. 28
Cincinnati, OH 45215
Buying and selling - Howdy Doody, Hopalong Cassidy, character paper dolls and coloring books, boardgames and character items.

Elmer & Viola Reynolds
c/o Character Toys
P.O. Box 2183
Clarksville, IN 47131
Buying only - Kewpies, all comic character toys, banks, tin wind-ups, bisques, Disneyana.

Antique Toy Museums To Visit

Memory Lane Antique Doll and Toy Museum
Olde Mistick Village
Mystic, CT 06355
Contact: Violet Meier

Perelman Antique Toy Museum
270 S. Second St.
Philadelphia, PA 19106
Contact: Leon J. Perelman

Margaret Woodbury Strong Museum
Rochester, NY

Schroeder's Antiques
Price Guide

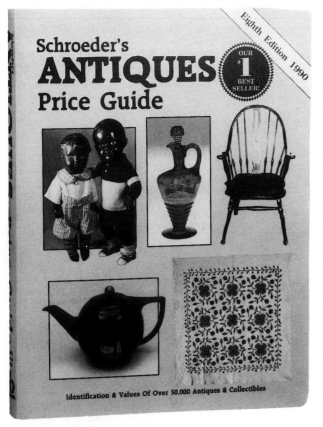

Schroeder's Antiques Price Guide has become THE household name in the antiques & collectibles industry. Our team of editors work year around with more than 200 contributors to bring you our #1 best-selling book on antiques & collectibles.

With more than 50,000 items identified & priced, *Schroeder's* is a must for the collector & dealer alike. If it merits the interest of today's collector, you'll find it in *Schroeder's.* Each subject is represented with histories and background information. In addition, hundreds of sharp original photos are used each year to illustrate not only the rare and unusual, but the everyday "fun-type" collectibles as well -- not postage stamp pictures, but large close-up shots that show important details clearly.

Our editors compile a new book each year. Never do we merely change prices. Accuracy is our primary aim. Prices are gathered over the entire year previous to publication, from ads and personal contacts. Then each category is thoroughly checked to spot inconsistencies, listings that may not be entirely reflective of actual market dealings, and lines too vague to be of merit. Only the best of the lot remains for publication. You'll find *Schroeder's Antiques Price Guide* the one to buy for factual information and quality.

No dealer, collector or investor can afford not to own this book. It is available from your favorite bookseller or antiques dealer at the low price of $12.95. If you are unable to find this price guide in your area, it's available from Collector Books, P.O. Box 3009, Paducah, KY 42001 at $12.95 plus $2.00 for postage and handling.

8½ x 11", 608 Pages   **$12.95**

COLLECTOR BOOKS
A Division of Schroeder Publishing Co., Inc.